Charlie Loram first travelled to India in 1992 having just graduated in geography from Newcastle University. Enchanted by the natural splendour and charming people of the western Himalaya he has returned as often as he can to explore the remoter valleys. In addition to several months in Ladakh researching this guide he has spent time studying the culture and environment of neighbouring Lahaul where he worked closely with local environmental organisations as co-ordinator of a research expedition.

Other journeys have so far taken him to South-East Asia, North America, Australia, New Zealand, Hawaii and through much of Europe. When at home in the UK he spends as much time as possible walking, climbing, cycling, surfing and sailing. He is at present training to become a teacher of the Alexander Technique.

Leh & Trekking in Ladakh
First edition 1996

Publisher
Trailblazer Publications
The Old Manse, Tower Rd, Hindhead, Surrey, GU26 6SU, UK
Fax (+44) 01428-607571

British Library Cataloguing in Publication Data
A catalogue record for this book is available from the British Library

ISBN 1-873756-09-7

© **Charlie Loram 1996**
Text, maps and photographs

The right of Charlie Loram to be identified as the author of this work has been
asserted by him in accordance with the Copyright, Designs and Patents Act 1988

The quotation from *A Journey in Ladakh* by Andrew Harvey is reproduced on p107
by permission of Jonathan Cape Ltd and Aitken Stone & Wylie. Quotations from
Getting Started in Ladakhi by Rebecca Norman are reproduced by permission of
Melong Publications.

Editor: Patricia Major
Typesetting: Bryn Thomas and Anna Jacomb-Hood
Cartography and index: Jane Thomas

Every effort has been made by the author and publisher to ensure that the
information contained herein is as accurate and up to date as possible. However,
they are unable to accept responsibility for any inconvenience, loss or injury sus-
tained by anyone as a result of the advice and information given in this guide.

Printed on chlorine-free paper from farmed forests by
Technographic Design & Print Ltd, Colchester, Essex, UK

LEH
&
TREKKING
IN
LADAKH

CHARLIE LORAM

TRAILBLAZER PUBLICATIONS

For Tor

Acknowledgements

This book couldn't have been written without the help of many kind and generous people. First, I'd like to thank Victoria Cornet – the best companion – who has contributed in so many ways from accompanying me on some of the treks, writing the section on p69, rearranging my rambling text into a more readable form and giving unwavering support from beginning to end.

I'd also like to thank several people who provided information which has made this guide all the more comprehensive: John Ayres (UK) and Andy Smith (UK) for all the laughs and for information on Nubra; Espen Skorstad (Norway) and Matthew Connor (Australia) for their notes on the route from Sumdah-Chenmo to Skiu; Josh Bridgens (UK) for the Stok Kangri route information and the map on p225; Fabian Kalambokis (Switzerland) for his company on the Leh to Nubra trek and help in Leh and Delhi; Claudia Bremer (Germany) for information on Zanskar; Jennifer Long (UK) for details on cycling between Manali and Leh; Lisa Kremer (USA) for various route ideas and for inviting a lone trekker to a gourmet dinner in the middle of the Rupshu wilderness; Rodney Aldis (UK) for much information on wildlife.

For patiently answering all my questions in Leh and advising me on things Ladakhi I'd like to thank Helena Norberg-Hodge of the Ladakh Project, Sonam Wangchuk and Terry Fundak of SECMOL, Sonam Dawa of LEDeG, Dr S Dawa Lonpo at the SNM Hospital and Sunder N Namgil at Footprints Adventure Company. Thanks also to Narendra Kothiyal at the India Tourist Office, Delhi.

I am very grateful for the help I received in such varied capacities from so many, in particular Rachel McEuilly (UK), Graham Cloke (UK), Matthew Wetherall (UK), Rosalind Rickaby (UK), Marco Vismara (Italy), Jason Myatt (UK) and Gudrun Schepokat (Germany).

Special thanks must go to both my brothers, Johnnie for starting the ball rolling and Adrian for computer advice, and to my mother and father for allowing my wanderlust to flourish.

Thanks also to Jane Thomas for editing the maps and compiling the index, Patricia Major for editing the text and Anna Jacomb-Hood for typesetting. Particular thanks to Bryn Thomas without whom none of this would have happened.

A request

The author and publisher have tried to ensure that this guide is as accurate and up-to-date as possible. Nevertheless things change, prices rise, rail services are extended or cut back, hotels open and close. If you notice any omissions or changes that should be included in the next edition of this book, please write to Charlie Loram at Trailblazer Publications (address on p2). A free copy of the next edition will be sent to persons making a significant contribution.

Front cover: Lamayuru Gompa

CONTENTS

INTRODUCTION

PART 1: PLANNING YOUR TRIP

With a group or on your own?
Organising the trek yourself 10 – Guided trekking groups 11
Trekking agencies 13 (Ladakh 13, UK 13, Continental
Europe 14, USA 15, Canada 15, Australasia 15)

Getting to India
Visas 16 – By air 17 – Overland 18

Budgeting
Costs in towns 18 – Independent trekking costs 19
Overall budget 19

When to go and for how long
Seasons 20 – Average temperatures and rainfall 21
How long do you need? 21

Route options
The Markha Valley trek (6-10 days) 22 – Likir to
Temisgam (2-4 days) 24 – Lamayuru to Alchi (4-6 days)
25 – Leh to Nubra (4-6 days) 26 – The Indus Valley to the
Rupshu (8-10 days) 28 – Stok Kangri ascent 29 – Other
possibilities 30 – Trekking in Zanskar 31 – Across Zanskar (15-
21 days) 32 – Other options in Zanskar 33

What to take
Keep it light 35 – Buying gear 36 – How to carry it 36
Footwear and foot care 37 – Clothes 38 – Medical kit 40
Finding out more 44 – Maps 46

Health precautions and inoculations
Who should avoid high altitude treks? 47 – Pre-trek preparations
48 – Inoculations 48 – Travel and health insurance 50

PART 2: INDIA

Facts about the country
Geographical background 51 – Climate 51 – Historical
outline 51 – Religion 53

Practical information for the visitor
Visa validity and extensions 56 – Trekking restrictions 56
Transport 57 – Language 60 – Time 61 – Money 61
Electricity 62 – Holidays and festivals 63 – Post and tele-
communications 65 – The media 66 – Food 66 – Drink 67
Things to buy 68 – Security 69

PART 3: DELHI & MANALI

Travel options map 70 – Travel options 71

Delhi
History 72 – Arrival and departure 73 – Orientation 75
Where to stay 76 – Where to eat 80 – Services 81
What to see 83 – Getting to Ladakh 86

Manali
Orientation 89 – Where to stay 89 – Getting away 91

PART 4: LADAKH

Geographical background 93 – Climate 94 – Historical outline 95
Economy 100 – Education 103 – People 103 – Religion 105

PART 5: LEH & BEYOND

Leh: Arrival 108 – Orientation 109 – Where to stay 109 – Where
to eat 115 – Services 117 – Nightlife 122 – Local transport 122
What to see 123 – Moving on 125 **Beyond Leh:** West of Leh 128
Leh to Srinagar road 130 (**map** 130) – Zanskar 131 – South-east of
Leh 132 – Leh to Manali road 133 (**map** 133)– Protected areas 136

PART 6: MINIMUM IMPACT TREKKING

Cultural impact 140 – Environmental impact 142 – Economic
impact 146 – **Organising your trek** 148 – Ponymen and pack
animals 148 – Local equipment 151 – Food for trekking 152
Preparing yourself 155

PART 7: TRAIL GUIDE AND MAPS

Using this guide
How to use the route maps 156 – Route map symbols 157

Markha Valley trek
Getting to the start 158 – Stok to Rumbak (alternative start) 158

Spituk to Jingchan 158 – Jingchan to Yurutse 161 – Yurutse to
Shingo 163 – Shingo to Skiu 166 – Skiu to Markha 166 – Markha
to Tahungste 170 – Tahungste to Chukirmo 172 – Chukirmo to
Karu 175

Likir to Temisgam
Getting to the start 178 – Likir to Yangtang 178 – Yangtang to Hemis-
Shukpachu 181 – Hemis-Shukpachu to Temisgam 181

Lamayuru to Alchi
Getting to the start 184 – Lamayuru to Wanla 186 – Wanla to Hinju
188 – Hinju to Sumdah-Chenmo 188 – Sumdah-Chenmo to Sumdah-
Choon 192 – Sumdah-Choon to Alchi 193

Sumdah-Chenmo to the Markha Valley
Sumdah-Chenmo to Chiling 198 – Chiling to Skiu 199

Leh to Nubra
Getting to the start 199 – Leh to Sabu 199 – Sabu Phu to the Digar La
200 – Digar La to Chumik Yogma 204 – Chumik Yogma to the Shyok
Valley 204 – Along the Shyok Valley to Rong 206

The Indus Valley to the Rupshu
Getting to the start 210 – Karu to the confluence of the Nimaling and
Markha rivers 210 – Confluence to the Zalung Karpo La 210 – Zalung
Karpo La to Sorra 211 – Sorra to Dat 215 – Dat to the Yar La 218 –
Yar La to Pogmar 218 – Pogmar to Pang 222

Stok Kangri ascent
Getting to the start 224 – Stok to the base camp, and to summit 224

Across Zanskar
Getting to the start 226 – **Part 1:** Lamayuru to Padum 226
(alternative: from Sengge La to Padum via Nera La and Zangla 229)
Part 2: Padum to Darcha 230 (alternative: from Tanze to Darcha via
the Phirtse La and Baralacha La 233)

APPENDICES

A Indian embassies 234
B Itineraries 235
C Health and mountain safety 236
D Flora and fauna 245
E Ladakhi words and phrases 247
F Glossary 250
G Mountaineering in Ladakh 251

INDEX

INTRODUCTION

Sandwiched between the vast ranges of the Karakoram and the Himalaya in the far north of India, Ladakh is the highest, most remote and least populated region in the whole country. The name is derived from *Ladags* which means 'the land of high passes'. Its corrugated, arid landscape is often described as a mountain desert which does not do justice to the inherent beauty of its chaotic ridges, twisted and exposed geological strata, snow-shrouded peaks, dark gorges and wide valleys. The eye is relieved from this relentless desolation by the vibrant green oases of the villages, where the resourceful inhabitants make up for the almost non-existent rain by channelling glacial meltwater across miles of precipitous mountainside to irrigate their barley fields and willow groves. It is a land of climatic extremes: fiercely hot days are followed by freezing nights just as the brief summer is followed by a long ice-bound winter, which completely isolates much of the region from the rest of the world for seven to eight months every year.

Until recently, Western visitors to Ladakh were rare. Its inaccessibility and hostile landscape initially kept them away and then, just when Ladakh's communications were improving, the Indian government imposed a ban on foreign tourists because of Ladakh's strategic position near the borders with Pakistan and China. Since this ban was raised in the 1970s Ladakh has become a popular destination for aficionados of wild mountain scenery and those interested in a unique culture. As much of the region is accessible only on foot, trekking is the ideal way to explore this fascinating land.

At various times in the past, Ladakh has been politically part of western Tibet and this influence is still prominent today throughout most of the region. Indeed it is said that Ladakh is a more accurate representation of Tibet before the Chinese invasion than Tibet itself. The Ladakhi people are principally of Tibetan origin and Tibetan Buddhism is still practised here, as it has been for hundreds of years. *Gompas*, or monasteries, overlook the valleys from their solitary positions on top of craggy hills and these religious institutions still play an active role in all Ladakhi life. Even deep in the mountains you are reminded that this is a Buddhist culture as you walk past *mani* walls and *chortens* at the entrance of every village, or over high passes where tattered prayer flags flutter from the summit cairn.

Trekking in Ladakh is very different from hiking in the West as the trails are the lifeline between villages. It's not unusual to find yourself sharing the trail with a *lama* on his way to a remote gompa, or a shepherd making his way up to a high pasture and it is this close interaction with the local people that makes it such an enriching experience. However, unlike the busy tea-house trails in Nepal, where you can guarantee food and shelter every day, in Ladakh you need to be totally self-sufficient. Villages are often several days apart and these subsistence communities grow only enough food to feed themselves. The best way to carry your camping equipment and food is to trek with a local who will bring along one or two pack-horses and will be only too happy to act as your guide and companion. All the necessary arrangements can be made both cheaply and easily in Leh, the atmospheric capital of Ladakh.

A trek is a rejuvenating experience. Day by day, mile by mile, you become leaner and fitter, slowly peeling away the constraints of modern life. Time for once is on your side and you have the privileged opportunity to immerse yourself in 'the naked mountains and the blessed sunshine and the merry rosy people'. (*The Himalayan Letters of Gypsy Davy and Lady Ba* by Robert and Katherine Barrett). The trekking industry is still young here and, at present, is free from rules and regulations. Each trekker must therefore accept his or her individual responsibility for ensuring that the magic of what the Barretts called these 'high quiet places' is never lost.

PART 1: PLANNING YOUR TREK

With a group or on your own?

Above all do not lose your desire to walk. Every day I walk myself into a state of well-being and walk away from every illness. I have walked myself into my best thoughts and know of no thought so burdensome that one cannot walk away from it. **The Buddha**

Foreign travellers have been following Ladakh's mountain trails for centuries. Since the beginning of this millennium, long rambling caravans of heavily-loaded pack animals accompanied the exotic traders from Central Asia, the Middle East and Tibet, as they made their way through the arid mountains before crossing over the Great Himalayan Range or the mighty Karakoram.

The first Western traveller in this region was a Portuguese by the name of Diogo d'Almeida who crossed the high passes in 1600. He was followed by a slow trickle of missionaries, merchants, explorers and adventurers ranging from an impoverished Transylvanian in the 1820's called Csoma de Koros, the self-styled pioneer of Tibetan studies, who wandered the remote trails dressed as a tramp, to the mildly eccentric Robert and Katherine Barrett, alias Gypsy Davy and Lady Ba, who trekked for a year in 1923-24 with a luxurious entourage of 'twenty or more ponies...eight menservants, a lot of coolies carrying loads from one village to the next, and always a village headman or two.' (*The Himalayan Letters of Gypsy Davy and Lady Ba*).

The trails fell quiet for a little over twenty-five years until 1974, when the previously imposed ban on foreign visitors was lifted. The popularity of trekking holidays has developed rapidly in the intervening decades but the basic approaches remain the same as those developed by the early pioneers. Today's trekker has several choices. You can experience the splendour of the mountains with the minimum of discomfort by joining a fully organised trek, complete with crew and a caravan of ponies; you can adopt a lightweight, sensitive and less costly approach (as advocated by the great explorer mountaineers, Eric Shipton and HW Tilman) by employing a local pony-man with a few pack animals; or you can trek completely independently, carrying everything you need on your back.

ORGANISING THE TREK YOURSELF

Backpacking

From the point of view of organising a trek, backpacking is simplest. This is the usual and preferred form of trekking in the West and one that is also common in Nepal, where the popular routes have a well established system of inns, or 'tea-houses', in which you can sleep and eat. However, it doesn't adapt quite so easily to the mountains of Ladakh.

First, the villages in Ladakh are often far apart and it's rare to be able to find food or somewhere to sleep along the trail. Therefore, on most treks you need to be self-sufficient for food and shelter. Secondly, there's the problem of route finding. Trails are frequently hard to follow, and there are few locals from whom to ask the way. Thirdly, the mountains are larger than anything in the West. Not only will you be walking uphill for several days on end, but you'll be doing so at altitudes in excess of 3500m/11,480ft – hard enough without a 15+kg pack on your back.

There are, however, one or two shorter and lower level treks that can quite easily be backpacked, but for the majority of routes this is an unnecessarily punishing way to walk. Despite this, there will be a few people for whom reading these sentences will only serve to whet their appetite for adventure. For those with a high level of fitness and experience, backpacking can be a very exciting way to explore the mountains. However, you should consider that for little extra cost and effort you could employ a pony-man who would enrich your experience even more, and by giving him work you'd be helping the local economy.

Pack animals and pony-men

Keeping to the principles of low weight, low cost and low impact does not mean you have to forgo all comfort. Ladakh is ideally suited to independent individuals or small groups making their own arrangements with a pony-man. (Ladakhis are caravan traders, not porters, and so this is a traditional means of carrying your gear into the mountains). The pony-man will not only provide the ponies or donkeys to carry your luggage (£3-6/US$5-9 per animal per day) but will also act as your guide for no extra charge and possibly your cook as well. This is an excellent way to travel particularly if you keep the size of the group small.

A party of up to about four people, along with the pony-man and two or three ponies can walk together at the same speed, pitch camp in the smallest of spaces, alter the itinerary with ease and, perhaps more importantly, will be welcomed into villages and houses along the way. A friendship between you and your guide will develop as you practise your Ladakhi and he practises his English (which will certainly be better than your attempts at his language), while both of you learn more about each other's cultures. Understanding and appreciation of what you are seeing will be greatly increased, while a huge weight is taken off your back.

Organising such a minimal outfit is simple (see p148) and need take no more than two or three days. Leh is the best place to buy food and hire any camping equipment that you need, while pony-men can be organised either there or at the village at the start of your trek.

GUIDED TREKKING GROUPS

There is a certain amount of overlap between the approach mentioned above and guided trekking groups; the distinction is really in how much organisation you are prepared to do yourself.

Local trekking agencies

As the size of a group increases, or the level of service you require grows, it begins to make sense to employ the help of a local trekking agency in Leh. While you may well use an agency just to help you find a pony-man, their real skill lies in organising a complete trek from start to finish. For those for whom cost is not of major importance, or those who would rather let someone else worry about where and how to pitch the tent, how far to walk each day and what to have for dinner, then a fully organised and guided trek is the answer.

Almost anything can be arranged from a simple but efficient trek with tents, food, ponies, guide and cook for as little as £13/US$20 per person per day, up to a luxury trek with excellent food, separate toilet, dining and kitchen tents plus a slick crew costing anything up to £55/$80 per person per day. The price becomes slightly cheaper per person the more people you have in the group.

This kind of organised group trek can easily be arranged when you arrive in Leh. It will take the agency between three and seven days to get everything together (the higher the level of service and the more complicated the itinerary, the longer everything takes), which gives you ample time to acclimatise and explore the local area.

If you are very short of time, require a very high level of service, or there are six or more of you (not to be recommended), it might be wiser to make preliminary arrangements before you reach India. Try contacting an Indian trekking agency from abroad via the state tourist office (see p83) but note that this can be a frustrating and time consuming business: allow at least a couple of months. Alternatively, sign up with an adventure travel company from your own country.

Foreign trekking agencies

The growth of adventure travel companies in the West over the last decade has been phenomenal. All the companies listed on p13 offer treks in Ladakh, many choosing the most popular routes, while others make a point of taking you off the beaten track, or even up a mountain or two.

• **What you get for your money** A complete pre-planned trekking package is laid on so that there is almost nothing left for you to organise: international flights, high quality hotels, most meals, guided tours, transfers and transportation are all included. On the trek itself everything is provided, all you have to do is keep placing one foot in front of the other. The success of the trip depends on the quality of the leader and the local ground-handling agents. Most companies employ Western leaders to accompany the group for the whole of the trip, while leaving the day to day logistics of the trek in the hands of an experienced local guide. A few companies use local representatives throughout.

• **Pros and cons** Booking a trip with a trekking agency in your home country is a sensible choice for those who want to cram as much as possible into a limited amount of time and who enjoy being looked after. No time is wasted finding hotels, booking transport or getting a trekking crew together; someone else is being paid to worry about all that. Another benefit is that if you don't fancy the idea of travelling on your own, then group treks are an excellent way to meet like-minded people.

However, not everyone finds it easy to travel with between five and 11 total strangers and rifts in the group are not uncommon. There can also be problems with sticking to such a fixed itinerary and always being with the group. There's little time to go off exploring on your own, to interact independently with the locals, to meet fellow trekkers or to take a rest day when you feel like it. Things can get more serious at high altitude, when in the interest of saving time, the group is forced to ascend rather more quickly than may be appropriate, causing unnecessary discomfort.

This is without a doubt one of the most expensive ways to trek. While this style suits some, there are others who book with a commercial group because they don't realise that arranging a trekking holiday to Ladakh themselves is really very easy.

On the trail with a trekking group

If you've always thought that camping is best left to those with masochistic tendencies, then trekking with a commercial group will come as a luxurious surprise. You are woken up in your spacious tent and snug sleeping bag with a cup of steaming tea, which is soon followed by a bowl of hot water for washing. You then tuck into a sustaining breakfast while the crew strikes camp and loads up the ponies.

Carrying just a small day-pack containing a jacket, camera and water bottle, you set off gently. There's plenty of time to take photos, catch your breath or just enjoy the scenery. A simple packed lunch gives you an excuse to sit down and recuperate, while your crew rushes on ahead to set up camp before you arrive. The afternoon's walking is much shorter and you arrive at camp in time for tea and biscuits. With several hours of daylight left you can explore around the campsite, relax in the sun or have a wash by a mountain stream. After a wonderful three-course dinner, miraculously prepared on a couple of kerosene stoves, most trekkers are only too happy to turn in early.

• **What to ask** If you do decide to trek with a commercial company, there are a few questions you should ask before parting with your money. Some companies attract a certain type of clientele so it's worth finding out who your fellow trekkers will be and whether you think you'll get along with them. The top companies now give audio visual shows so that you can meet other people interested in going on trips and so that you get an idea of what trekking with that company is like.

Try to find out who will be leading your trip and what experience he or she has of leading groups, travelling in India and Ladakh, and of walking that particular route. A knowledgeable leader can teach you so much about a region. Ask for a detailed itinerary of your trek, how difficult it is and how big the group will be. Good indicators of the level of comfort that you can expect are the sort of food you will be eating and the standard of equipment that you will be using.

Perhaps most importantly, you should enquire about how comprehensive their medical kit is, whether the trek will be accompanied by anyone with medical training and what the policy is if someone falls ill, especially with Acute Mountain Sickness (AMS, commonly known as altitude sickness, see p238). Have they worked out emergency descent routes and will it be possible for someone to escort the AMS sufferer back to lower altitude if it's necessary?

TREKKING AGENCIES

Trekking agencies in Ladakh

Making arrangements with local trekking agencies in Leh is best left until you arrive as trying to make contact from abroad can be hard. One exception, however, should be mentioned: Students' Educational and Cultural Movement of Ladakh (SECMOL, see p119) run what they call Friendship Tours. They are not a trekking agency and all proceeds go towards SECMOL's work. The students at SECMOL run a maximum of five tours a year with the aim of encouraging beneficial interaction between locals and foreigners. The easy five or six day treks are led by students trained as trekking guides and are usually in the Indus Valley. They are much more of a cultural exchange than a wilderness experience and you will be put up in villagers' houses each night. It is hoped that the students and villagers will benefit as much from the experience as the visitors. If you are interested write no later than March (for a trek that summer) with details of how many people will be in your group, when you are coming and what sort of itinerary you would like, to: SECMOL Friendship Tours, PO Box 4, Leh, Ladakh, 194101, India.

Trekking agencies in the UK

Most UK trekking agencies quote prices including return airfares from London, all accommodation in India, all transport and a fully guided and equipped trek. Prices range from about £1200 for a 16 day trip, to £2500 for 30 days away. Some companies also offer other adventurous activities in Ladakh, such as mountaineering, white-water rafting and mountain biking, and where this is applicable these have been mentioned.

• **Camp One (Himalayan Adventure)** (☎/fax 01677-426114) Unit 7, Enterprise House, Bridge St, Bedale, North Yorkshire DL8 2AD. Trekking and mountaineering itineraries in Zanskar.

• **Exodus** (☎ 0181-675 5550, fax 0181-673 0779) 9 Weir Rd, London SW12 0LT. Trekking, mountaineering and mountain biking.

• **ExplorAsia/Abercrombie and Kent** (☎ 0171-730 9600, ☎ 0171-973 0482, fax 0171-730 9376) Sloane Square House, Holbein Place, London SW1W 8NS.

• **Explore Worldwide** (☎ 01252-319448, fax 01252-343170) 1 Frederick St, Aldershot, Hampshire GU11 1LQ.

• **High Places** (☎ 0114-275 7500, fax 0114-275 3870) Globe Works, Penistone Rd, Sheffield S6 3AE. Trekking and mountaineering.

• **Himalayan Folkways and Chandertal Tours** (☎ 01323-646604, fax 01323-725482) 10 Station Parade, Eastbourne, East Sussex BN21 1BE. Trekking, mountain biking, rafting, pony-trekking and motorcycling.

• **Himalayan Kingdoms** – Treks: (☎ 0117-923 7163, fax 0117-974 4993) 20 The Mall, Clifton, Bristol BS8 4DR. Mountaineering: (☎ 0114-276 3322, fax 0114-276 3344) Adjacent The Foundry, 45 Mowbray St, Sheffield S8 8EN.

• **KE Adventure Travel** (☎ 017687-73966, fax 017687-74693) 32 Lake Road, Keswick, Cumbria CA12 5DQ. Trekking, mountaineering and mountain biking.

• **Peak International** (☎/fax 01296-624225) 15 Moor Park, Wendover, Aylesbury HP22 6AX. Trekking, mountaineering, rafting and cycling.

• **Roama Travel** (☎ 01258-860298, fax 01258-861382) Shroton, Blandford Forum, Dorset DT11 8QW. Specialise in organising individual treks, but also run set treks from Lamayuru to Padum.

• **Worldwide Journeys and Expeditions** (☎ 0171-381 8638, fax 0171-381 0836) 8 Comeragh Rd, London W14 9HP.

Trekking agencies in Continental Europe

• **Belgium Divantoura** (☎ 03-233 1916) St Jacobsmarkt 5, 2000 Antwerpen. (☎ 09-223 0069) Bagattenstraat 176, B-9000 Gent. **Boundless Adventures** (☎ 02-426 40 30, fax 02-426 03 60) Verdilaan 25, 1083 Brussels - Ganshoren.

• **Denmark Inter-Travel** (☎ 33-15 00 77) Frederiksholms Kanal 2, DK-1220 Kobenhavn K. **Topas Globetrotterklub** (☎ 86 89 36 22, fax 86 89 36 88) Bakkelyvej 2, 8680 Ry.

• **Germany Explorer Fernreisen** (☎ 0211-99 49 02, fax 0211-37 70 79) Huttenstrasse 17, 40215 Dusseldorf.

• **Ireland** **Maxwells Travel** (☎ 01-677 9479, fax 01-679 3948) D'Olier Chambers, 1 Hawkins Street, Dublin 2. Agents for Explore (UK). **Silk Road Travel** (☎ 01-677 1029, fax 01-677 1390) 64 South William Street, Dublin 2. Agents for Exodus (UK).
• **Italy** **Agiata SRL** (☎ 02-86 12 30, fax 02-86 90 617) Corso Di Porta Romana 6, 20122 Milano.
• **Switzerland** **Suntrek Tours** (☎ 01-462 6161) Birmensdorferstr. 187, CH-8003 Zurich. **Exodus GSA Switzerland** (☎ 064-22 76 63, fax 064-23 10 84) Rain 35, POB 2226, 5001 Aarau.

Trekking agencies in the USA
North American trekking agencies quote land-cost only. Sample costs are US$2400 for a 21 day trip and US$3400 for 32 days.
• **Adventure Centre** (☎ 800-227 8747, fax 415-654 4200) 1311 63rd St, Suite 200, Emeryville, CA 94608. Agents for Explore (UK).
• **Journeys** (☎ 313-665 4407, ☎ 800-255 8735, fax 313-665 2945) 4011 Jackson Road, Ann Arbor, MI 48103.
• **Snow Lion Expeditions** (☎ 800-525 TREK, ☎ 801-355 6555, fax 801-355 6566) Oquirrh Place, 350 South 400 East, Suite G2, Salt Lake City, UT 84111. Trekking and mountaineering.
• **Wilderness Travel** (☎ 510-548 0420, ☎ 800-368 2794) 801 Allston Way, Berkeley, CA 94710.

Trekking agencies in Canada
• **Adventure Centre** (☎ 416-922 7584) 17 Hayden St, Toronto, Ontario M4Y 2P2. Agents for Explore (UK).
• **GAP Adventures** (☎ 416-922 8899, fax 416-922 0822) 264 Dupont Street, Toronto, Ontario M5R 1V7.
• **Trek Holidays** (☎ 800-661 7265), agents for Explore (UK), have offices in **Calgary** (☎ 403-283 6115), 336 14th St NW, Calgary, Alberta T2N 1Z7, and **Edmonton** (☎ 403-439 0024).

Trekking agencies in Australia
• **Adventure World**, agents for Explore (UK): **Adelaide** (☎ 231 6844) 7th floor, 45 King William St, Adelaide SA 5000; **Brisbane** (☎ 800-177 508, ☎ 229 0599), 3rd floor, 333 Adelaide St, Brisbane Qld 4000; **Melbourne** (☎ 800-133 322, ☎ 03-9670 0125), 3rd floor, 343 Little Collins St, Melbourne Vic 3000; **Perth** (☎ 800-621 300, ☎ 221 2300) 2nd floor, 8 Victoria Ave, Perth WA 6000; and **Sydney** (☎ 800-221 931, ☎ 956 7766) 73 Walker St, North Sydney NSW 2059.
• **Exodus** (☎ 02-251 5430, fax 02-251 5432) Suite 5, Level 5, 1 York Street, Sydney NSW 2000. Agents for Exodus (UK).
• **World Expeditions** has branches in **Brisbane** (☎ 07-236 4388, fax 07-229 5602) 1st floor, 145 Charlotte Street, Brisbane QLD 4000, **Melbourne** (☎ 03-9670 8400, fax 03-9670 7474), 1st floor, 393 Little

Bourke Street, Melbourne Vic 3000 and **Sydney** (☎ 02-264 3366, fax 02-261 1974) 3rd floor, 441 Kent Street, Sydney NSW 2000. Trekking and mountain biking.

Trekking agencies in New Zealand
• **Adventure World** (☎ 09-524 5118, fax 09-520 6629) 101 Great South Rd, Remuera, PO Box 74008, DX 69501, Auckland. Agents for Explore and Exodus (UK).
• **Himalaya Trekking** (☎ 06-868 8595, 025-466 465), 54a Darwin Rd, Gisborne. Organises individual itineraries.
• **Suntravel** (☎ 09-525 3074, fax 09-525 3065) PO Box 12-424, 407 Great South Road, Penrose, Auckland. Trekking, mountain biking and rafting. **Venturetreks**, agents for World Expeditions (Australia), are a division of Suntravel.

Getting to India

VISAS

Unless you are from either Nepal or Bhutan you won't get into India without a visa. Tourist visas come in three and six months durations only and there is an important distinction between the two. Three-month visas are valid from the day you first enter India (provided that date is within three months of the date of issue), whereas six-month visas are valid from the date of issue, not the date you arrive. Both can theoretically be extended once you get to India (see p56).

Get your visa from the Indian embassy or consulate in your home country (see p234) if at all possible. Taking your passport in person is by far the quickest method. In the UK, for example, your visa will be processed by the next working day, but if you apply by post it will take between five weeks and three months. If you have no choice but to apply in a foreign country, expect to wait longer and to pay more. The cost of the visa depends on your nationality. The British currently pay £13 for a three-month visa, or £26 for six months. US citizens pay double this.

On the visa application form you are asked how many entries into India you are going to make. It costs no more to request a multiple entry visa and this will give you the option of crossing over into Pakistan or Nepal. Very occasionally, travellers who specify on the form that they are going to Ladakh are given a visa stamped with a 10 day restricted area pass for Ladakh; no use if you were planning on a 20 day trek. Since most of Ladakh ceased to be a restricted area years ago there seems to be no logical reason for this. While most people encounter no problems by specifying Ladakh, it might be wiser not to mention it.

BY AIR

There are numerous carriers to Delhi, the nearest international airport to Ladakh; but book early. For the best deals check the travel pages of newspapers and magazines and phone as many travel agents as you can – a couple of hours' research can save you a lot of money. Although it's occasionally worth contacting the airlines themselves for special offers, the best deals will usually be through an agent. When you find an attractive price, check the restrictions on the ticket, the flight route and timings. You may find it's worth paying a little extra for a more convenient flight or for the security of using a more reputable travel agency. Some airlines increase their prices for flights to Delhi in July, August and December. Many offer discounts to students and people under 26.

From the UK

Prices of return flights start from £310 for an off-season flight with an Eastern European or Central Asian airline (with dubious safety standards and lengthy stop-overs in inhospitable airports), or from about £500 for a high season direct flight with a well-respected carrier. Search for bargains in London's listings magazines such as *Time Out*, or check the travel pages of the Sunday papers. Recommended travel agents include:

• **Campus Travel** who have many offices throughout the country and accept telephone bookings on ☎ 0171-730 8111 (London); ☎ 0161-273 1721 (Manchester); and ☎ 0131-668 3303 (Edinburgh).

• **Quest Worldwide** (☎ 0181-547 3322) 29 Castle St, Kingston, Surrey KT1 1ST.

• **STA Travel** have many branches in Britain and can be contacted for telephone sales on ☎ 0171-361 6262 (London); ☎ 0161-834 0668 (Manchester); ☎ 0117-929 4399 (Bristol); ☎ 01223-366966 (Cambridge); ☎ 01865-792800 (Oxford).

• **Trailfinders** have offices in London (☎ 0171-938 3366, 42-50 Earls Court Rd, London W8 6FT),

---

Getting to Ladakh from Delhi
See p86 for details of how to get to Ladakh from Delhi. It's easy to make travel arrangements once you've arrived in India, but for those on a very tight schedule, who are planning to fly into or out of Leh, it is possible to book Indian Airlines domestic flights from your home country through the same travel agent with whom you booked your international flight (although not every travel agent will do this for you). It is recommended that you only reserve a flight, paying for it once you've arrived in India, as several travellers have turned up at the Indian Airlines office in Delhi to find that their 'confirmed' ticket did not exist. If all the flights seem to be fully booked, don't panic – it's usually easier to get a seat once you've arrived in India.

Birmingham (☎ 0121-236 1234, 22-24 The Priory, Queensway, Birmingham B4 6BS), Bristol (☎ 0117-929 9000, 48 Corn St, Bristol BS1 1HQ), Glasgow (☎ 0141-353 2224, 254-284 Sauchiehall St, Glasgow G2 3EH) and Manchester (☎ 0161-839 6969, 58 Deansgate, Manchester M3 2FF).

• **United Air Travel** (☎ 0171-930 4161), 26 Oxendon St, London SW1.

From USA and Canada

Flights from the west coast cost from around US$1400 return, and are slightly cheaper from the east coast. The independent travel specialists, **STA Travel**, have offices throughout the USA and can usually offer some very competitive prices. Contact the New York branch (☎ 212-627 3111), 10 Downing St, NY 10014, for details of other offices. Try **Travel Cuts** in Canada (☎ 416-979 2406, 187 College St, Toronto, Ontario M5T 1P7).

From Australasia

Return flights start from around A$1300 from Australia and NZ$1800 from New Zealand. **Trailfinders** have Australian offices in Cairns (☎ 070-41 1199, Hides Corner, Shields St, Cairns, Queensland) and Brisbane (☎ 07-3229 0887, 91 Elizabeth St, Brisbane, Queensland). **STA Travel** have several offices in both countries. Contact the following offices for details of the others: in Australia (☎ 02-212 1255, 1st Floor, 732 Harris St, Ultimo, Sydney NSW 2007); in New Zealand (☎ 09-309 9995, 10 High St, Auckland).

OVERLAND

The classic overland route to India from the UK is much harder than it was in the '60s, but plenty of travellers are still undertaking this fascinating journey. The most popular route goes through Hungary, Romania, Bulgaria, Turkey, Iran and Pakistan. It's quite possible to organise independently, using either public transport or your own vehicle. There are also several specialist overland companies in the UK who will transport you in their well-equipped trucks: **Dragoman** (☎ 01728-861133, fax 01728-861127) 96 Camp Green, Debenham, Stowmarket, Suffolk IP14 6 LA; **Encounter Overland** (☎ 0171-370 6845, fax 0171-244 9737) 267 Brompton Road, London SW5 9JA; **Exodus** (see UK trekking agencies above); **Top Deck Travel** (☎ 0171-370 4555). Prices start from £1195 and the trips range in length from nine to fifteen weeks.

Budgeting

Costs in towns

India is one of the cheapest countries in which to travel. A basic double room with communal bathroom in Delhi, which is one of the most expensive places in India, will cost you about £3/US$5 a night, whereas in Manali and Leh you will get far nicer double rooms with a common bath from £1.50/US$2.50. Very comfortable rooms with attached bathroom and running hot water in an upmarket hotel will cost you about £8-15/US$13-$24 a night.

Expect to pay from around £1.50/US$2.50 for a good evening meal and about £1/US$1.60 for a bottle of beer. Restaurant prices in Leh and Manali are pretty uniform but in Delhi you can pay far more than this for a meal in a top restaurant.

If you're really counting the pennies, then it's quite possible to find a room for under £1/US$1.60 and to eat an evening meal for less than £0.60/US$1. Many people who have brought their own trekking stoves find that cooking their own meals makes an interesting change and is a good way to keep the costs down; some wonderful organic vegetables can be bought in the bazaars.

Independent trekking costs
If you're organising the trek totally independently and have all your own equipment, the main costs will be pack animals and food. Each trekker should expect to pay £3-6/US$5-9 per day for pack animals and a pony-man, and about £2-3/US$3-5 a day for food and fuel. A fully organised trek, arranged in Leh, costs from about £13/US$20 per person per day.

There is very rarely anything to buy on the trail apart from the occasional packet of biscuits or bar of chocolate. Expect to pay camping charges of about £0.40/US$0.60 per tent each night.

Your overall budget
Budget travellers should reckon on spending £50-90/US$80-150 a week, which will cover food and accommodation, local travel, sightseeing, trekking and pocket money for chocolate, paperbacks, a few cheap souvenirs and the odd phone call home.

Travel from Delhi to Ladakh and back again will cost about £50/US$80 if you go by bus, £110/US$175 by plane, or £80/US$130 if you take the bus one way and fly the other.

Once you've calculated how much you will need for the trip, bring a little more in case you get ill and require a doctor and a quick flight back to Delhi, or if you get tempted into going rafting on the Indus, or by a 'very good price' Kashmiri rug!

When to go and for how long

Ladakh is surrounded by a ring of high mountains and snow-covered passes which, before the airport was built at Leh, effectively cut it off from the rest of the world for seven or eight months every year. Although the modern visitor can now fly into Leh at any time of the year, trekking is restricted to the five months when the region is free from the grip of winter. The great advantage of Ladakh as a trekking destination is that it is one of the only Himalayan regions in which it is possible and pleasurable to trek from late June to mid-September, when most other areas are suffering from the constant deluge of the monsoon.

SEASONS

Ladakh's four seasons are not as even in length as those of Europe and North America, the year being dominated by the long, cold winter which is separated from the short but hot summer by a brief spring and autumn. In many ways, spring and autumn are little more than the end and the beginning of winter, and can hardly justify being called separate seasons.

June, July and August
The trekking season begins in about the middle of June. This is a nice time to come as there won't be many visitors, but you may have to fly in to Leh if the roads haven't opened yet and restrict your trekking to the lower altitudes if there is too much snow on the high passes.

Ladakh is at its busiest from the middle of July to the end of August when the Manali to Leh road is most likely to be free of snow. The weather at this time of year is ideal for trekking, as the days are hot and the nights refreshingly cool. The only drawback is the relative number of visitors. The popular trails may be quite busy and it can sometimes be hard to get a room in the guest house of your choice in Leh.

September and October
September is one of the best months to come trekking, as the number of people both on the trails and in Leh begins to tail off towards the end of August and if you come at the beginning of the month your stay will coincide with the Ladakh Festival (see p64). There won't be any problems finding good accommodation and the locals will have much more time for you. The temperatures are pleasantly warm during the day, without being too hot, but you should come prepared for cold nights, particularly when you're in the mountains.

The roads into Ladakh are usually open until mid-September, but from then on you can't be quite so certain. Although they can often remain open throughout October you should be prepared to consider flying. It's usually possible to trek right up until the end of October, although you will need to be suitably equipped for freezing temperatures after the sun has gone down.

November to March
At the beginning of November the lasting snows of winter begin to fall and the streams freeze over for five months. The coldest month is January when temperatures fall as low as -40°C, but by March this savage cold has gone. For experienced and well-prepared winter mountaineers and ski

tourers this season can provide some exciting possibilities. Read Guy Sheridan's account of a winter journey from Kargil to Manali, through Zanskar and Lahaul, in his book, *Tales of a Cross Country Skier*.

April and May

It is still quite cold during these months and snowfall is not uncommon at the beginning of April, but by now the ground has begun to thaw and activity has resumed in the villages. Trekking is really only feasible on low altitude routes, such as from Likir to Temisgam, and as the roads will still be closed, flying in is your only option.

AVERAGE TEMPERATURES AND RAINFALL

Delhi

Month	Jan	Feb	Mar	Apr	May	Jun	Jul	Aug	Sep	Oct	Nov	Dec
max °C	21	24	30	36	41	40	35	34	34	35	29	23
min °C	7	10	15	21	27	29	27	26	25	19	12	8
rain mm	25	22	17	7	8	65	211	173	150	31	1	5

Leh

Month	Jan	Feb	Mar	Apr	May	Jun	Jul	Aug	Sep	Oct	Nov	Dec
max °C	-3	1	7	12	17	21	24	24	21	14	8	2
min °C	-14	-12	-7	-1	3	7	10	10	6	-1	-7	-11
rain mm	13	8	13	5	5	2	15	18	10	5	2	8

HOW LONG DO YOU NEED?

Despite its remoteness, Ladakh can be reached remarkably quickly from the West, and it's quite possible to fit an exciting and rewarding trekking holiday into three weeks. A typical itinerary might be: Day 1: fly to Delhi; Day 2: fly to Leh; Days 3 to 5: acclimatising, organising your trek and sightseeing; Days 6 to 14: trekking; Day 15: in Leh; Day 16: fly to Delhi; Days 17 to 20: sightseeing; Day 21: fly home.

If you are on a tight schedule and have to be back home by a certain date, you should be aware that buses and planes to and from the region occasionally get cancelled or delayed by the weather. You must allow yourself a few days' leeway to get back to Delhi from Leh.

A schedule that works well for those short of time is to get up to Ladakh as soon as possible after arriving in India and to leave your exploration of Delhi until the end of your holiday. Aim to fly back from Leh about five days before you are due to fly home. If all goes well, this will give you plenty of time to see Delhi and maybe fit in a trip to the Taj Mahal in Agra as well. If, on the other hand, your flight from Leh is cancelled, you still have plenty of time to make it back to Delhi by road.

If you are one of the lucky few who has no need to be back home by a set date, then there's almost no end to the number of trails that can be walked and discovered in Ladakh.

Route options

Ladakh is criss-crossed by a complex network of mountain trails which, even in these days of motorised transport and roads, still provide the only link between the majority of valleys, villages and high pastures. Some of these were the highways of the centuries-old caravan trade, while others are hardly ever used except by a few shepherds each year. These provide the trekker with wonderful routes ranging from gentle undulating hikes to demanding expeditions over wild mountain passes. A wide cross-section of routes is provided in this book and these include the most popular 'classic' treks as well as less travelled routes into remote areas.

Planning your route

This section provides a brief outline of the routes described in greater detail later in this guide, which should help you plan your trek according to the amount of time you have, your ability and where your interests lie. Don't make the common mistake of trying to cram too much into too little time. You are on holiday after all, and the trip will be much more pleasurable if you allow yourself time to stop and soak up the atmosphere. The number of days it takes to walk each trek is given as a rough guide only and doesn't take into account the all-important rest days. For sample itineraries see p235; for the **Route Planning Map** see inside back cover.

The dedicated trekker can create even more routes by combining treks or exploring less frequented trails with the help of a local guide. Some of these possibilities are also outlined below.

THE MARKHA VALLEY TREK (6-10 DAYS)   pp158-178

This is Ladakh's most popular trek attracting about 60% of all trekkers. Its length, accessibility and variation of landscape have ensured its classic status. People usually take eight or nine days to complete it; doing it in less time would involve some very long days and being well-acclimatised before you start. It can be walked any time from mid-June to mid-October providing there isn't too much snow on the passes.

Direction

The trek is usually walked from west to east, beginning in either Spituk or Stok and finishing in Karu (near Hemis). This way the first two days are relatively gentle, taking you to the lowest point of the Markha Valley and making acclimatisation easier. Only consider starting at the other end if you are fit and well-acclimatised, as the steep and difficult route from Karu to the Gongmaru La takes you quickly to 5100m/16,730ft.

The route
Spituk or Stok are a short bus or taxi ride from Leh. Karu is about an hour and a half to the east of Leh and can also be reached by bus or taxi. If you are starting from the west you have two options: the most popular is to start from Spituk and ascend the Jingchan Nala; the other is to begin in the village of Stok, cross the Stok (or Namling) La (4800m/15,750ft) and then descend to Rumbak where the two trails converge. The latter involves a steep ascent and descent of the Stok La and usually takes an extra day if you're acclimatised and longer if you're not.

The trail crosses the high but gentle Ganda La (4850m/15,910ft) and descends via a magnificent gorge to the Markha Valley. The next few days are spent following the Markha River upstream, passing through small and under-populated villages until you climb to the high-altitude valley of Nimaling, where villagers graze their livestock beneath the snow covered peak of Kang Yaze. You then cross the Gongmaru La (5100m/16,730ft), which reveals views as far as the Karakoram, and descend back down to the Indus Valley.

Safety
A tent and enough food to last the whole trip are essential on this trek. During the main trekking season of July and August it's sometimes possible to supplement your supplies with chocolate, biscuits, instant noodles and cigarettes bought from the tent restaurants/shops which set up along the trail, but you can't depend on these as they are not always there.

Backpacking with over a week's food and camping equipment while walking at high altitude is only for fit and experienced trekkers. Even a French mountain guide from Chamonix, whom I once met, was finding backpacking this route extremely hard work and not very enjoyable. It makes sense to hire pack animals.

Route finding is generally easy, although it can become difficult over the passes if there's been recent snowfall. If you are travelling without pack animals (which you can hang onto or ride) take either a stick or some rope to cope with the river crossings. These are usually straightforward but demand extra care if there has been any rain.

Altitude, as always, is a problem. Whichever direction you decide to start from you have to cross a high pass to gain access to the Markha Valley. The only answer is to allow enough time in your itinerary to acclimatise before each pass. Beginning in Spituk helps because the altitude gain is not so rapid, and after crossing the Ganda La you descend to the lower end of the Markha Valley.

Pros and cons
This is one of the easiest treks to organise because of its proximity to Leh. Practically all the local pony-men and guides know the route, so finding one to suit your needs is easy. The scenery is stunning and very varied.

You pass close to two of the most regularly climbed peaks in Ladakh, Stok Kangri and Kang Yaze, and most of the trek is within the Hemis National Park which means you are likely to see some wildlife (see p245). The trek can be linked with others to make it as long as you wish: you can combine it with the Lamayuru to Alchi trek by crossing the Zanskar river at Chiling, and with the trail to Pang by continuing up the Markha River above Hankar rather than going to Nimaling. There is also much of cultural interest at Spituk, Stok and Hemis as well as some small monasteries along the route.

All this contributes to its main drawback: it can get crowded in July and August.

LIKIR TO TEMISGAM (2-4 DAYS)   pp178-184

This short, low altitude trek through historical villages is an easy intro-duction to trekking in Ladakh. It is the only trek for which a tent is not essential as guest houses are becoming established in a few of the vil-lages. It is possible to complete in two days, but taking longer would allow you to make side trips and have time to explore each village prop-erly. The best months to walk this route are May, June, September and October, when the temperatures are cooler.

Direction
It is usually walked from Likir to Temisgam (east to west) because there are guest houses in Likir but none in Temisgam. However, as far as walk-ing is concerned, there's no reason why you shouldn't go from west to east.

The route
Likir, the usual start of this trek, is a two-hour bus ride from Leh. The trail runs parallel to, but north of the Leh-Srinagar highway, passing through six relatively prosperous villages and over five low passes. It follows part of the old Leh to Khalsi road between Likir and Temisgam, which was the main pony trail along the Indus Valley before the motor road was built. You can add on a side trip to Rizong Gompa and an extra stage by extend-ing the trek to Khalsi.

Safety
This is the only trek in Ladakh where it is possible to stay overnight in rudimentary guest houses. However, this method of trekking is in its infancy and most trekkers still prefer the flexibility of camping. If you intend to trek without a tent, careful planning and a local guide who knows people you can stay with are necessary.

The shops on the trail have very limited supplies so bring enough food for the entire trip. If you are staying in someone's home you will be provided with an evening meal and breakfast. Generally this is a safe and easy walk with no large gains in altitude or dangerous river crossings but as always in the mountains you should be prepared for the worst.

Pros and cons
Its short length and low altitude (under 4000m/13,120ft) make this trek an ideal proposition for the novice trekker or for those looking for a short acclimatisation trek. With gompas at Likir, Rizong, Hemis-Shukpachu and a ruined fort at Temisgam there's plenty of cultural interest and it's a good way of seeing village life at close quarters. For those with more experience it is perfectly possible to complete this trek without the usual paraphernalia of guide, ponies and bulging rucksack. It can also be walked at any time of year making it suitable for off-season visits.

Points against it are that it can get very hot in mid-summer and it doesn't offer much in the way of dramatic mountain scenery, great adventure or solitude.

LAMAYURU TO ALCHI (4-6 DAYS)   pp184-198
High passes, rough ground and some complicated route finding make this a short but challenging trek through stunning mountain scenery. It's possible to walk in four long days but the pony-men prefer to take at least five. One commercial trekking company takes nine days over this trek so, as always, it depends very much on the individual. It can be walked from June to October as long as there isn't too much snow on the passes.

Direction
It's best to tackle this trek from west to east as this gives you longer before you have to climb your first major pass, allowing you to gain height gently. If you need further persuasion, one look at the mountain barrier behind Alchi should send you hurrying on to Lamayuru. Starting at Alchi would involve an immediate, steep climb of nearly 2000m/6560ft with no good places to camp until you're over the pass and down the other side, a minimum of 10 hours walking. In addition it is easier to find guides and pack animals in Lamayuru than in Alchi.

The route
The traditional start is Lamayuru, at least six hours from Leh by bus or truck. The first section follows the well worn trail between Lamayuru and Phanjila going over the Prinkiti La (3700m/12,140ft) and through Wanla. This is also the start of a popular route into Zanskar. From there it branches up the secluded Ripchar Valley to the Konzke La (4900m/16,080ft) and then descends to the isolated village and monastery of Sumdah-Chenmo. (It is possible to continue east into the Markha Valley from here via the Dundunchen La, crossing the Zanskar River on a cable-car at

Chiling, see p198). The route to Alchi goes down the narrow and complicated Sumdah Chu and then heads north-west to Sumdah-Choon with
its beautiful monastery perched above the village. It's a long, hard climb
over the Stakspi La (4950m/16,240ft), from which you descend to Alchi.

Safety
You will need a tent and all your food with you as there is nowhere after
Wanla where you can re-stock. You'll be thankful if you hire pack animals in Lamayuru as the two major passes involve stiff climbs of over
1000m/3280ft and the pony-man can also act as a guide on the more complicated sections. The trail can be hard to follow between Sumdah-
Chenmo and the Stakspi La.

There are several rivers to be forded and gorges to walk through so
extreme care should be taken if there is any rain.

If you plan this trek properly you can camp below 4000m/13,120ft
every night. However, much of the walking is above this and there are
two passes of almost 5000m to cross. If you should get any altitude related problems after crossing the first major pass, quick evacuation is almost
impossible, so careful acclimatisation is essential and is made easier if
you start in Lamayuru.

Pros and cons
This is a wonderful way to get between the two historical sites of
Lamayuru and Alchi. The scenery is dramatic and never dull and there are
several beautiful villages and gompas which can be visited along the
route. If all you need is pack animals and a guide, then organising the trek
yourself in Lamayuru is straightforward. However, if you want an organised trek with food, tents, guide and cook included, it is best to make
arrangements in Leh. Because it is some distance from the capital, this
trek avoids the intense visitor pressure that the Markha Valley attracts.

Although it can be strenuous and difficult at times, going with a good
guide and taking your time makes this a most rewarding trek.

LEH TO NUBRA (4-6 DAYS)   pp199-210
Now that the restrictions on visiting Nubra have been lifted, trekking
routes into this area are beginning to be discovered. This route follows a
trail often used by the inhabitants of eastern Nubra as a way of getting to
and from the markets of Leh. In the past it was used by the caravans when
the shorter trail over the Khardung La was blocked by snow: the English
explorer, William Moorcroft, followed the same route during his travels
in the early 1820s. It provides an exciting way into the area and explores
the remote and rarely visited Shyok Valley. It's a tough trek involving
rapid ascent to high altitude which is usually walkable from July to
September, depending on how much snow is on the Digar La.

Direction

The route is best walked from east to west, starting from Sabu. This direction involves less ascent and also makes organising the trek much easier. Guides and pack animals are very hard to find in Nubra so it makes more sense to arrange these in Leh.

The route

From Leh, you can either walk over the hills to Sabu (3 hours) or take a 20 minute bus ride. The route from Sabu follows the small Sabu River up through pastures then climbs steeply to the Digar La (5250m/17,230ft). From here you descend gradually to the pretty village of Digar and then down to the barren floodplain of the Shyok River. The route continues west along the river, sandwiched between the Ladakh Mountain Range to the south and the Eastern Karakoram to the north. Eventually you reach the fertile village of Rong; and it's a short climb to the Leh-Khalsar road.

Safety

You need to be completely self-sufficient as the villages you pass through have only enough for themselves. A tent is essential, as many of the camps are in exposed and remote places. The route is used mainly by locals rather than trekkers, so finding pony-men and guides who know the way can be hard. However, with time, perseverance and perhaps some help from a trekking agency, you should be able to find someone.

The main problem on this trek is the rapid altitude gain at the beginning. From Leh you go quickly up to over 5000m/16,410ft and so you need to be acclimatised to these altitudes before you embark on this trek. It's best to do an easier trek before this one or to spend a couple of nights acclimatising at Pulu before crossing the Digar La. If you get problems with the altitude you can quickly descend back to Leh. If you experience AMS on the other side of the pass (unlikely if you've acclimatised properly) then you can descend rapidly to the Shyok River at 3300m/10,830ft.

There are no difficult river crossings but some of the walking is very strenuous. The Digar La is both steep and high, whilst the Shyok Valley has long, tiring sections across sandy alluvial deposits. This latter stage can also get very hot because of the lower altitude. This is exacerbated by the shortage of places where you can find potable water. Route finding can be a bit tricky up to the Digar La but after that it is quite straightforward.

Pros and cons

It's a little travelled route through remote and challenging country passing only two small and isolated villages. On this trek you experience the harsh but majestic landscape of Nubra close up.

Trekking in Nubra is complicated by the need for a permit (see p120). Few guides or pony-men know the route well, and, since the road back to

Leh is generally only open during August, September and October, the only other way out is to trek back again. For those who are physically prepared and have the time to deal with the logistics, it's a wonderful way to experience a side of Nubra that most travellers don't see.

THE INDUS VALLEY TO THE RUPSHU (8-10 DAYS, pp210-223)

The Rupshu region in the south-east of Ladakh is the western fringe of the Chang Tang, a huge plateau that spreads hundreds of kilometres east to the province of Qinghai in China. It's an area sparsely inhabited by nomadic and semi-nomadic peoples. Their simple winter villages and tented summer encampments are the only signs of civilisation you will see. This demanding high-altitude trek through vast valleys, deep gorges and barren deserts takes a minimum of eight days. It should be possible to walk this route from June to October but this depends on how much snow is on the passes.

Direction
For logistical reasons this route is usually walked from north to south, beginning near Hemis, as the start is easily reached from Leh. If you wanted to start in the south, at Pang, there is nowhere nearby where you can arrange pack animals, guides and supplies.

The route
From Leh you take a bus, truck or taxi to Karu, which is near Hemis. The first part of the trail follows the end of the Markha Valley trek, climbing steeply to the Gongmaru La (5100m/16,730ft) and then over into the high altitude pastures of Nimaling. The scenery gets wilder as you progress south over the Zanskar Mountains via the Zalung Karpo La (5050m/16,570ft) and from here the trail stays above 4000m/13,120ft, following remote valleys and passing a few tiny winter settlements.

There are two more passes, the Yar La (4850m/15,910ft) and the Pogmar La (4800m/15,750ft), to cross before you descend to the vast plain of Kanchuthang which is often dotted with the black yak hair tents of the Changpa nomads, who come to graze their livestock on the summer pastures. The Leh-Manali road crosses this area and the trail follows it to Pang. From here you can either continue south to Manali by bus or truck, or return to Leh. This trek can be used as an interesting way out of Ladakh as it cuts out a considerable part of the road journey between Leh and Manali.

Safety
This is a long trek through isolated country. The first climb up to the Gongmaru La is probably the hardest and from then on the walking itself is not particularly difficult. The altitude and remoteness, however, make this a serious undertaking and a guide and pack animals are essential.

Almost the entire route is above 4000m/13,120ft and there is no practical way of descending to lower altitude if AMS should strike. You need to be completely self-sufficient and confident that you can cope if an emergency arose – help is a long way away. Not only are the villages deserted during the summer, but very few people travel through this area. There are a number of river crossings to be made, but as long as there hasn't been any rain they shouldn't be too difficult. The trail is often vague and sometimes non-existent and with no locals to ask for directions, a good guide is invaluable.

Finding a guide who knows this route is harder than for the more popular treks. It is often members of the Tibetan community in Leh who know this area best because of trading connections with the Chang Tang region.

Pros and cons

This is a trek for those who like wild and remote places. In this little known region of Ladakh you are unlikely to pass many other people apart from the occasional nomadic Changpa. Compared with the other treks, there is little of cultural interest along the way, apart from the tiny gompa at Dat. You walk through a landscape that combines the dramatic scenery of the Zanskar Mountains with the gentler plains of the Rupshu.

You need to be well acclimatised, equipped and experienced before you set off because of the constant high altitude and isolation. If you combine this route with the Markha Valley trek then you have a wonderful long distance trek with the added bonus that it allows time for acclimatisation. Finding guides can be a problem, but the reputable trekking agencies in Leh should be able to help you with this.

STOK KANGRI ASCENT (4 DAYS MINIMUM) pp224-225

This 6153m/20,188ft peak, which is also known as Kang La Cha, is the highest peak visible from Leh. It's an ideal introduction to Himalayan mountaineering and has been included here because in good conditions the summit is within the grasp of experienced trekkers. From the summit there are views all the way to K2 in the Karakoram.

Although the climb is technically straightforward you will need to be able to use crampons and an ice axe, and occasionally conditions will demand the use of a rope as well (see p121). In addition you will need glacier glasses and good sunblock. If the weather is on your side, it's simply a tough walk up snow slopes with short sections of scrambling. Make no mistake, though, this is the Himalaya and conditions at this altitude can deteriorate rapidly turning your ascent into a serious climb. Even in mid-summer you can sometimes get over a metre of snow, freezing winds and blizzard conditions that will wipe away any trace of your ascending footsteps. Coping with this at 6000m calls for a high level of experience.

Unfortunately mountaineering has not escaped the jaws of Indian bureaucracy. Theoretically you need to apply to the Indian Mountaineering Foundation (IMF) for a permit to climb any peak in the Indian Himalaya, whether it's a 4000m bump or 7000m giant. The cost escalates with height but not with the size of group (see p251). Heavy fines are imposed on those caught climbing without a permit.

Stok Kangri has recently been designated as one of four 'trekking peaks' within India. All that this means is that you don't need a liaison officer to accompany you, though you still require a permit. Nevertheless, some climbers get away without one each year and the general opinion in Leh is that if you are a small independent party, you are less likely to be noticed on the mountain. The main contributing factor for this permissiveness is that you can only get the permit at the IMF offices in Delhi! Don't believe anyone who says that you can get a permit in Leh, they are just after your money. Registered mountaineering guides can be hired through the trekking agencies in Leh for Rs600 per day.

OTHER POSSIBILITIES

Spituk to Stok via the Stok La (3-4 days)
This short trek follows the two alternative starts to the Markha Valley trek. From Spituk you walk up to Rumbak via Jingchan, cross the 4800m/15,750ft pass and descend to Stok. Being short and close to Leh it is easily organised and is an ideal acclimatisation trek to see how you cope with trekking at high altitude.

Treks in the restricted areas
As these areas were only opened to tourists in 1994, few trekking routes have been established yet. Trekking is complicated by the need for a permit (see p120), a maximum stay of seven days and few guides or ponymen who know these areas well. However, one or two trek operators in Leh are beginning to explore the trekking potential in Nubra and also around Tso Kar and Tso Moriri, two lakes that lie to the east of the Leh-Manali road in the area known as the Rupshu.
• **Nubra** In addition to the Leh to Nubra trek, there are various possibilities for other routes across the Ladakh Range. From Sakti cross over the Wari La, descend to Agham and follow the route described in the Leh to Nubra trek west along the Shyok River to Khalsar (5-7 days). Alternatively start to the west of Leh, either from Phyang or Basgo, then cross to Hundar and continue along the valley floor to Deskit (5-7 days).
• **Rupshu** The main limitation to treks here is that there is no public transport. You must therefore arrange for a jeep to take you, or to collect you. Possible routes are from Rumtse to Tso Kar via the Kiameri La (3-4 days) and then on to Tso Moriri (3-4 days). Or extend the Indus Valley to the Rupshu trek to Tso Kar and Tso Moriri.

Combining treks

Many of the treks in this guide can be linked to provide longer routes. One of the most obvious is to link the Lamayuru to Alchi trek with the Markha Valley trek as explained on p198. This in turn, can be combined with the route to Pang (see p210), making an interesting but demanding 11 to 15 day traverse of the Zanskar Mountains from Lamayuru in the west to Pang in the east. You can of course come down to the Indus Valley anywhere in between: Nimu, Spituk, Stok or Hemis. There are all sorts of other combinations which are only dependent on your imagination and how much time you have.

TREKKING IN ZANSKAR

Events in the summer of 1995 cast a shadow of doubt over the future of trekking in Zanskar. Having allegedly been neglected by the state government for some years the Zanskaris are now calling for greater political autonomy and the construction of a road up the Zanskar Gorge linking Padum with Leh, thereby allowing continuous winter access to Zanskar for the first time. At present road access is limited to three months of the year via Kargil and the Pensi La. Snow blocks the passes for the other nine months effectively cutting off the region from the rest of the world. To attract the attention of the state government to these demands the Zanskaris instituted a ban on tourists entering the region, to be lifted only when their demands were met. Anyone who tried to enter was turned back at the first Zanskari village they reached. The protest culminated in 17 trekkers being 'detained' in Padum for a day.

The most important issue to come out of this action was that the Zanskaris felt that they couldn't lose by targeting tourists and trekkers. Not only would they receive more publicity but they were making the fundamental point that almost all of the benefits from tourism went to outsiders. All the Zanskaris receive is loss of grazing, pollution and disturbance.

This highlights the key role trekkers play in making sure we don't destroy the very thing we have come to see. We must realise that our actions have wide ranging consequences and it's time we took more individual responsibility for them (see p139).

Unfortunately for the Zanskaris their protests seem to have had little effect. However, it's encouraging to see local people exercising their right to control what goes on in their own region. Whether similar tactics will be tried again is not known but it would be wise to check locally before visiting Zanskar and to have a back-up plan if you are denied access.

At the risk of stating the obvious, this is in no way connected to the atrocities being carried out by terrorists in the Vale of Kashmir. The protest in Zanskar is a far more peaceful affair and there have been no reports of anyone coming to any harm.

ACROSS ZANSKAR (15-21 DAYS)   pp226-233

This classic trail is two treks combined into one. The first half is from
Lamayuru to Padum (8-11 days) and the second from Padum to Darcha
(7-10 days). Despite its popularity, it is not an easy trek. There are eight
passes to cross between Lamayuru and Padum which gives this section a
reputation for being particularly difficult. The trek can be done as soon as
the passes are free of snow, from the middle of June through to October.

Direction
Each half can be walked in either direction. Pack animals and guides can
be hired in Lamayuru and Padum, and if you are starting from Darcha
then you can arrange them in Manali. If you're travelling up from Himachal Pradesh, using this trek as a way into Ladakh makes a lot of sense.
Trekking gives you more control of your rate of ascent than travelling by
bus, and ponies tend to be cheaper to hire in Manali than in Ladakh.

The route
Lamayuru is at least six hours by bus or truck from Leh. The beginning
of the trek is gentle from here to Wanla and on to Hanupatta. It then starts
getting more strenuous as the trail winds its way over the convoluted
Zanskar Mountains, passing through small villages and crossing several
passes, the highest of which is the Sengge La (5000m/16,410ft). The trail
runs parallel to the Zanskar River, finally meeting it just before the tiny
village of Hanumil. It then follows a wide flat valley to Padum past
Karsha Gompa, the largest in Zanskar.

If you want to explore off the beaten track there are a couple of alternative trails you can use instead of following the main trail all the way.
Rather than taking the trail to Wanla, you can take a more difficult route
up the Shillakong River and then over the Snigutse La (5050m/16,570ft)
to meet the main trail after Hanupatta. The second alternative leaves the
main route as you descend from the Sengge La. You then follow a
demanding trail to Padum on the east side of the Zanskar River via the
Nera La (4800m/15,740ft) and Zangla.

The second half of the trail from Padum to Darcha continues south-
east along the Tsarap River to the magnificent gompa at Phuktal. You then
have a choice of whether to take the usual route over the Shingo La
(5100m/16,730ft) to Darcha or the less frequented trail over the Phirtse
La (5450m/17,880ft) which brings you down at Sarchu Bridge on the
Manali-Leh road.

Safety
Bring a tent and all your own food because it is only possible to re-stock
at Padum. It is sensible to take pack animals with you: not only is carry-

---

(**Opposite**) Looking towards Zanskar from the Zalung Karpo La (see p211).

ing food for 10 days masochistic but the pony-man can also act as a guide, particularly necessary for the Lamayuru to Padum stretch. Zanskar's rivers are notorious for being difficult to cross so you may want to bring some rope or trekking poles.

High altitude is encountered early on whichever end you start at and evacuation from this remote area is difficult. Particular care must be taken if you're starting in Darcha (3300m/10,830ft) and have just come from Manali (2050m/6730ft) as the process of acclimatising will have only just begun. Spend a couple of days in Darcha and take it slowly up to the Shingo La.

Pros and cons
This is one of the longest treks in the region and an exciting way to travel between Leh and Manali. If you don't have the time to complete the whole route you can start or finish in Padum. You pass through a wide cross section of Himalayan cultures and scenery from Ladakh in the north to Lahaul in the south, while Zanskar itself has some fascinating villages and gompas.

Its length, plus several difficult and demanding sections, means that you need to be in pretty good physical shape before setting off. It's also a very popular trek, particularly with large commercial groups; if you're looking for solitude avoid the peak season (mid-July to mid-August).

OTHER OPTIONS IN ZANSKAR
Rangdum to Heniskot, Lamayuru or Khalsi (4-7 days)
This is a little-travelled route through remote country with some difficult sections. It's a much shorter way out of or into Zanskar than the well-travelled Lamayuru to Padum trail and may well be preferable to the tedious and uncomfortable bus journey. The best time to walk it is at the start of autumn when the streams are not so powerful but it can still be done throughout the summer providing the passes are free of snow.

For the first three days all the routes follow the same trail from Rangdum to Kanji. You then have to decide whether to drop down to the Leh-Srinagar road near Heniskot (4-5 days); continue over the Yogma La and then follow the Shillakong stream to Lamayuru (6 days); or from the Yogma La carry on over the Snigutse La to join up with the main trail to Padum. From here you can either follow this via Wanla to Lamayuru (6-7 days) or to the Leh-Srinagar road near Khalsi (6-7 days).

The route from Rangdum to Kanji initially follows the Kanji Nala to the base of the Kanji La (5-7 hours). It then follows a difficult trail through a gorge to the top of the pass (5200m/17,060ft), from which you

(**Opposite**)   **Top:** The reward of a dawn start: sunrise on the Zanskar Mountains above Sumdah-Chenmo (see p192). **Bottom:** Tea stop before the Rohtang La, Manali - Leh Highway.

descend to the Kong Nala (7-8 hours). The trail follows this stream to Kanji (3-4 hours), and from here you can reach the main highway just to the west of the Fatu La in less than 4 hours, via some stunning gorges. The small village of Heniskot is just north of the main road, while Lamayuru (see p129) is an hour's bus or truck ride to the east.

If you want to continue your trek on to Lamayuru or Khalsi from Kanji, cross the Yogma La (4700m/15,420ft) and camp by the Shillakong River (5-6 hours). You can follow this downstream, through more beautiful gorges until it joins the trail between Lamayuru and Wanla. This route involves a lot of river crossings. Alternatively, carry on east over the Snigutse La (5050m/16,570ft) and then pick up the Lamayuru to Padum trail (see p226) to Hanupatta (8-9 hours). It's another long day to Lamayuru or Khalsi from here.

Zangla to the Markha Valley via the Zhumlam (5-6, 9-11 days)

This trek takes five to six days from Zangla to the Markha Valley or nine to 11 days from Padum to the Indus Valley. Passing through uninhabited country, it has the reputation of being one of the hardest treks in the whole of Ladakh, and rightly so. Not only are there high passes to cross, but there are many complicated gorges to navigate, and over 100 stream crossings to be made. It is really only safe to attempt at the end of August or during September when the streams are at their lowest and before the winter cold sets in. If you attempted it any earlier you could get stranded in the gorges, unable to cross the raging torrents. A local guide is essential as there is a complicated section through the gorges where it would be easy to become thoroughly lost.

From Zangla you head east over the Charchar La (5000m/16,410ft) and then down through an extremely narrow gorge, where at one stage your pack animals may have to be unloaded to get through. By the time you reach Tilut Sumdo (3 days) you will already have made around 50 river crossings, but this difficult terrain continues until you reach the Markha River. You can either gain access to the Markha Valley by going over the Ruberung La (5000m/16,410ft) and then down the Char Cham Chu to Markha, or carry on over the Zalung Karpo La (5050m/16,570ft) and descend the Luntung Chu to Hankar (both 2-3 days). You are now on a well-trodden route (see p171) and can go north-west to Spituk and Stok (4-5 days) or east to Hemis (3-4 days).

Padum to Phuktal to Padum (5-7 days)

Although this looks an appealing circuit, it is in fact a very hard and dangerous trek. Between Tantak gompa and Phuktal it is impossible to use pack animals as the route passes through narrow gorges with numerous river crossings. A guide is essential.

From Padum go north-east to Thongde and from there head south-east over the Thongde La (5150m/16,900ft) to Shade, which is up a side valley to the north (3 days). (There's a rarely travelled route leading north from here that takes you to Zangla). Having returned to the main valley, continue south-east past the tiny gompa of Tantak and then swing south to the Tsarap River which you follow to Phuktal. From Phuktal follow the main route back to Padum.

Alternatively, there's another remote route that leads from Tantak in a south-easterly direction and eventually meets the Leh-Manali road. The route goes via Murshun and Yurshun but is not suitable for pack animals as there are rope bridges to cross and a long cliff face path to negotiate.

Padum to Zangla to Padum (3-4 days)
This is an easy trek around the principal villages of central Zanskar. It is quite possible to walk this route without camping equipment by staying in village guest houses or with villagers. The route basically goes up one side of the Zanskar river and comes back the other via Thongde, Zangla and Karsha. For route details see the Lamayuru to Padum trek (p226).

The Chaddar/Ice Path (5-8 days)
During the middle of winter, when the passes are blocked by snow, the only way in and out of Zanskar is along the frozen Zanskar River, between Nimu and Padum. This is a very difficult and dangerous journey for which you must be physically and mentally prepared. Temperatures regularly drop below minus 30°C at night and the solidity of the ice can change rapidly. You need to be flexible with your time so that you can wait for the best conditions and should be aware that if the ice melts you could get stranded in Zanskar until the passes open in late spring.

Animals cannot travel on the ice so all your supplies have to be carried. You must be completely self-sufficient as the villagers will not be able to spare any of their food which only just sees them through the winter. The route is possible only when the river is at its coldest, this is for about 6 weeks during January and February. During this time quite a few locals make the journey so it shouldn't be too difficult to find someone who will act as your guide either in Leh or Nimu. Don't attempt this without a local companion.

What to take

Keep it light
How much you take with you is a very personal decision. Some trekkers love to travel as light as the locals (rarely more than a shoulder bag), while others are only happy when they have countless bits of equipment for every possible occurrence, most of which they'll never use. It takes experience to know what you'll find useful but if you are in doubt about

anything on your list, then be ruthless and leave it at home. Even if you are planning to hire ponies for your trek, you've still got to get your luggage to Ladakh. You'll find that you'll be much freer with a light pack as it allows you to wander easily around towns or to jump on a bus with the minimum of fuss. If you are going on an organised trek with a company from your home country, you'll be given an exhaustive equipment list when you book. How much you take is not so important since taxis or mini buses will be arranged to get you around.

Buying gear

Equipping yourself for a trek can cost a considerable amount of money and if you don't really know what you are looking for, you can make expensive mistakes. Mail order catalogues are an excellent way of getting an idea of what's on the market and how much it will cost (in the UK try Field and Trek ☎ 01277-233122; Cotswold ☎ 01285-643434; Taunton Leisure ☎ 01823-331875). However, there is no substitute for a really knowledgeable mountaineering shop where all your questions can be answered and you can see the items. If this trek is not a one-off then it's usually a false economy to go for the cheapest products. Stick to respected and well-known manufacturers and use price as a reasonably reliable guide to quality, although you should be careful not to buy something packed full of features that you are unlikely ever to need – they simply add cost and weight.

How to carry it

Backpackers will obviously need a **large rucksack** (65-80 litres capacity) in which to carry all their camping gear and food. This should have a stiffened back system and be fully adjustable for a perfect fit. The idea is to have the load high and close to the body with a large proportion of the weight carried on the hips by means of a padded hip belt. It's also handy to have a **bum/waist bag** or a light day-pack in which you can carry your camera, guidebook etc when you're sightseeing.

If you will be hiring ponies or going on an organised trek a **large hold-all** will do the job just as well as a rucksack when you are trekking but it's not quite as convenient for carrying your luggage around town or to the start of the trek. You'll also need a **day-pack** for carrying the things you need with you throughout the day, such as your camera, a water bottle, some food, waterproofs and a fleece or jumper. All this takes up quite a lot of room, so a day-pack of 30-40 litres will probably be about right.

Pack similar things (such as clothes, washing things, camping equipment) in separate **stuff-sacks** so that they are easier to pull out of the dark recesses of your rucksack. All of these can be put inside a **waterproof rucksack liner**, or tough plastic bag, which then slips inside your pack. Everything will then be well protected from rain or leaking kerosene, a hazard of Asian bus travel.

Footwear and foot care

• **Boots** Your boots are probably the single most important item of gear that can affect the enjoyment of your trek. Most of the trails in Ladakh involve crossing fairly rough and steep ground from time to time. You should therefore look for a boot which provides good ankle support, has a reasonably stiff sole, has an upper which is substantial enough to provide protection from knocks, and is waterproof enough for crossing shallow streamlets and walking through late lying snow on high passes. If you are carrying your own pack you will need even more support.

Leather boots are generally more supportive, offer greater protection, are more reliably water resistant (if regularly treated), and will last longer than Gore-tex or Sympatex fabric boots. However, the latter will be instantly comfortable, lighter and require less 'walking in' – the choice really depends on where your priorities lie. Whatever the material of the upper, you should have few problems if you choose a well made, three-season hill-walking boot from a respected company.

The most important thing is to make sure they fit properly. When fitting boots, try lots of different makes and models, and wear the same socks as you would when walking. Make sure you have enough room in front of your toes (so that they don't keep hitting the end when you descend a steep slope), by pushing your foot forward in the boot before lacing up and checking that you can easily slide a finger down between your heel and the back of the boot. Then slide your foot to the back, lace them up and pace around the shop to get a feel of what they are like in action. If your heel lifts off then they are too loose but if you feel pressure points they may be too tight. Before assuming they are the wrong size, try lacing them up in a different way first. Once you've bought them, wear them in thoroughly before trekking; this is very important.

• **Insoles** Good quality boots either have a dual density sole or a shock absorbing insert in the heel to reduce the effects of jarring with each step. However, Sorbothane insoles can be bought to reduce the shock even more and can be useful for taking up any excess room in the boot.

• **Socks** The traditional wearing of a thin liner sock under a thicker wool sock is no longer necessary if you choose a high quality modern sock specifically designed for walking. The ones with thick spongy pads around the ball and heel of the foot, such as those made by Thor-Lo, are particularly comfortable. Three pairs are ample.

• **Extra footwear** If you're hiring pack-animals you can afford the extra weight of a pair of sports sandals. These are invaluable for crossing the countless streams you will come across and are good for lounging around camp. It also means you have an alternative to wearing your hiking boots in Delhi and Leh. Lightweight trainers are a good substitute.

• **Foot care** Keeping your feet dry and clean is the best way to keep them healthy and blister-free. When you stop for lunch, take off your boots and socks and pull the footbeds out of the boots so you can let everything dry in the sun. Washing your feet every evening will prevent any nasty flora growing, so will keeping your socks reasonably clean. (See p242 for information on how to deal with blisters).

Clothes

There has been a revolution in outdoor clothing over the last decade or so (in technology as well as in fashion) and finding an outfit than can cope with the wide range of conditions that you can expect in Ladakh (see p94) is easy and doesn't have to weigh a ton. Most trekkers pick their clothes according to the versatile layering system, which consists of a base layer to transport sweat away from your skin; a mid-layer or two to keep you warm; and an outer layer or 'shell' to protect you from the wind, rain and snow.

You must take care to wear clothes that don't offend the local people, see p139 for further guidance.

• **Base layer** This is the least exciting layer but is important if you want the system to work well. Too much moisture next to the skin is not only uncomfortable, but can rapidly cool your body, making you feel cold. A cotton T-shirt, for instance, will absorb your sweat and trap it next to your skin. A thin thermal layer made from a synthetic material, on the other hand, will draw that moisture away and keep you dry. A thin and light-weight **thermal top** can therefore keep you cool and dry when worn on its own, (modern designs are now styled with this in mind), or warm and dry when worn under other clothes. The other major advantages are that the material still feels warm when wet and it dries extremely quickly. This means that you can wash it often and let it dry on you if the weather is reasonably warm. Buy one with long arms and a collar if at all possible, as this will help keep the sun off. As this shirt will be worn all day every day it's nice to have something clean to put on in the evenings. Another thin thermal is ideal, but if your budget doesn't run to that, then a light **cotton shirt** or T-shirt is useful.

• **Mid-layers** These layers provide the insulation and so anything that is warm will do. From July to late August a medium thickness woollen jumper, or a **mid-weight fleece top**, along with another thinner layer (a thin jumper or a **lightweight fleece top**) will suffice. If you really feel the cold or will be trekking at other times in the year, substitute the thinner of these layers with a **down jacket**. These are expensive, but provide unbeatable warmth for very little weight. They are wonderful in the cold evenings and can substantially boost the warmth of your sleeping bag. A cheaper and less effective alternative is a fibre pile jacket or pullover.

• **Outer layer** This is the final layer between you and the elements and so must be capable of keeping out the wind, rain and snow. The emphasis nowadays is on **jackets** made from waterproof, windproof and breathable fabrics (such as Gore-Tex, Aqua Dry, Triplepoint Ceramic etc), which prevent the build up of condensation on the inside of the jacket. However, as this technology doesn't come cheap (£150/US$225 or more) and since it's unlikely to rain that much when you're in Ladakh, a cheaper neoprene or polyurethane coated nylon jacket will suffice.

If you go for the latter option then consider bringing a **windproof top** (made from Pertex or a similar fabric) as well, as these are highly breathable while keeping out the wind and protecting you from a light shower. They weigh next to nothing, take up hardly any room and can also be used as a rather inefficient but adequate towel. Many trekkers swear by an umbrella or poncho but as both become worse than useless in a high wind with driving rain or snow, their value in high mountains is limited.

• **Leg wear** It can get quite chilly at night and at high altitude, so a pair of thermal **longjohns** or thick tights is pretty much essential. Cotton **trousers** and skirts are easily bought or made up for you in India and are great for trekking. Poly-cotton trousers, as made popular by Rohan, are even better as they are extremely light, hard wearing, relatively windproof and dry very quickly. Jeans are not so good as they take ages to dry.

Many women find long **skirts** useful, as they are more culturally acceptable than trousers. They also have the advantage that they can double as a 'port-a-loo' when there aren't any bushes to crouch behind.

A lightweight pair of **waterproof over-trousers** can help keep you warm as well as dry but is not vital, particularly if you've got quick drying poly-cotton trousers.

• **Other clothes** A **sunhat** that protects the back as well as the front of your head and **sunglasses** which offer 100% UV protection are necessary to combat the strong sunlight during the day (glacier glasses with side protection flaps are useful when there's a lot of snow around). A warm **woolly hat** and a pair of warm mittens or **gloves** are welcome accessories for the cold evenings and cooler days. If you are prone to bathing in freezing streams bring a **swimsuit** – you must never swim or wash in the nude. **Towels** never dry when trekking and soon start to smell awful. Many trekkers find that a tea-towel, light sarong or even an item of clothing is just as handy and takes up far less room in your pack. A large **handkerchief** or bandanna has many uses from mopping your brow to keeping the sun off your neck. Don't forget your **underwear**! Three pairs are fine.

Sleeping bag
A good quality sleeping bag is indispensable as many guest houses don't have blankets and the ones for hire in Leh are usually dirty and lacking in

insulation. The temperatures plummet at night, even in Leh, so your bag should be warm. A three-season bag is fine for July and August, but if you are trekking before or after this you will find a four-season bag preferable, unless you have an excellent circulation. Any bag can be upgraded simply and cheaply by wearing more clothes when you're in it.

Down filled bags are far superior to synthetic ones, because for the same warmth, a down bag will pack down smaller, will be much lighter and although it's initially more expensive will far outlast a synthetic bag. Their only drawback is that they lose most of their insulating properties when wet and take an age to dry; keep yours in a sealed plastic bag.

A cotton, silk or synthetic sleeping bag **liner** helps keep the bag clean and is useful on its own for Delhi's hot and humid nights.

Toiletries

On seeing the contents of many trekkers' rucksacks, you could be forgiven for thinking you were looking at a travelling pharmacist, rather than a lover of the great outdoors getting back to the simple things in life. Most toiletries (soap, shampoo, toothbrushes, toothpaste, loo paper, razors, sanitary towels and washing powder) can be bought in Delhi and Leh, so there is no need to worry about how much you need. A small amount of what you usually use should be ample: one bar of **soap** in a plastic container (or film canister); a few sachets of **shampoo**; a small tube of **toothpaste** and a **toothbrush**; one roll of **loo paper** in a plastic bag, along with a **lighter** for burning after use (if the left-hand-and-water method does not appeal); a **razor** and a tiny bottle of **shaving oil** is much more compact than foam; **deodorant**; **tampons/sanitary towels**, bring plenty of your own as the local brands are antiquated; good quality **aftersun** and **lip balm** to combat the drying effect of the sun and dry air; a high factor **sun screen** or **sun block** is vital and should be liberally applied at high altitude (it's hard to find in India so bring enough); and finally **condoms/contraceptive pills**.

Medical kit

Deciding what to include in a medical kit for remote areas is never easy and no two people will agree. If you don't have much experience in this area have a look at a good book on the subject (see p45) or talk to an expert. The problems you're most likely to encounter are discussed in the health section on p236. The list below should be seen as a basic kit to which you may want to add.

If you're trekking with an organised group the company will probably have their own extensive medical kit. Check to see what it includes in case you want to bring along any extra items.

• **First aid** Ready-made **first aid kits** for outdoor activities are a sensible investment, as they solve the problem of deliberating about what to take and should include detailed and clear instructions on how to cope with the most common emergencies. If you want to make up your own, then it should include **plasters/Band-Aids** for minor cuts; **moleskin** or **Second Skin** for blisters; **bandages** for holding dressings, splints and limbs in place, and for supporting a sprained ankle or a weak knee; various-sized **sterile dressings** for wounds; **non-adherent dressings** for burns; porous **adhesive tape**; **antiseptic wipes**; **antiseptic** cream, liquid or spray; **safety pins**; **tweezers**; **scissors**; and a **thermometer**.

• **Pills and potions** Bring **paracetamol** or **aspirin** for treating mild to moderate pain; **loperamide** (Imodium) for emergency relief of diarrhoea; *ciprofloxacin* and *metronidazole* for treating diarrhoea; *acetazolamide* (Diamox) for altitude sickness; and a broad-spectrum antibiotic such as *co-trimoxazole* for urinary tract, skin, sinus and throat infections. Don't forget your **anti-malarial** tablets and bring along a small amount of **insect repellent** to keep the mosquitoes away while you are in Delhi (the best available contains a high percentage of diethyl-toluamide – DEET). Some travellers like to bring **multi-vitamin tablets**, particularly if they fear they won't be eating healthily for a while; and **oral rehydration powder** can be useful if you become dehydrated.

Note that the drugs in italics need a doctor's prescription in the UK and USA. All these drugs are available in Delhi and you can usually buy the antibiotics in Leh. They are available without a prescription and are much cheaper than in the West. However, you should be warned that counterfeit drugs are not uncommon in India and it's therefore much safer to buy them in the West before you leave. Wherever you decide to buy them, you should have discussed your requirements with your doctor first, as these drugs have side effects and can be dangerous if taken by some individuals.

• **Aids avoidance kit** Important for anyone travelling to developing countries, the kit should be carried with you at all times to reduce the risk of your contracting blood-borne diseases. It contains syringes, needles and suture material and is designed to be given to a qualified person looking after you in an emergency. The kits are sold by travel clinics and some pharmacies in the West.

• **Water purification kit** No water in India can be considered safe to drink unless you have purified it yourself. The various methods are described on p236 and you should choose whichever appeals the most. None of these treatments is available in Leh, so make sure you bring enough plus some extra in case of breakage or loss.

General items
Other essential items include a litre **water bottle** (see camping gear below); a watch with an **alarm** for catching those early buses; a

torch/flashlight, the head torches made by Petzl are the most convenient as your hands are left free (don't forget a spare battery and bulb, as Indian batteries are next to useless and tend to only come in AA and C sizes); a longlife **candle** (but take extreme care if using it in your tent – put it in a saucepan so that it won't set the tent alight if knocked over, keep a bottle of water and an open penknife handy so you can cut your way out of the tent if it does go up in flames); **matches** or a reliable **lighter**; spare **boot laces** or a length of **cord**; a **sewing kit**; a small **padlock** for locking your room with the knowledge that you are the only one with the key, and for safeguarding your luggage on buses; a **compass** for following some of the directions in this guide and for exploring off the beaten track; and a Swiss Army **penknife** which will become your friend for life.

There are lots of other odds and ends that some people find indispensable and others totally useless: a **Frisbee** is a good way to integrate with the local kids and can also be used as a plate; **ski/trekking** poles (which can usually be hired in Leh, see p121) can significantly decrease the stress on joints and the spine, especially if you are carrying your own pack (one manufacturer calculates a 250 ton reduction in an eight-hour hike), and they can also help you power over those high passes – whether you use one or a pair is up to you; some people find an **umbrella** useful as it can be used to protect you against rain, wind, sun and fierce dogs, or as a walking stick; a **collapsible bucket** is convenient for washing clothes and yourself in the mountains without polluting streams; writing a **diary** is the best way for keeping memories fresh; a paperback **book** will help you wile away the time on long bus journeys, as will pocket **games** or a pack of **cards**; and lastly, an **altimeter** is a fun, if expensive, way to disprove the heights I calculated for this book!

Photographic equipment

Modern compact cameras are the answer for those who don't want to fuss with all the paraphernalia of an SLR or be lumbered with its weight. Those taking an SLR will have to keep their equipment to a minimum to keep the weight down. Whatever your camera, treat it to a padded carrying case so that it is protected from all the knocks it will inevitably get. Bring a spare set of batteries as they are hard to come by in India. Lens tissues and a brush are vital in Ladakh's dusty and dry atmosphere and a polarising filter can be useful in the bright light. Slide and print film can sometimes be found in Leh, but as you have no idea how they have been treated it is better to bring all you need from home. Airport X-ray machines are generally considered safe in the West, but you should be more cautious in India. The airport officials are usually prepared to check film by hand and it's worth packing the canisters in a clear plastic bag so that they can see the contents. You could even consider leaving your camera at home – you'd be surprised how liberating it can be.

Camping gear

It's possible to arrive in Leh without any camping equipment and make do with what's available there (see p151). However, if you've got good equipment already, then definitely bring it along with you, as it will perform far better than anything you can obtain in Leh.

• **Tent** As rain or light snow is quite possible, some kind of shelter is necessary. A few ultra-lightweight trekkers make do with a Gore-Tex bivi bag or a basha (a waterproof sheet that can be used to rig up a make-shift shelter), but a tent provides much more privacy, comfort and safety, and as most people hire ponies, weight is not of utmost importance. A three-season tent is fine for Ladakh as heavy snowfall is very rare.

• **Sleeping mat** This is essential. Not only will it make sleep more comfortable but it'll also insulate you from the cold ground. Closed-cell foam mats are fine, but for the ultimate in five-star luxury try a Thermarest self-inflating pad.

• **Cooking equipment** If you are hiring a cook then there's no need for this equipment, as he will either have his own, or you can buy it cheaply in the bazaar if he doesn't.

It is almost impossible to buy gas canisters in Leh or Delhi so you are reliant on either **kerosene** or **petrol** for fuel. As both fuels are dirty and of low quality, you need a **stove** which can be easily cleaned and is fully maintainable in the field. One of the best on the market, which has proved its worth over the years is MSR's XGK stove. Take along a **maintenance kit**, a small **funnel** for filling up the fuel bottle and some coffee **filter papers** for filtering the fuel (also useful for getting rid of sediment in river water). Buy good quality **fuel** and **water bottles**, cheap ones tend to leak. Aluminium bottles made by Sigg and MSR are the best. Filled with boiling water at night (with a sock over the bottle to prevent burns) you'll have a hot water bottle plus ready-made drinking water in the morning.

Unless you enjoy knocking up cordon bleu meals in the wilds, one **pan** and one **frying pan** that can double as a lid/plate is fine for two people. You'll also need a **mug**, **spoon** (more useful than a fork), **pan handle**, and a **wire scrubber** for the washing up (there's no need for washing up liquid). Also bring along lots of **plastic food/freezer bags** for dividing up and storing your food and some little **plastic bottles**, as made by Nalgene, which are excellent for storing things like coffee, tea bags, sugar, jam, cooking oil and peanut butter.

Mountaineering equipment

If you are planning to climb Stok Kangri you can equip yourself in Leh. Serviceable ice axes, rope and articulated crampons (make sure your boots are stiff enough to accept them) are all available; but if you need anything more specialised for harder climbs, bring your own.

Money and documents

Travellers' cheques are the best way to carry your money as they are much safer than cash and you get a better rate of exchange in the banks. Buy cheques from a well-known company such as Thomas Cook or American Express in either US dollars or pounds sterling, as other currencies can be hard to change outside big cities. It's sometimes worth having cheques from two different companies as some banks don't accept some makes of cheque (for instance, the bank in Manali won't change Visa travellers' cheques).

A **credit card** can be useful in Delhi and for buying souvenirs elsewhere but there is nowhere in Leh to get cash advances on cards.

Keep your **passport** with you at all times as there are several army and police checkpoints along the major roads and close to any border areas. If you are considering driving or riding a motorbike then bring an **international driving licence**.

All these things can be kept reasonably safe in a **money belt**, or a pouch that goes around your neck. You should, however, make photocopies of any important documents in case you do lose them.

FINDING OUT MORE

Books

• **Guidebooks** Lonely Planet's new guide to the region, *Indian Himalaya – a travel survival kit*, should be out soon, replacing their *Kashmir, Ladakh and Zanskar*. The best general guides to the whole of India are Lonely Planet's *India – a travel survival kit* and Rough Guides' *India*. For seeing the potential for trekking throughout the Himalaya you should get hold of Hugh Swift's wonderfully anecdotal *Trekking in Pakistan and India*, or Lonely Planet's *Trekking in the Indian Himalaya*. Two guidebooks published by Artou are *Hiking in Zanskar and Ladakh* by Chabloz and Cremieu, which contains 13 separate treks throughout the region written on individual pull-out sheets, and *Ladakh, Zanskar* by Charles Genoud, which is a good introduction to the region. Both of these books can usually be bought in Leh if you have difficulty finding them in the West.

• **Flora and fauna** The only guide directly relevant to the area is *The Wildlife of Ladakh* by JN Ganhar which you are unlikely to find outside India. Ornithologists will find the various books by Salim Ali useful (*Indian Hill Birds; A Pictorial Guide to the Birds of the Indian Sub-continent*; and *Field Guide to the Birds of the Eastern Himalayas*), or Charles Vaurie's *Tibet and its Birds. The Book of Indian Animals* by SH Prater is good for identifying mammals, as are *Mountain Monarchs – Wild Sheep and Goats of the Himalaya*, and *Stones of Silence*, both by GB Schaller.

The best book for the botanist is *Concise Flowers of the Himalaya* by Oleg Polunin and Adam Stainton.

• **Phrasebooks** *Getting Started in Ladakhi* by Rebecca Norman is the best introduction to the language and is widely available in Leh. Those wanting to delve deeper may like to try the *Ladakhi – English/English-Ladakhi dictionary* by Helena Norberg-Hodge and Gyelong Thupstan Paldan, which again is available in Leh or from the Ladakh Project (see below). Lonely Planet's *Hindi/Urdu phrasebook* is very useful for the rest of India.

• **Medical books** Trekking in Ladakh can take you a long way from medical help and although only large scale expeditions can afford to take extensive medical supplies, even the lightweight backpacker can carry a book which will help diagnose the more common medical emergencies. One of the best self-help books on the subject is *Medicine for Mountaineering and Other Wilderness Activities* by James Wilkerson. At half a kg it's a little on the heavy side for the backpacker but that's not much of a price to pay for peace of mind. *Travellers' Health – How to stay healthy abroad* by Richard Dawood, is a useful book to read before you go, but its self-help advice doesn't really go deep enough for use on the trail. An excellent little book that takes up hardly any room in your pack is Stephen Bezruchka's *Altitude Illness – Prevention and Treatment*, which makes diagnosing this potentially lethal sickness relatively easy.

• **Other books** One of the most readable and informative books on Ladakh's history and culture is Janet Rizvi's *Ladakh – Crossroads of High Asia*, but if you are after a really in-depth guide to the main monasteries in Ladakh and Zanskar get hold of *The Cultural Heritage of Ladakh* by David Snellgrove and Tadeusz Skorupski.

Another important book is *Ancient Futures – learning from Ladakh*. This is written by the founder of the Ladakh Project (see below), Helena Norberg-Hodge, who describes how traditional Ladakhi culture is being changed by modernisation, while using the example of Ladakh to challenge the Western notion of development.

One of the best known travel books to the region is *A Journey in Ladakh* by Andrew Harvey, which is as much about the author's spiritual journey as it is about his travels. *Zanskar – the hidden kingdom* by Michel Peissel, describes a trek the

> **The Ladakh Project**
> The Ladakh Project (☎ 0117-973 1575, fax 0117-974 4853, 21 Victoria Sq, Clifton, Bristol BS8 4ES, UK; or ☎ /fax 510-527 3873, PO Box 9475, Berkeley, CA 94709, USA) is a small international organisation interested in sustainable and equitable ways of living with particular reference to Ladakh, which works closely with the Ladakh Ecological Development Group in Leh (p000). It publishes a newsletter and sells books, cassettes and videos with a similar theme.

author made through the region soon after Zanskar was opened to foreigners in the mid 70s. *Nomads of Western Tibet – the survival of a way of life* by Melvyn Goldstein and Cynthia Beall is a fascinating book on the lifestyle of the Chang Tang nomads and much of the information, as well as many of the superb photographs, are in their article in *National Geographic* (June 1989).

William Moorcroft and George Trebeck's *Travels in the Himalayan Provinces of Hindustan and the Panjab* is the classic account of what Ladakh was like in the early 19th century, while *Himalayan Tibet and Ladakh* by A. Reeve Heber and Kathleen Heber, *The Himalayan Letters of Gypsy Davy and Lady Ba* by Robert and Katherine Barrett, and *Peaks and Lamas* by Marco Pallis are all interesting accounts of treks at the beginning of the 20th century.

There are several coffee-table books full of wonderful photographs of the region, most of which you can buy in Delhi or Leh. Olivier Follmi's photographs are hard to beat and he has several books on the region. *Zanskar – a Himalayan Kingdom* is the most widely available.

Maps

The largest scale maps available for Ladakh are the Leomann Trekking Maps at a scale of 1:200,000. They include brief trekking information on the reverse side, mark the principal trekking routes and name most of the mountains, but they are not entirely accurate with trails or the position of villages. The relevant sheets are: Sheet 2 – *Kargil, Zanskar and Nun Kun Area*; Sheet 3 – *Nubra Valley, Leh and Zanskar Area*; and Sheet 5 – *Kulu Valley, Parbati Valley and Central Lahaul*.

For navigation purposes the US Army Map Service series U502 (1:250,000) are by far the best. They are not entirely accurate either and are certainly very out of date with many of the new roads not marked, but the contours give you a better feel for the land, and most villages, trails and rivers are accurately marked. Most of the treks are included on sheets NI 43-8 *Leh* and NI 43-12 *Martselang*, but you may also need NI 43-11 *Anantnag* and NI 43-7 *Kargil* for western Zanskar, and possibly NI 43-16 *Palampur* for the southern end of the 'Across Zanskar' trek. Sheets NI 44-9 *Pangong Tso* and NI 44-13 *Tso Morari* could be useful if you wanted to explore these two lakes. A few of the maps in this series are currently out of print, but it is sometimes possible to obtain photocopies of these from a specialist map library. In the UK try the Royal Geographical Society (☎ 0171-589 5466) 1 Kensington Gore, London SW7 2AR.

Artou publish a good overview map, *Ladakh – Zanskar* (1:350,000), which covers the most popular treks and some less known routes.

If your local travel bookshop can't get hold of any of these maps try Stanfords in London (☎ 0171-836 1321, fax 0171-836 0189), who have a mail order facility.

India tourist offices
The Government of India's foreign tourist offices are good for general background information and glossy brochures: **Australia** (☎ 02-232 1600) Level 1, 17 Castlereagh St, Sydney, NSW 2000; **Canada** (☎ 416-962 3787) 60 Bloor St West, Suite 1003, Toronto, Ontario M4W 3B8; **France** (☎ 01-42 65 83 86) 8 boulevard de la Madeleine, 75009 Paris; **Germany** (☎ 069-23 5423) Baseler Str 48, 60329, Frankfurt-am-Main 1; **Italy** (☎ 02-80 4952) 9 Via Albricci, Milan 20122; **Netherlands** (☎ 020-620 8991) Rokin 9-15, 1012 KK, Amsterdam; **Spain** (☎ 91-345 7339) Avenida PIO XII 30-32, Madrid 28016; **Sweden** (☎ 08-21 5081) Sveavagen 9-11, S-III 57, Stockholm 11157; **Switzerland** (☎ 022-732 1813) 1-3 Rue de Chantepoulet, 1201 Geneva; **UK** (☎ 0181-812 0929) 7 Cork St, London W1X 2LN; **USA** (☎ 212-586 4901) 30 Rockefeller Plaza, 15 North Mezzanine, New York; (☎ 213-380 8855) 3550 Wiltshire Blvd, Suite 204, Los Angeles.

Health precautions and inoculations

Travelling to Ladakh does not necessarily involve any greater risk to your health than life in the West, but many of the risks that you may be exposed to will be different from those you are used to dealing with. Most risks are totally avoidable – it's simply a matter of learning what they are and taking the relevant precautions.

WHO SHOULD AVOID HIGH ALTITUDE TREKS?

Travel to Ladakh demands a little more respect than many other high altitude destinations because the whole region is considerably higher to start with (all above 2600m/8860ft). Therefore there is no way of reaching lower altitudes without going over a high pass first. In addition to this, when you are on your trek, you will almost certainly be several days away from the nearest hospital (Leh). People in reasonably good health should not get alarmed by this but the altitude and lack of medical facilities can create problems for certain groups. If you have a medical condition such as high blood pressure, heart or lung disease, before going you should get the advice of a doctor who is familiar with the effects of altitude.

Infants and young children are more likely to be susceptible to altitude than adults and it is usually recommended that if they are to go above 3000m or 10,000ft, there should be a means of getting them rapidly and easily to lower altitude if the need arises. As this is not possible anywhere in Ladakh it is best to find a more suitable destination. Teenagers are also more at risk than adults and should allow a few extra days for acclimatisation.

People on specialist medication should check with their doctor before travelling to altitude. Probably the greatest risk is not being able to replace your medication should you lose it or run out. If you have got any niggling complaints that are worrying you, then get them examined by a doctor before you go, if only to put your mind at rest. The effects of altitude on pregnancy are not known, but if you are at all concerned it is better not to go.

PRE-TREK PREPARATIONS
Getting fit – before or during your trek?
Being fit will not lessen your chances of getting altitude sickness, in fact it may well increase the risk as fitter people are more likely to climb higher and faster than those who aren't so well prepared. Having said that, you will enjoy your trek far more if you are in good physical shape. Walking for up to seven hours a day each day is demanding anywhere in the world but in high mountains it is even more so. Anyone going trekking in Ladakh will greatly benefit from an exercise programme starting about three months before you go. If you are used to a sedentary life, then start gently, build up gradually and try to get out every other day for at least 20 minutes. Any exercise will do, swimming, jogging, aerobics, cycling are all good, but the best of all is to go for long walks in hilly country.

Plenty of people go trekking with no physical preparation at all, but if you spend your whole holiday in agony you've only yourself to blame. If your body is used to a bit of exercise before you leave, you can build on this throughout the trek and come home feeling wonderfully fit and healthy.

Visit your dentist
Few people think about their teeth before going away, but as dental care in Ladakh is rudimentary and dental problems can develop because of the altitude (the lower pressure can cause air in cavities to expand), you would be well advised to get a check up before you leave. Allow enough time for any treatment that may be necessary.

INOCULATIONS

Officially you do not need any inoculations before entering India unless you have just come from a country where yellow fever is endemic (Africa and South America). You would be very unwise, however, not to get yourself vaccinated against some of the diseases listed below.

Up-to-date information on what the recommended vaccinations are for Delhi and Ladakh is best got from specialist travel clinics who are usually better informed than your local doctor. As they keep most vacci-nations in stock they can provide on-the-spot inoculations. **British Airways** have travel clinics throughout the UK (phone 0800-600 900 for the nearest), or try **Trailfinders** in London (☎ 0171-938 3999, 194 Kensington High St). Prices vary, so shop around and compare the prices of travel clinics to your local doctor's surgery.

As some inoculations cannot be given at the same time and others need boosters to be fully effective, you should start making enquiries about two months before you leave. Make sure the inoculations are recorded in a booklet which you should be given at the time.

• **Hepatitis A** This is prevalent in areas of poor hygiene and it is essential that you are vaccinated against it. The newer vaccine, Havrix, gives long term immunity (up to 10 years) and is less painful than the gamma-glob-ulin injection, but it is more expensive and requires two initial injections and a booster a year later. Gamma-globulin should be given as close to the departure date as possible and will last for two to six months depend-ing on the size of dose.
• **Typhoid** This disease is caught from contaminated food and water and is prevalent in India. Vaccination is highly recommended.
• **Meningitis** Epidemics of this disease regularly break out in India and so vaccination is recommended.
• **Tetanus-Diphtheria** A low dose diphtheria vaccine is now available combined with tetanus. You should check that your protection against both of these easily preventable diseases is up-to-date. You may need a booster before you travel.
• **Polio** Boosters are recommended every 10 years so check your records.
• **Rabies** There is a minimal risk of being bitten by a rabid animal and you may wish to consider the vaccination, particularly if you are going for a long time. The course of three injections is expensive and you will still need a course of follow-up injections should you get bitten.
• **Cholera** The vaccination only gives limited protection and is not nec-essary unless you are travelling on to a country which demands evidence of vaccination on entry.

Malaria prophylaxis
This serious and potentially fatal disease is caused by a parasite that is transmitted to humans by the bite of an infected *Anopheles* mosquito. Malaria transmission does not take place above 2000m or 6500ft, so Manali and Ladakh are theoretically safe. Unfortunately, malaria is prevalent in Delhi and lowland India, so you will be exposed to the risk while you travel to Ladakh. Delhi airport, in particular, is noted for its clouds of mosquitoes.

Anti-malarial drugs are a sensible precaution against the disease. The drug of choice for different areas changes as the parasite becomes resistant to the drugs, so you should check which is being recommended before you leave. It is essential that you begin taking the drugs one week before entering a malarial zone and for four weeks after leaving it. It's therefore highly likely that you will have to continue taking the drug throughout your stay in Ladakh, in order to ensure that you are still protected when you go back to the lowlands. As the drugs can cause nausea they are best taken last thing at night.

Anti-malarials are not 100% effective, so it is vital that you take adequate precautions to stop yourself from being bitten. The *Anopheles* mosquito is active only between dusk and dawn, so you should cover up as much of your body as possible during those times and use a powerful insect repellent on any exposed skin.

TRAVEL AND HEALTH INSURANCE

Trekkers should seriously consider a combined travel/health insurance cover. Some companies rate trekking in the Himalaya as a hazardous sport which will mean you won't be covered if you haven't paid an extra premium, so check this before you part with your money. Also ensure that you are covered for emergency helicopter evacuation. The military helicopters which operate emergency airlifts won't leave the ground unless they are guaranteed payment of their operational costs (see p245). In view of this, it is also wise to register with your embassy in Delhi as they will often be contacted to see if anyone will cover the cost.

For further health information, see p236.

Warning

Owing to continued militant activity, it is advised that you do not visit **Kashmir** – in other words, anywhere west of the Zoji La, Ladakh's western boundary. In recent years foreigners have been involved in kidnappings, robbery and murder. In 1994 two Britons were kidnapped in the Vale of Kashmir, while an American tourist was shot dead in Srinagar and then in 1995 five Western trekkers were kidnapped and a Norwegian member of the group was subsequently executed. Frequent demonstrations and bomb blasts in Srinagar and Jammu make this an unsafe place to travel. A few travellers are still continuing to go there, but as you are restricted as to where you can go, there seems little point in taking the risk.

Ladakh is not affected by these troubles in any way but, if you are travelling there by road, it would be safer to go via the Kullu Valley and Manali, rather than via Jammu and Srinagar. Flights via Srinagar or Jammu are reasonably safe because security at these airports is some of the tightest in the world.

In 1995 political activists banned trekkers and other tourists from entering **Zanskar** (see p31). Whether this kind of activity will continue in future years is unknown, but if you are considering trekking in Zanskar it would be wise to have an alternative plan should you not be allowed entry. Up-to-date information on the situation is only available in Leh and from Manali trekking agencies who operate in the area, so check there before finalising your itinerary.

PART 2: INDIA

Facts about the country

GEOGRAPHICAL BACKGROUND

India's 3,287,590 sq km can be split into three distinct geographic zones. Running across the far north of the country, along the borders of China, Nepal and Bhutan, are the mountains of the Himalaya, which effectively separate most of India, excluding Ladakh, from the Tibetan Plateau. South of this mighty mountain range is the Indo-Gangetic plain which stretches from Pakistan in the west to Bangladesh and Burma in the east, while encompassing the Thar Desert and the drainage basins of the River Indus (mostly in Pakistan but from which India derives its name), the River Ganges and the Brahmaputra River. To the south of this is the huge Deccan Plateau which is flanked by two lines of hills called the Western and Eastern Ghats.

CLIMATE

The climate of most of India, apart from Ladakh (see p94) and to a lesser extent Lahaul and Spiti, is governed by the monsoon. This arrives in the south-west of India at the end of May and slowly moves up the country reaching the north by July. Although it rains heavily, it doesn't rain incessantly, with most areas getting one or two heavy downpours a day interspersed with bright sunshine. The south-west monsoon begins to withdraw in September, then follow a few months of comfortably cool weather between October and January. This is the best time to visit anywhere south of the Himalaya, although the extreme south-east of the country is affected by a brief north-east monsoon. The heat increases from February to May, when it's almost intolerable – temperatures of 40°C and above are common, and everyone awaits the beginning of the monsoon to start the cycle again.

HISTORICAL OUTLINE

The people in the Indus Valley (now in Pakistan) formed India's first important civilisation. This incredibly ordered and stable culture survived for 1000 years before its rapid decline in the wake of the Aryan invasion in about 1500 BC. It was during this Aryan civilisation that Hinduism evolved, although during the following Mauryan Empire (321BC to 184BC) and the beginning of the Gupta dynasty (fourth to sixth century AD) it was largely superseded by Buddhism, until Hinduism gained many followers once again, at the end of their reign.

Muslim raiders invaded northern India in the twelfth century and managed to unify much of India from their sultanate in Delhi. A subsequent Muslim invasion heralded the beginning of the great Mughal Empire (1526 to 1761), and the start of a golden age for building, arts and literature, as epitomised by the Taj Mahal. It was during this era that various Europeans began to arrive: the Portuguese, British, French, Danes and Dutch. As the Mughal Empire began to collapse, the British East India Company and the French started to fight for a hold on Indian trade. British supremacy was established in 1757 after Robert Clive's victory at the Battle of Plassey.

British India

Throughout the next century power gradually moved from the East India Company to the British Government. Those areas directly controlled by the new imperial power became known as British India, while the rest was administered by a number of compliant Indian princes.

Among the achievements of British India were the creation of a stable system of government and law, and a massive rail infrastructure. However, their main raison d'être for colonising the country was to increase wealth for the British Empire. Their trading arrangements had a damaging effect on the Indian economy by allowing British goods into India duty free while imposing high tariffs on Indian exports to Great Britain. Other policies helped to create a landless population of peasants in many parts of the country, and these, coupled with the widespread enforcement of English as the main administrative language, provoked social and political unrest. The Indian Mutiny of 1857-59, also known as the First War of Independence, in which about 35,000 Indian soldiers rebelled, developed into a bitter war between the British and the Indians. When the conflict was finally resolved, the East India Company handed its remaining administrative powers over to the British government. There then followed a slow transition of more and more power to the Indian people. In 1919 an elected parliament was formed, which allowed the Indian National Congress greater freedom to demand home rule. This independence movement gathered momentum under Mahatma Gandhi's non-violent policy of civil disobedience, which led to his frequent imprisonment. Congress refused to support the British during World War II unless their demands for independence were granted.

Independence

Independence finally came in 1947 but not without bloodshed. The majority of Muslims, under the leadership of the Muslim League, wanted a separate state for themselves. The problems of such a split were immense but as no other solution seemed possible the creation of Pakistan was reluctantly approved. Millions of Hindus and Muslims moved east and west across the border and in the bloody process about 500,000 people were slaughtered. The maharaja of one of the last remaining princely states, Kashmir, couldn't decide whether to join India or Pakistan, and it wasn't until he was pressed by their two advancing armies that he chose India. Ever since, the region has been the scene of conflict between the two countries, Pakistan claiming it is geographically and culturally theirs with its mainly Muslim population, while the Indian government believe it legitimately and politically belongs to India. This intractable problem still simmers away, made worse by the likely funding and arming of Kashmiri militants by Pakistan and unconfirmed reprisals by the Indian military. The militants' demands have now escalated to one of complete independence for Kashmir from both India and Pakistan, one that is not popular with either nation.

Modern India

India's Prime Ministers, Jawaharlal Nehru, Indira Gandhi and Rajiv Gandhi have all been dogged by the inherent difficulties of dealing with the world's second largest population of over 900 million people in a country that has more officially 'poor' people than anywhere else, surrounded by economic difficulties, inefficient administrations, corruption and the continued threat from separatist and terrorist organisations. This is, however, a country that can feed its rapidly expanding population without relying on outside help, is the tenth greatest industrial power, and perhaps most significantly, is the world's largest democracy.

The general election in May 1996 left no party capable of forming a majority government, and Prime Minister Narasimha Rao resigned. He has been replaced by HD Deve Gowda heading a fragile coalition; it is unlikely that this government will last a full term in office.

RELIGION

All the world's major religions can be found in India. As well as about 700 million Hindus there are also about 100 million Muslims, 20 million Christians, 18 million Sikhs, 6.5 million Buddhists and several other minor religious groups including Jains and Zoroastrians.

Hinduism

Hinduism has developed from about 5000 years of continuous cultural evolution. As a result it has no formal creed but has instead absorbed much wider influences, including those of Christianity, Islam, Buddhism and Sikhism and is, therefore, one of the most tolerant of religions in theory if not in practice.

Central to Hinduism is the belief in *karma* – the sum of your life's good and bad actions that determines whether you'll be reincarnated at a higher or lower level of life, a rich businessman or an ant. Hindus also adhere to a rigid caste system. The four main castes consist of the Brahmins at the top, traditionally the priestly caste; Ksatriyas or warriors; Vaisyas, the merchants; and Sudras, the serfs and artisans. Outside these castes are the 'untouchables' or Dalits, who carry out menial and unclean chores.

Countless rebirths lead to eventual release, or *moksha*, from the constant cycle. However, depending on your karma, you can as easily move further away from moksha with each life as closer towards it. Hindus, therefore, try to increase their karma in a variety of ways: by good deeds, through meditation or asceticism, or by worshipping a popular god. The three main gods (*Trimurti*) are Brahma the creator, Vishnu the preserver and Shiva the destroyer and god of reproduction. Most Hindus are either Vaishnavites following Vishnu or are Shaivites following Shiva.

Islam

Muslims, as the followers of Islam are called, believe in only one God, Allah, whose prophet, Mohammed, founded the religion in the seventh century AD in Arabia. The visions that Mohammed received are recorded in the Muslim holy book, the Koran, which also sets out the basis of Islamic belief, practice and law. Much of the Koran relates to parts of the Bible, particularly the Books of Moses and the Gospels of Christ, and Muslims believe that Moses and Jesus were prophets of Allah.

Muslims must follow five basic obligations: to state and believe that there is only one God, Allah, and that Mohammed was his prophet; to recite the five daily prayers at set times, facing Mecca; to make the pilgrimage, or *haji*, to Mecca at least once a lifetime; to fast and abstain from sex during the month of Ramadan; and to pay a tax for charity.

Originally, believers in Islam were obliged to spread the religion by means of *jihad*, or holy war. As a result, the powerful Arabian armies managed to carry Islam quickly throughout the Middle East and North Africa in the seventh and eighth centuries AD, from where it spread to sub-Saharan Africa, India, China, SE Asia, the Balkans and Spain. Early on in its history, Islam divided into two major sects which still remain today, the majority Sunnites, the rest Shiites.

Sikhism

With their beards and turbans, Sikhs are one of India's most unmistakable peoples. They are recognisable by their five outward symbols, or *Kakkars*, which stem from the belief in *Khalsa*, a chosen race of warrior holy men. In addition to uncut hair (the reason for the turban) and beard, they include shorts, a sword, a comb and a steel bracelet.

The religion was founded by Guru Nanak in the 15th century with the aim of combining Hindu and Islamic ideals. Sikhs reject the Hindu caste system and the vast pantheon of gods, believing instead in one universal God, but they believe in karma, reincarnation and that devotional singing, the repetition of God's name and meditation can all help free the self from the endless cycle of rebirths. Since the sixteenth century, when Guru Gobind Singh militarised the religion, the majority of Sikhs have taken the surname Singh, meaning lion.

Buddhism

Buddhism is more of a philosophy for life than a religion as it does not worship a god. It was founded in the sixth century BC in north-east India by the Indian prince Gautama Siddhartha who was later given the title, Buddha, or awakened one. He was brought up in a life of royal luxury but by his late twenties had become disenchanted with this indulgent lifestyle.

Endeavouring to find the reasons behind the endless suffering of human life, he abandoned his wife and son to become an ascetic. For six years he deprived himself of all comforts until he eventually came to the realisation that this too was not the path to real happiness. Frustrated, he sat down alone under a banyan tree in what is now Bodhgaya in Bihar to meditate on his predicament. In meditation he discovered the Middle Way, moderation in all things, and in so doing attained enlightenment. For the rest of his life he taught the principles of enlightenment, *dharma*, to his disciples around northern India.

The Buddha's teachings Central to Buddhism is the belief that all living things can reach enlightenment. Unfortunately we are all tied to the endless wheel of existence and therefore, through reincarnation, are stuck in a cycle of rebirth. Like Hindus, Buddhists also believe that karma determines your next life. The only way to be set free from constant rebirth is to cease to desire for it is desire that makes us permanently dissatisfied. If we cannot obtain what we desire we are unhappy, but if we get what we desire we soon grow bored with it and turn to something else. This is inevitable because, as the Buddha taught, all things are impermanent, including ourselves.

The Four Noble Truths These are: that life is characterised by suffering; that desire causes this suffering; that it is possible to bring an end to this suffering; and that this can be achieved by following the Eight-Fold Path of right understanding, right thought, right speech, right action, right livelihood, right effort, right mindfulness and right meditation.

By thorough comprehension of the Four Noble Truths we can gain enlightenment and reach *nirvana*, a state in which we are free from the cycle of rebirth and in which desire and the self are annihilated.

Theravada and Mahayana Buddhism Over its long history Buddhism has split into many schools. The two main branches are Theravada and Mahayana. **Theravada** is the old conservative school of Buddhism, also known as the Hinayana (or 'lesser vehicle'), which is popular in Sri Lanka and South-East Asia. This school maintains that the only way to enlightenment is through your own efforts as a monk. **Mahayana** on the other hand is more adaptable, believing that everybody will eventually gain enlightenment. So that this can be achieved a few enlightened beings called *bodhisattvas* refuse the bliss of nirvana so that they can return again and again to the world in order to help all other living things gain enlightenment. This feature has widened the appeal of the Mahayana school because gods from other religions can be incorporated into Buddhism as bodhisattvas. This is the school of Buddhism which is dominant in Ladakh (see p105) and also in Nepal, Tibet, Mongolia, China, Korea and Japan.

Practical Information for the visitor

VISA VALIDITY AND EXTENSIONS

If you have any doubt about how long you may stay in India, then apply for a six-month visa in the first place. Although visas are theoretically extendible, it can be hard to achieve in practice. If you do succeed, the amount of time granted is in the hands of the official you are dealing with, and it can vary from a couple of weeks to three months. Apply to the Foreigners' Registration Office in Delhi (☎ 331 9489, Hans Bhavan, Tilak Bridge, open 9.30am-1.30pm and 2pm-4pm Monday to Friday) or in Bombay, Calcutta and Madras, or alternatively to the superintendent of police at any district headquarters (see p122 for Leh).

If you stay in India for more than 180 days you are required to get an income tax clearance exemption certificate from the foreign section of the Income Tax Department in Delhi, Bombay, Calcutta or Madras before you leave the country. You will need to take along your passport, visa and bank encashment certificates.

TREKKING RESTRICTIONS

There are few restrictions on trekking in Ladakh, which comes as a pleasant surprise in a country which is usually over-keen on wrapping things up in red tape. Apart from a few sensitive border areas (see below), trekkers are free to walk where they like and for as long as they like, providing they have a valid visa.

The Inner Line The restricted areas in Ladakh (or protected areas as the government now likes them to be known) are all beyond what is known as the Inner Line. Travellers are not allowed to cross this without special permission. The position of this line sometimes alters but at the time of going to press it runs parallel to but 1'/2km north of the Zoji La-Drass-Kargil-Khalsi road in the west of Ladakh; it then moves 6km to 8km north of the Khalsi-Nimu-Leh-Upshi road to allow visitors to reach the various monasteries in that area; and in eastern Ladakh the Inner Line runs along the Upshi to Manali road, thereby restricting access to all the areas further to the east.

Since 1994 the government has opened up several of these areas to tourists – Nubra, Pangong Lake, Dha-Hanu, Tsomoriri and Tsokar. You still need permission to visit them but this is easily arranged in Leh (see p120) as long as you comply with certain conditions: you must travel in a group of four or more; you can't stay longer than seven days; and you should stick to the identified tour circuits. Permission to enter the other Inner Line areas is rarely granted to foreigners but if you want to try contact the Ministry of Home Affairs (☎ 461 1984) Lok Nayak Bhavan, Khan Market, New Delhi, well in advance of your intended visit.

LOCAL TRANSPORT

Air

Indian Airlines, the government-run domestic carrier, has an extensive network of routes throughout India (timetables available from IA offices) and is the only airline flying to Leh. Air India planes fly between Bombay, Delhi, Calcutta and Madras, and there are also a number of smaller operators, of whom Jagson and Archana are the most useful for the Himalayan-bound trekker, as they fly from Delhi to Kullu.

There are Indian Airlines offices or agents in most major towns and cities and making a booking is a simple affair provided there are seats available. Many routes, Leh-Delhi being one of them, get heavily booked, so try to plan as far ahead as possible. If you don't manage to get a confirmed flight you can be put on the waiting-list. You can be wait-listed for up to four different flights, so make the most of this until one is confirmed. The waiting-list works in mysterious ways – even if you're told that there are a couple of hundred people ahead of you on the list, you may still get a confirmed seat in the end.

Tickets must be paid for in hard currency (cash or travellers' cheques) in Leh, or by hard currency or credit card elsewhere. There is an excellent youth fare entitling you to 25% off if you are aged 30 or under, children under 12 get a 50% discount, while those under two pay 10%. If you cancel your ticket before your flight you will get a full refund, but Indian Airlines will not refund you if your ticket is lost. You have been warned! You can also lose all rights to your ticket if you are not at the airport at least 30 minutes before the flight is due to leave, so it is advisable to turn up at least an hour before departure. As Indian Airlines has a habit of changing its flight timings without warning it's a good idea to check flight details a day or two before you fly. Finally, don't pack batteries or knives in your hand luggage; they will be confiscated.

Train
Travel by rail is one of the great Indian experiences. Unfortunately Himachal Pradesh and Ladakh are two of the few regions that aren't served by the railway. If you're planning to go, or come back, via Kashmir you can use the trains that run between Delhi and Jammu and then catch a bus between there and Srinagar. **Note the warning on p50**.

Bus
The bus system in India can get you almost anywhere cheaply and generally quickly (barring, of course, breakdowns). Buses come in varying degrees of dilapidation and comfort. On rock-bottom priced 'ordinary' or 'B class' buses you will be squashed onto a hard seat with as many people as possible but the journey will be an entertaining insight into local life. At the other end of the scale is 'deluxe' or 'supercoach', which are a bit faster and have reclining seats. On some popular long distance routes, such as between Delhi and Manali, and Manali and Leh, you will find 'luxury' tourist buses operating. While these are comfortable, if a little expensive, they don't provide quite the same level of cultural exchange as a bus full of locals.

For the faster and longer distance services you'll usually need to book in advance; tourist buses insist on it but for local services you just need to turn up and pay on the bus. At large bus stations, as at railway stations, women should make use of the separate, faster ticket queue for them. If there doesn't appear to be one then you can go straight to the front of the existing queue. Luggage goes on the roof of the bus (no charge), along with any passengers who can't fit inside. The cramped seats on some services help explain why the roof 'seat' is the most favoured by many Westerners but you should realise that it is illegal to be up there and if you are asked to come down, do so, as the conductor can be fined. Keep an eye out for low power cables and branches if you want to stay on!

City buses, particularly in Delhi, are horrendously crowded and trying to find out which buses run on which routes is difficult if your Hindi isn't good enough to translate the timetables. As a result, most visitors opt for the more expensive but less complicated auto-rickshaws.

Taxi
The main vehicle used for the job is the classic Hindustan Ambassador, a copy of the Morris Oxford, complete with sofa-like bench seats. In Delhi they are easily identified as they are painted yellow and black. In the mountains you will also find a number of Gypsy and Mahindra jeeps

which cope better with the more difficult roads. Taxis in Delhi have a meter, rarely switched on for tourists even if it is working. The best policy to adopt is to agree on a price before getting in. If the driver won't agree on a fair price, find another. In Leh fares are set by the Taxi Operators' Union and there is a list available detailing these.

Auto-rickshaw

These three-wheeler scooters are much cheaper than taxis and faster for short distances in traffic. You are guaranteed an exhilarating ride. You may occasionally be able to persuade the driver to use his meter but expect to pay more than the fare indicated as the meter is unlikely to have been recalibrated to the latest tariff, or so they say. It's often easier to follow the same advice as for taxis. There are no auto-rickshaws in Leh.

Tempo

The auto-rickshaws' big brother, with seating for up to eight people, tempos are often propelled by the front half of a Harley-Davidson. They are mainly found in Delhi where they operate along fixed routes.

Cycle-rickshaw

These operate in Old Delhi and are a cheap, environmentally sound but slow way of getting around. While you may feel pity for the rickshaw wallahs' physically demanding work, it is far better to use their services than to deny them your money. Always agree on a price before setting off.

Hire car

If you are looking for a more independent way of travelling around it is possible to hire self-drive cars in Delhi and other major cities but once you've seen the conditions on the road you'll understand why most people hire a car with driver. This can be done either through a specialist firm (ask the tourist office or your hotel), or with a taxi driver. It's an expensive way to travel long distances, often costing more than flying, but it does allow you to stop wherever you like.

Motorbike

India is a dream for the classic motorcycle enthusiast and the lure of the stunning high altitude road between Manali and Leh is too much for many to resist. Hundreds of travellers each year tour around on hired or bought Indian Enfield 350cc or 500cc Bullets, copies of the British Royal Enfield Bullet. There are also smaller bikes available, such as scooters and the ubiquitous 100cc Japanese two-strokes. You'll find the widest range of bikes for sale in Delhi but hiring them in Manali or Leh shouldn't be a problem either. If you plan to buy a bike start your enquiries at a mechanic's or look on the noticeboards of popular traveller's hang-outs. It also makes sense to employ the skills of an 'auto consultant' who can guide you through the maze of bureaucracy that is involved.

Bicycle

Cycling is an excellent way to explore local areas and it's possible to hire bikes in Leh and Delhi. For those with more time there can be few better ways of travelling further afield. You are totally free to go where you like; it costs you next to nothing and should your legs give up on you, it's a simple matter to put the bike onto a bus, train or plane. Those after the ultimate challenge should consider cycling between Manali and Leh along the world's second highest road (see p88) or even continuing up and over the Khardung La above Leh, the 'highest motorable road in the world'. For this sort of adventure you will need to bring your own machine but for riding in the less hilly areas you could do far worse than buy a strong, heavy, single-geared Indian bike for about £25/US$38 (new!). It'll come complete with strong carrier to which you can lash your rucksack, fat tyres, sprung saddle and rod brakes, making it virtually indestructible.

The CTC (Cyclists' Touring Club) (☎ 01483-417 217, fax 01483-426 994) Cotterell House, 69 Meadrow, Godalming, Surrey, UK produce fact sheets covering almost every aspect of cycle touring, including India.

Hitching

This is not an easy option and the only people likely to stop for you are truck drivers. Expect to pay as much as you would on the bus and make sure you agree on the amount before you set off. You should also find out when the driver expects to reach your destination. He may be planning to spend the night at a village just down the road, or popping in to visit friends or relations on the way. While a night in the cramped cab of an Indian truck with the driver and his crew may make a good travel story, it's not conducive to a good night's sleep. Women should never hitch alone in India. The Western 'thumb-up' gesture that says 'give me a ride' is not understood in India. The way to stop any vehicle is to pretend you're a one-winged bird trying to fly, a gentle up and down waving of the hand and arm.

LANGUAGE

The most widespread spoken language in India is English and it is perfectly possible for the traveller to get around without any knowledge of any of India's other languages, although a few words of Hindi are useful. Officially India has 14 languages, but if minor languages are included this rises to over 700. There have been attempts to make Hindi, which is the most widely spoken of Indian languages, into the official national language but so far this has not succeeded.

The Ladakhi language is a form of Tibetan. While much of the spelling is the same, the words are pronounced so differently that Ladakhis and Tibetans can find it hard to understand each other. The

Ladakhi language is hardly ever written down in the same way as it is spoken, because the 'correct' written language is a scholarly Tibetan, comparable to Shakespearean English. As a result very few people outside of monasteries read or write in their own language.

English is commonly understood, particularly around Leh, as is Urdu (similar to Hindi) but trekkers should try to learn a little Ladakhi so that they can talk to people particularly in rural areas. You'll provide a great source of entertainment for those listening. It's not hard to pick up a few basic words (see p247), and to help you learn, buy a copy of Rebecca Norman's excellent little yellow book, *Getting started in Ladakhi*, which is widely available in Leh.

TIME

Indian Standard Time is 5 hours 30 minutes ahead of Greenwich Mean Time (GMT). Time calculations for the following cities are:
- London: -5 hours 30 minutes (Oct to Mar)
  -6 hours 30 minutes (Apr to Sep)
- New York:-10 hours 30 minutes
- Los Angeles: -13 hours 30 minutes
- Sydney: +4 hours and 30 minutes
- Auckland: +6 hours and 30 minutes

MONEY

Currency

There are 100 paise (p) in the Indian rupee (Rs). Coins come in denominations of 5, 10, 20, 25, 50 paise and 1, 2 and 5 rupees. Notes come in denominations of 1, 2, 5, 10, 20, 50, 100, and 500 rupees. Make sure the notes you are given have no ripped edges, as you will find it almost impossible to get rid of them again. Holes left by staples do not matter.

Changing money

This can be time consuming and frustrating, especially in smaller towns. The best solution is to change as much as you feel happy carrying before you leave Delhi. You'll get a better rate of exchange than in Leh or Manali and you will be able to change most foreign currencies or travellers' cheques – pounds sterling and US dollars are often all you can change outside the capital or other big cities.

American Express, Mastercard and Visa **credit cards** can be used to obtain cash rupees in several banks but there is nowhere in Leh

Rates of exchange
There's a slightly better rate of exchange for travellers' cheques than for cash. Current exchange rates for travellers' cheques are:

	Delhi	Leh
£1	Rs52	Rs48.35
US$1	Rs34	Rs31.40
A$1	Rs24.40	Rs22.50
DM1	Rs21.50	Rs19.50

that offers this facility. Credit cards can also be used in large hotels, restaurants and shops. There are several **foreign banks** which have branches in India; ANZ Grindlays has the most branches.

Hang on to the **encashment certificates** that the banks give you, because you will need them if you want to change more than Rs1000 back into hard currency when you leave. Taking rupees out of or into India is illegal.

Black market

Changing money on the black market is illegal and does nothing to help India's national debt. Now that the Indian rupee is a convertible currency you will get only a marginally better rate than at the bank, your best chances being with US$100 or £50 bills. The black market in Leh is almost non-existent, though it is alive and well in Delhi.

Baksheesh

This is the term used for giving small amounts of money as a 'thank you' for good service, to help get things done or to beggars. Baksheesh applies equally to Indians as to visitors, so don't assume you are being picked on just because you are a Westerner. Although it is not really necessary to tip taxis, cheap restaurants or small hotels, it is often expected and the small amount of five rupees will keep everyone happy. A similar amount to whoever helps you with your bags will be appreciated, while those who achieve the seemingly impossible deserve a little more. Large restaurants and hotels will expect 10%.

Genuine pleas from desperate beggars are an inevitable, heart rending, part of travel in India. These people depend to a large extent on donations from the public (there is no social security) and the best course of action seems to be to follow what other Indians do and give them your small change. Alternatively you can give to the various charities who help the poor. Giving to children who reserve their pestering for tourists, demanding 'one pen', 'one bon-bon' or 'one rupee' should on no account be encouraged (see p142).

Bargaining

This is an important part of buying souvenirs or things from a market and some negotiating will also take place when you are hiring a pony-man. Approach it as a light-hearted game and not as a means of getting the lowest possible price. You should have an idea of how much you are prepared to pay for an item before you begin haggling and never begin bargaining if you are not interested in buying the item. Once you've quoted a figure you are committed to it, there's no backing out. Although bargaining is important, don't lose sight of the fact that £0.10/US$0.20 is nothing to you, but could be a lot to the vendor.

ELECTRICITY

The voltage is usually 220 volts AC, 50 cycles but some areas also have DC supply. Always check the voltage before plugging in. Socket sizes vary but the most commonly found are two or sometimes three round pin type. Take a universal adaptor if you're going to be using the supply.

Electricity has not affected the majority of Ladakh and is generally restricted to Leh, Kargil and a few villages along the Indus Valley. Leh's inadequate supplies are provided by the Hydroelectric Project at Stakna and a couple of diesel generators in the town which you can hear humming away at night. Power cuts are very common so always have a torch or some candles on you after dark. Even when it's working properly, the light given off by the bulbs can be so dim that it's hard to read at night.

HOLIDAYS AND FESTIVALS

Opening times

All **shops** are generally open between 10am and 5pm, Monday to Saturday but many keep longer hours. **Banks** are open 10am to 2pm Monday to Friday, 10am to 12pm on Saturday. **Post offices** are open 10am to 5pm on weekdays and 10am to 12pm on Saturday, while **government offices** are open 9.30am to 5pm Monday to Friday and 9.30am to 1pm on Saturday (sometimes closing on alternate Saturdays).

In Leh some shops are open on Sundays as well. Official times sometimes alter during winter in Ladakh.

National Public Holidays

• **Republic Day** (26 January) This is in celebration of the day India became a republic in 1950. The main events are in New Delhi and include a huge parade to the Red Fort.

• **Independence Day** (15 August) Marks the anniversary of India's independence from Britain in 1947.

• **Gandhi's birthday** (2 October)

• **Christmas Day** (25 December)

Festivals

There is a festival somewhere in India almost every day of the year. They are colourful and noisy occasions to which visitors are generally welcomed. The principal Hindu, Buddhist and Islamic festivals are listed below. The dates are complicated to work out as they change each year. Buddhist, Hindu and Sikh festivals being determined by the lunar calendar, while Islamic festivals are determined by the Islamic year which is shorter than the Gregorian calendar (contact a tourist office for dates).

• **Id-ul-Fitr** (December – February) The end of Ramadan, the month in which Muslims have to abstain from sex and must not eat, drink or smoke between sunrise and sunset, is celebrated with a large feast and festivities.

• **Tibetan New Year** (late February or early March) While most Tibetans will be celebrating their New Year now, the Ladakhis will have beaten them to it by two or three months. (See Losar).

• **Holi** (March) A slightly anarchic Hindu festival that marks the end of winter and the beginning of spring. Don't wear your smart clothes today as the streets are full of people throwing coloured powder and water. Tourists are a popular target but it's all good fun.

• **Rama Navami** (March – April) The Hindu festival which celebrates the birthday of Rama, the main character of the epic *Ramayana*. It is auspicious to read from and act episodes of this great story.

• **Id-ul-Zuha** (March-April) The Muslim festival commemorating Abraham's attempt to sacrifice his son on the command of God. Animals are sacrificed and mutton traditionally eaten.

Monastic Festivals in Ladakh
Ladakh's monasteries put on spectacular dramatic festivals each year to re-enact the story of each gompa's particular divinity. These used to take place in the winter when they provided a much needed diversion from the drudgery of the long cold months. In a shrewd financial move, however, several have changed their dates to make the most of the summer visitors. The most famous of these masked dance festivals is the one at Hemis but Lamayuru, Phyang and Tak Tok all now have their festivals in the tourist season. The dates of the most important festivals are given under the entry for each gompa (see p127).

• **Buddha Purnima** (1 June 1996, 22 May 1997, 10 June 1998, 30 May 1999) The Buddhist festival that conveniently celebrates Buddha's birthday, enlightenment and attainment of nirvana, all at the same time. Full celebrations are held in Leh.

• **Ladakh Festival** (1-15 September) This cultural festival takes place mainly in Leh. It's a good opportunity to see polo matches, archery, music recitals, crafts and other things Ladakhi and succeeds in its aim of extending the short tourist season a few more weeks.

• **Janmashtami** (August-September) Krishna's birthday celebrated by Hindus all over the country.

• **Dussehra** (September-October) This popular 10 day Hindu festival celebrates the triumph of good over evil, usually represented by Rama's destruction of Ravana, or the goddess Durga's victory over the demon Mahishasura. Try to be in Kullu (just south of Manali) for this festival, where it is celebrated in great style.

• **Diwali** (October-November) Rama's homecoming after 14 years of exile is celebrated by Hindus all over India by the lighting of oil lamps and firecrackers. It ranks as India's noisiest and brightest festival.

(**Opposite**) Many Ladakhis dress up in their finery for the annual Ladakh Festival. This woman is dressed in the traditional *goncha* (long coat) and *tibi* (hat), while the woman in the background is wearing a turquoise-studded *perak* (head-dress).

• **Nanak Jayanti** (October-November) The major Sikh festival which celebrates the birthday of Guru Nanak. It is marked by processions and the continuous reading of the holy book.

• **Losar** (Dec 11 1996; Dec 30 1997; Dec 19 1998; Dec 8 1999) Ladakhis celebrate the Tibetan New Year before the actual new year (in February) because of a decision made by the Ladakhi king, Jamyang Namgyal, at the beginning of the seventeenth century. The impatient king was keen to lead a military campaign to western Ladakh but was advised to wait until after the new year celebrations. Rather than waste a couple of months he decided to bring the date of the celebrations forward. Ever since then, the Ladakhis have been out of step with other Tibetans.

POST AND TELECOMMUNICATIONS

Postal services

The Indian postal service is generally reliable, with letters from Europe taking one or two weeks to arrive, even to Leh. Most travellers use the Poste Restante service at all main post offices to receive mail. Letters should be addressed with your surname in capital letters and underlined (so that it is sorted properly), Poste Restante, GPO, the name of the town and the state. If you can't find a letter that you were expecting, check under the first letter of your first name, in case it's been mis-sorted. Airmail rates are currently Rs11 for a letter, Rs6.50 for an aerogramme and Rs6 for a postcard.

Sending parcels home is a convenient way to shed some of the weight in your pack. The parcel needs to be wrapped in cheap white material and then stitched up. Most tailors will perform this service for you. Leave one end open so that the post office can inspect what you're sending. This way you can also take things out, or put things in the parcel so that it fits into the kilogram bracket (0-1kg, 1-3kg, 3-5kg etc) that gives you the best value for your money. Take a needle and thread to the post office so that you can sew it up. If you want to be extra safe seal the seams with wax (available at stationery shops).

Phone and fax

Telephoning anywhere from India is simple at one of the many private STD/ISD offices available in every town. Many of these now have fax machines which you can use as well. The international **dialling code** for India is 91, Delhi is 011, Kargil is 01985, Leh is 01982, Manali is 01901 and Srinagar is 0194 (leave off the first 0 if calling from outside India).

(Opposite) The elaborate Buddhist iconography at Sankar Gompa is similar to that found in gompas (monasteries) all over Ladakh, much of which is hundreds of years old.

THE MEDIA

Newspapers and magazines

Indian newspapers are excellent value, rarely costing more than Rs2. The *Times of India* and the *Indian Express* are the most popular English language papers. Also available are the *Hindustan Times*, the *Independent* and the *Statesman*. Look out for *Ladags Melong* (Rs20) in Leh. This excellent magazine is the only locally produced journal and covers a wide range of topics. Most articles are written in English, but the magazine has also taken on the admirable task of trying to extend the use of written Ladakhi beyond religious texts. It therefore includes a few articles in Ladakhi that are written as closely to the spoken language as possible. The other regional papers are the *Kashmir Times* and the *Daily Excelsior* but as both are based in Srinagar they carry little news relevant to Ladakh.

Radio and TV

All India Radio broadcasts news in English at 9pm every night while Doordarshan, the national TV channel, broadcasts news at 9.30pm.

Satellite TV has hit India by storm. Programmes from BBC World Service TV and numerous American soaps are available. The effect of rose-tinted images of the West, as portrayed by *Baywatch* and *Beverly Hills 90210*, on remote areas like Ladakh remains to be seen.

BBC World Service radio is on short wave frequencies between 6am and 8.30am on 15310, 11955, 9580; between 8.30am and 5pm on 17790, 15310, 11750; and between 5pm and 11.30pm on 15310, 9740, 5975.

FOOD

Indian

India is rightly famed for its unique cuisine but that wonderful food is really only available in smart restaurants and private houses. Make the effort to eat in a really good restaurant once in a while as the food is incomparable. Such a meal may take a large chunk (£7/US$10) out of your daily budget yet it's superb value when compared with the cost of a restaurant meal in the West. Travellers generally make do with the run-of-the-mill food that is pro-

---

Popular Indian dishes

- **Bhindi bhaji** – fried okra or ladies' fingers
- **Biryani** – a mild dish of saffron- or turmeric-coloured rice with meat or vegetables
- **Dal bhat** – India's basic meal of lentils and rice
- **Dhansaak** – meat and lentil curry with rice
- **Dum alu** – potato curry
- **Kofta** – vegetable or meat balls with curry
- **Korma** – a mild curry with a yoghurt sauce
- **Malai kofta** – lamb in a rich and creamy sauce
- **Mattar panir** – peas and cheese
- **Pakoras** – small deep-fried batter balls filled with vegetables
- **Pulau** – mildly spiced rice
- **Rogan josh** – classic mild Kashmiri lamb curry
- **Saag alu** – spinach with potatoes
- **Samosas** – fried triangles of pastry filled with curried meat or vegetables
- **Tandoori chicken** – marinated chicken cooked in a clay oven, mild and dry
- **Vindaloo** – vinegar-marinated meat in hot curry

vided by small restaurants and *dhabas*, the cheapest and most numerous of India's eateries. The basis of the meal is a plate of rice or Indian bread such as *chapatis*, *rotis*, *parathas* or *puris* to which is added *dal* (lentils) and a vegetable curry. This is filling and tasty and shouldn't set you back more than Rs30. Meat dishes are sometimes available and cost a little more, but the meat (usually mutton) often consists of little more than bone. There is no need to worry if you can't stand hot and spicy food as there are several milder dishes which are generally available. Beer is the great healer for a burning mouth.

Chinese
Chinese food, or at least attempts at it, is widely available in Delhi; fried rice or chow mein can make a pleasant change from curry. Most of Leh's restaurants also offer a wide selection of Chinese dishes.

Western
In restaurants popular with Western travellers spaghetti, pizzas, pancakes, porridge, muesli and other Western dishes are on all the menus. Elsewhere, chips and omelettes are usually easy to find and you will almost always be able to get toast and jam for breakfast.

Ladakhi/Tibetan food
The Ladakhi staple is roasted barley flour called *ngamphe* or *tsampa*. The raw barley is roasted in hot sand (to prevent it from burning) until it pops. It is then separated from the sand and ground to a fine flour. This can be mixed with tea, put into soup, or made into a porridge.

One of the most popular Tibetan delicacies is *momos*. These are like miniature Cornish pasties filled with meat, cheese or vegetables. The dough is steamed rather than baked and they are often served in a soup called *renuchutsuey*. Fried momo are called *khotay* and are particularly delicious when they have been put into a simmering soup until all the soup has been absorbed by the momo. Soups figure heavily on any Tibetan menu; the most common is *thugpa*. Others include *tsam-thuk*, which is tsampa in a soup and *than-thuk*, flat noodle soup.

DRINK

If you want to stay healthy in India, it is safest to assume that all water needs to be purified before it's safe to drink (see p236). Reasonably safe bottled mineral water (Rs15 to Rs30) is available almost everywhere but make sure the seal hasn't been tampered with. Most of it is simply treated tap water and as the bottles are generally not recycled it's far cheaper and more environmentally friendly to purify your own.

India grows some of the best tea in the world though lovers of English tea may be disappointed when they drink a glass of sweet and milky *chai* (Rs2 to Rs5). This ubiquitous beverage is made by boiling water, tea, milk powder and sugar (and occasionally cardamom or ginger) together in a pot and straining the resulting liquid into a glass. It's a safe, cheap and refreshing drink that's available everywhere, so it's worth learning to like it. Other teas such as lemon and ginger, jasmine, mint, and cardamom make a delicious change when you are sick of chai. Coffee is also popular but by far the best is made in south India. The favourite Ladakhi hot drink is butter tea, or *gur-gur cha*, which is made by adding salt, soda and brick tea together, and a little butter after it has boiled. This is churned in a special cylindrical barrel with the onomatopoeic name *gur-gur*. Well-made butter tea is delicious; think of it as weak soup rather than as tea.

Soft drinks (Rs7 to Rs12) are safe thirst quenchers. Coke and Pepsi are inevitably found in most places, as well as a range of interesting domestic makes such as Limca, Thums Up, Campa Cola and Gold Spot. There are also lots of fruit juices available either in bottles, such as the delicious apple juice in Ladakh (Rs21 for a large bottle), or cartons, such as mango, lemon and apple flavoured *Frooti* (Rs6). *Lassi* is a traveller's favourite; you should be aware that the curd is often mixed with ordinary tap water, so if you wouldn't drink the water, don't drink the lassi.

Beer is widely available in India with Kingfisher and Godfather being popular brands. It's comparatively expensive (Rs30 to Rs60), probably just as well as the wide use of chemical additives will ensure a heavy head the next morning if you drink too much. Indian imitations of whisky, brandy and rum are also available and usually drinkable though they bear little resemblance to the originals. William Moorcroft pointed out in his *Travels* in the 1820's that the Ladakhis were 'apt to be addicted to intoxication' and large quantities of *chang*, a delicious and mild home-brewed barley beer, are always consumed at any excuse for a celebration.

THINGS TO BUY

Delhi, Manali and Leh are literally brimming with irresistibly cheap things to buy. Silks, textiles, carpets, rugs, metalwork, woodwork, ceramics, leather, paintings, musical instruments, books and even cassettes of Indian or Western music can all be bought at bargain prices. However, it's best to wait until the end of your stay before you splash out, otherwise you'll end up lugging the contents of a souvenir shop across the Himalaya with you. Once the initial euphoria has worn off, you'll also have a better feel for what's available and what a sensible price is. During the tourist season, Manali and Leh fill up with Kashmiri and Tibetan souvenir sellers whose wares can often be found cheaper in Delhi. Having said that, each region also has its own specialities which are certainly best bought locally – shawls, woollen goods and Kullu pill-box hats in Manali, or butter tea churners, Tibetan carpets, *thankas*, traditional Ladakhi clothes and locally knitted woollens in Leh. Wherever you buy, make sure you bargain.

SECURITY

India is a reasonably safe country to travel in and big cities are certainly less violent than those in the West. As with travel anywhere you should be particularly aware of theft; travellers have been popular targets throughout history and things haven't changed. Keep the receipt for your travellers' cheques, details of your insurance policy, some spare cash and a photocopy of the personal information and Indian visa pages of your passport in a very safe place, so that you're not completely stuck if your wallet and passport get stolen. Pickpockets abound in busy places such as railway and bus stations and on buses and trains. Keep hold of your valuables at all times. Bring a padlock to safeguard your luggage on buses and trains and also securely lock your hotel room. Unfortunately you are probably as much at risk from fellow travellers as from anyone else.

Ladakh, however, has an extremely low crime rate and when trekking you are far more at risk from the natural elements than from man. There have been occasional thefts from unattended tents in frequently trekked areas, such as around Padum and in the Markha Valley, so even in the mountains it's best to keep your valuables on you all the time.

Hashish (*charas*) is widely produced in the Himalaya and is readily available. It is illegal, however, as are all other drugs. Possession carries a minimum 10-year sentence. Police in tourist areas are particularly vigilant; if you're arrested you may spend months in jail simply waiting for your case to come to trial. This is a travel experience that is best avoided.

Women travellers

Women in Ladakhi society are generally quite well respected. An outward symbol of this is that they are the guardians of the family wealth in the form of their turquoise-studded head-dresses (*peraks*) and other jewellery which is passed down from mother to daughter. Ladakhi women may be shy of Western men, but with women they are friendly and helpful and can give you a much better insight into Ladkahi life than you might get from a man.

The increasing exposure to Western-style television programmes has led many Indians to believe that all Western women are easy to get. As a result of this, you may experience unwanted attention. This rarely amounts to more than a quick grope but it is, of course, extremely annoying. If you are hassled, a yell for help will probably frighten them off and other people around will generally come to your aid.

There are a few simple ways you can avoid unnecessary scrapes and at the same time help to restore Western women's image. If you dress modestly you will not only achieve the above, but will also gain more respect. Avoid sleeveless tops that show your shoulders, and short skirts and trousers that show too much leg. Going without a bra will not be appreciated either. If you buy local clothes, wear them as locals do; for example, Indian draw-string skirts are actually sari petticoats. Other things to bear in mind are that if you return someone's stare it may be interpreted as flirtatious, as may getting into a long conversation with a man.

With regard to trekking it is best not to go alone as you will rarely see local women on their own outside their village. If you are travelling alone, hire a guide for your trek or team up with other Westerners in Leh. **Tor Cornet** (UK)

'The external boundaries of India on this map have not been authenticated and may not be correct'

■ Town served by airport

PART 3: DELHI & MANALI

En route to Ladakh

TRAVEL OPTIONS

Regular flights to Leh have made it all too easy to forget that Ladakh is still one of the most remote regions in the Himalaya. Travel to such a place is bound to have inherent difficulties and although most visitors have no problems, it's not unknown for planes to be delayed because of bad weather and buses to be held up because of landslides or snow.

Most travellers choose either to fly directly from Delhi to Ladakh, or to go by bus via Manali. Continued unrest in Kashmir means that the once popular route via Srinagar is now less appealing and this way into Ladakh is not recommended until the situation changes (see p50). If you have the time and are not averse to a little discomfort, then the three-day bus journey via Manali is a must. Although you get superb views of the Himalaya from the air, it is only by travelling overland that you can fully appreciate the awesome scale of the mountains, the variety of scenery and cultures that are found here, and just how cut off from the rest of India Ladakh really is.

Many travellers find that the best combination is to fly one way and take the bus the other. Whichever way you decide to travel, you must take your rate of ascent into account to prevent the onset of altitude illness (see p238 for more information). If travelling to Ladakh by road, use the altitude figures on the map on p133 to plan your journey.

Delhi

Delhi is the ideal gateway into India for Himalayan-bound trekkers. The city is well served by international flights and also by a vast network of road, rail and domestic air services, which make onward travel to Ladakh straightforward.

The capital of India is steeped in history and culture which reflect the diversity of the subcontinent. This provides travellers with many fascinating sightseeing possibilities, while enabling them to put India's disparities into context. With its many national and international services and shops, it's also a convenient place to make any final arrangements. However, Delhi's pollution, noise, and crowds can quickly become too much to bear, and summer trekkers heading for Ladakh will be keen to exchange the heat and humidity of the city for the cool of the mountains as soon as possible.

HISTORY

The site of the modern city of Delhi encompasses more than eight previous sites under various names. The first recorded city is that of Indraprastha, which is thought to have been near the Purana Qila until the 4th century AD and is the city of a similar name mentioned in the Hindu epic poem *Mahabharata*. The city officially recognised as the first Delhi was that of the Tomora and Chauhan kings (8th and 12th centuries) which was first called Lal Kot and then became Qila Rai Pithora. Muslim invaders from Afghanistan established a Sultanate here at the beginning of the 13th century.

The prosperous 14th century commercial city of Siri, near modern-day Hauz Khas, was the next to be built, followed rapidly by the fortress of Tughlaqabad to the south-east, which was only inhabited for five years before being replaced by Jehanpanah, also near Hauz Khas.

All these cities were situated to the south of modern Delhi. The next 'Delhi' was founded in 1354 to the east of Connaught Place on the banks of the Yamuna, and was called Ferozabad after the sultan Feroz Tughlaq. With the coming of the Mughals the capital was moved to Agra, but the second Mughal emperor, Humayun, moved it back to Delhi in 1534, where he built the Purana Qila as his fortress. However, he was soon ousted by the Afghan Sher Shah who added to the fort and renamed it Shergarh. Humayun regained power in 1555. After his death, his son Akbar moved the capital back to Agra.

Delhi came back to prominence in 1638 under the great monument builder, Shah Jehan, who founded Shahjehanabad (officially the seventh city of Delhi). Today's Old Delhi has grown around this former city and much of it, such as the Red Fort and the Jama Masjid, is well preserved. New Delhi became the eighth Delhi, conceived by the British when they decided to move their capital from Calcutta in 1911. However, it wasn't inaugurated as the capital until 1931, so the British colonial enjoyment of the grand buildings was short lived.

Delhi has remained the administrative and political capital of India since Independence in 1947 and has now become one of India's fastest growing commercial centres. As is common in many Third World cities, social and environmental problems, such as pollution, traffic congestion, overcrowding and poverty have followed in the wake of this rapid economic growth. Delhi's population of over ten million continues to rise daily as people are lured by the prospect of work and money yet almost one third of these people live in the pitiful conditions of the shanty towns on the outskirts of the city, largely unnoticed by the Western visitor or the Delhi élite.

INTERNATIONAL ARRIVAL AND DEPARTURE

Arrival

Indira Gandhi International Airport is 20km to the south-west of the city centre. You pass through immigration and customs into the arrivals hall where there are **foreign exchange counters** (State Bank of India and Thomas Cook), open 24 hours. There's also a **hotel reservations counter** where you can book accommodation in the more up-market hotels, and a **Government of India tourist counter** (☎ 32 9117) for any other information. If you have a confirmed flight within the next 24 hours then you can get a bed in the airport retiring rooms at either the international terminal (Terminal 2, ☎ 565 2011) or the domestic terminal (Terminal 1, ☎ 329 5126). These operate on a first come first served basis, so phone to check if any are available. It's about a ten-minute bus or taxi ride between the two terminals.

The cheapest way to get into Delhi is by **bus**. The most reliable is the Ex-Servicemen's Airlink Transport Service (EATS) who have a desk in the arrivals hall where you should buy your ticket. Buses leave every half-hour from the international terminal, going via the domestic airport to Connaught Place, (Rs25, 45 mins) and they will usually drop you off at the major hotels if you ask. Otherwise there are Delhi Transport Corporation buses which go via the domestic terminal, Connaught Place and the railway stations, to the Inter State Bus Terminus.

Your other option is to get a **taxi**, which will be marginally quicker. Ignore all the taxi drivers who demand your custom and go straight to the pre-paid taxi desk in the arrivals hall, where you pay a fixed rate for your destination (between Rs200-300).

Warning

Many international flights arrive in Delhi late at night which can pose a few problems for the unaware traveller. Most of the budget guest houses are closed from midnight to sunrise so either check into a more upmarket hotel for your first night or hang around the airport until it gets light. If you are taking a taxi in the early hours of the morning be on your guard for unscrupulous taxi drivers who may take you for a ride in more ways than one. The usual con trick is to be told that it's not possible to go to the hotel of your choice and instead you will be taken to a hotel where the taxi driver gets paid a commission and you get badly ripped off. One way of avoiding this is to telephone your hotel in advance from the airport to make sure they are open and have a vacancy. Once you've got into the taxi act as if you know Delhi like the back of your hand, even if this is your first time in Asia.

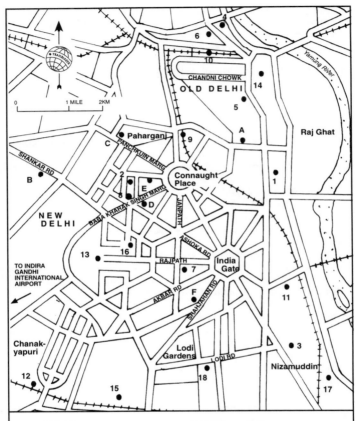

DELHI

1 Feroz Shah Kotla
2 Foreign Post Office
3 Humayun's Tomb
4 Inter State Bus Terminus (ISBT)
5 Jama Masjid
6 Kashmir Gate
7 National Museum
8 GPO (New Delhi)
9 New Delhi railway station
10 Old Delhi railway station
11 Purana Qila

12 Rail Transport Museum
13 Rashtrapati Bhavan
14 Red Fort
15 Safdarjang Airport
16 Sansad Bhavan
17 Sarai Kale Khan bus terminal
18 Tibet House

A Tourist Camp
B Master Paying Guest House
C Yatri Paying Guest House
D YWCA Blue Triangle Family Hostel
E The Connaught
F Claridges

Departure

Don't forget to confirm your flight 72 hours before leaving. EATS (☎ 331 6530) have buses that go first to the domestic and then on to the international airport (Rs25, 45 mins). They leave from their small office, just past Wimpy in Connaught Place, regularly from 04.00 to 23.30. If you are leaving at night it's easier to take a taxi (Rs200-300, 30 mins); make sure you book it the previous afternoon as it's almost impossible to find one in the middle of the night.

You'll need to arrive at the airport two hours before your flight leaves and pay a **departure tax** (currently Rs300 – Indian currency only). In the departure hall there are foreign exchange counters at the State Bank of India and Thomas Cook, a useless book shop and a very over-priced food counter.

ORIENTATION

Delhi is situated on the west bank of the River Yamuna and is two cities in effect, New Delhi and Old Delhi.

The most important landmark for getting your bearings is **Connaught Place** (officially renamed Rajiv Place, although still generally referred to by its former name) in the north of New Delhi, around which runs a busy ring road called **Connaught Circus** (officially renamed Indira Circus). Among the beautiful colonnades of Connaught Place you will find banks, shops, airline offices, restaurants, hotels, tourist offices and a host of other services useful to the traveller.

Running south from here is the important tree-lined road called **Janpath**, along which you will find the Government of India tourist office, a few more airline offices and plenty more guest houses and hotels.

Further south from here are the government buildings centred around **Rajpath** and among the parks and wide avenues are the expensive residences of the Delhi élite. Far out to the south-west, about halfway between Connaught Place and the airport, is the diplomatic area called Chanakyapuri where most of the embassies can be found.

North of Connaught Place, the streets get narrower and more crowded as you approach Old Delhi. Between the two cities is the New Delhi railway station and **Paharganj**, where there are lots of popular budget guest houses.

The main street of Old Delhi is **Chandni Chowk**, a seething mass of noise, smells and colours, off which run the narrow alleys and bazaars that this part of the city is famous for. The Red Fort and the Jama Masjid are here and just to the north is Old Delhi railway station and the main Inter State Bus Terminus. (Note that there's now a second bus terminus, Sarai Kale Khan, in the south of New Delhi, for buses to Agra).

WHERE TO STAY

Hotel areas
• **Connaught Place** There is a wide range of places to stay near Connaught Place, including budget guest houses around the top of Janpath, the YMCA and YWCAs around Sansad Marg, moderately priced hotels in Connaught Place itself and five-star international hotels slightly further south. The main reason for staying here is its proximity to Delhi's main shops, airline offices, banks, tourist offices and restaurants. Although very popular with budget travellers, the cheaper guest houses are over-priced and cramped when compared with similar accommodation in Paharganj.

• **Paharganj** This area around the Main Bazaar is about a ten-minute walk from Connaught Place and has a large selection of budget guest houses which attract Indian and Western travellers alike. The busy and narrow streets are conveniently located near the New Delhi railway station and give the traveller a better understanding of Indian city life than by staying in the more sedate and commercially orientated area around Connaught Place. When the Main Bazaar's noise, exhaust fumes and chaotic traffic of rickshaws, cows, bicycles and people get too much, it's always possible to retreat to a shady rooftop restaurant.

• **Other areas** There are several guest houses and hotels in other areas of Delhi which offer excellent value if you are just biding time in the city. They are not so convenient, however, if you've got a lot of organising or shopping to do in the centre.

Prices
Prices given below are for single/double rooms, with common (com) or attached (att) bathrooms, and air-conditioning (AC) as indicated. Rooms without air-con almost always come with a ceiling fan, which is essential in summer. The 'budget', 'moderate', and 'expensive' categories are based on the price of the cheapest double room. As is often the case with capital cities, accommodation in Delhi is far more expensive than elsewhere in the country and not nearly as good value for money.

Camping
The popular **Tourist Camp** in Old Delhi (on Jawaharlal Nehru Marg, near Delhi Gate, and opposite the JP Narayan Hospital, or Irwin Hospital, as it is sometimes called) has ample lawn space for pitching your own tent and at Rs30 per tent it's one of the cheapest places to stay in Delhi. There are clean communal washing and toilet blocks, a restaurant, laundry service and left luggage facility on site, and if you don't have a tent, you can stay in the very basic huts for Rs80/110 (com), or 'delux' for Rs100/140. The main drawback of the camp is that it's about 2km from all the facilities in Connaught Place.

Budget guest houses and hotels (£7/US$10 or less)

Places to stay below are [keyed] to the Central Delhi map on p79. For hotels that are not keyed refer to the main Delhi map on p74.

• **Connaught Place** At the top of Janpath, down a side street heading off to the east, are two very popular budget hang-outs. The first is the **Ringo Guest House** [9] (☎ 331 0605, 17 Scindia House), where you can offer your body to the mosquitoes on the open roof for Rs50, stay in a cramped dorm for Rs60, have a single for Rs90 (com) or a double from Rs160 (com) or Rs210 (att). The **Sunny Guest House** [8] (☎ 331 2909, 152 Scindia House), a little further on, offers much the same. Just around the corner from here is the slightly more expensive but rather dirty **Asian Guest House** [10] (☎ 331 3393, 14 Scindia House) above the Air France offices. All rooms have attached bathrooms and start from Rs175/215, or Rs300/350 if you want air-conditioning.

If you are after something quieter try looking down the small residential street called Janpath Lane, on the west side of Janpath. At No. 3 is **Mrs Colaco's** [6] (☎ 332 8758), where a dorm bed will cost you Rs55 and a double Rs130 (com), and further down Janpath Lane, at 7 Pratap Singh Building, is **Mr SC Jain's Guest House** [4] costing Rs130/200 (com) for simple rooms. In Connaught Place, at 85 M Block, is **Hotel Bright** [12] (☎ 332 0444) where decent sized, though gloomy, rooms cost Rs200/300 (com) and Rs300/400 (att). A little further round in D Block is the pleasant **Hotel Palace Heights** [13] (☎ 332 1419) which has a nice terrace to sit out on. Rooms are Rs275/325 (com) or Rs550 for air-con doubles with attached bath.

• **Paharganj** All the places to stay in this area fall into the budget category. Starting at the east end of the main bazaar (by New Delhi railway station) and heading west, you come first to **Hotel Kanishta** [17] (☎ 52 5365) which has clean double rooms for Rs150 and Rs200 (att). Not far after, on the other side of the road, is the very clean and pleasant **Traveller Guest House** [18] (☎ 354 4849). It is one of the more expensive places to stay in Paharganj with doubles for Rs160-225 (att) and all but the cheapest rooms come with a TV. Almost next door are the **Kailash Guest House** [19] (☎ 777 4993) with rooms costing Rs75/125 (com) or Rs160 for a double with bath, and the similarly priced **Kiran Guest House** [20] (☎ 52 6104) Rs85/105 (com), or a double with bath for Rs150. Both are cheap but OK.

Further west, the **Camran Lodge** [21] (☎ 52 6053) offers cheap and interesting accommodation with its vaguely Mughal-look decor for Rs60/120 (com) and attached doubles for Rs150. The redeeming feature of the overpriced, dirty **Hotel Payal** [22] (☎ 52 0867) is the friendly staff. Rooms cost Rs100/150 (com), Rs120/180 (att). Towards the west end of the Main Bazaar is the popular, grubby **Vivek Hotel** [23] (☎ 777 7062), which has plenty of large rooms at Rs100/120 (com), Rs130-200/150-225 (att), and Rs375/450 (att, AC). Down a side alley to the left is a very popular travellers' haunt called the **Hare Rama Guest House** [24] (☎ 751 8972), where rooms with common bathroom are a very reasonable Rs80/130, doubles with bath are Rs160, or Rs350 with air-con as well. Part of its appeal is the busy open-air restaurant on the roof. The **Anoop Hotel** [25] (☎ 52 6256) also has a rooftop restaurant with great views over Delhi. The clean rooms are similarly priced at Rs150 for doubles with shared bath, Rs120/190 for rooms with attached bath, and Rs300/350 for air-con rooms.

Moderately priced guest houses and hotels (£7-20/US$10-30)
• **Connaught Place** **Janpath Guest House** [5] (☎ 332 1935, fax 332 1937, 82-84 Janpath) is conveniently situated near the tourist office and Connaught Place. The carpeted rooms are reasonable value at Rs325/375 (att), or Rs500,775/625,950 (att, AC). If you don't want air-con then choose a room with a window as the others get very hot in summer.

Around Sansad Marg there are two YWCAs and one YMCA, all of which accept men and women. Despite the institutional atmosphere in these places they're extremely popular. The **YMCA** [3] (☎ 31 1915, fax 374 6032, Jai Singh Road) has large, airy and clean rooms for Rs260/440 (com) and Rs525/880 (att, AC). A free breakfast is provided and there's a swimming pool (Rs50). The **YWCA International Guest House** [1] (☎ 31 1561, fax 334 1763, 10 Sansad Marg) is similar, but all rooms have attached bathrooms and air-con and cost Rs416/695. The large **YWCA Blue Triangle Family Hostel** (☎ 31 0133) on Ashoka Road is a bit further away from Connaught Place than the other Ys and has clean, reasonably priced rooms: Rs325 for a single (att) or Rs400 with air-con, and between Rs475-530 for a double (att) or Rs575-750 with air-con (att).

In Connaught Place is the **Hotel Metro** [11] (☎ 331 3805, 49 N Block) which despite the grotty entrance hall has surprisingly nice rooms with attached bathrooms for Rs650/800 and Rs800/1000-1200 with air-con. At 55 H Block, Connaught Circus, is the fully air-conditioned **Hotel fifty five** [16] (☎ 332 1244) where attractively decorated, clean rooms cost Rs600/850 (att). There's a lovely balcony on the top floor, an ideal place to enjoy your breakfast and read the morning papers.

• **Other areas** If you don't mind the inconvenience of being further away from Connaught Place and are looking for a bit of peace and quiet, then there are two wonderful guest houses that deserve a mention. The first is the homely **Master Paying Guest House** (☎ 574 1089) at R 500 New Rajendra Nagar, which is a few km west of Connaught Circus. Immaculately clean rooms are Rs250-450 for a single and Rs450-600 for a double, all with shared baths. The other is the **Yatri Paying Guest House** (☎ 752 5563) which is only 1km to the west of Connaught Place

CONNAUGHT PLACE & PAHARGANJ

A American Express
B ANZ Grindlays
C Bank of America and Banque Nationale de Paris
D British Council
E Central Cottage Industries Emporium
F Delhi Tourism
G Ex-Servicemen's Airlink Transport Service (EATS)
H Government of India tourist office

I IDTC
J New Delhi railway station
K Nirula's
L Sona Rupa
M The Cellar
N The Host
O Thomas Cook
P United Coffee House
Q Wimpy
R Zen

1. YWCA International GH
2. Hotel Imperial
3. YMCA
4. Mr SC Jain's GH
5. Janpath GH
6. Mrs Colaco's
7. Park Hotel
8. Sunny GH
9. Ringo GH
10. Asian GH
11. Hotel Metro
12. Hotel Bright
13. Hotel Palace Heights
14. Hotel Marina
15. Nirula's Hotel
16. Hotel fifty five
17. Hotel Kanishta
18. Traveller GH
19. Kailash GH
20. Kiran GH
21. Camran Lodge
22. Hotel Payal
23. Vivek Hotel
24. Hare Rama GH
25. Anoop Hotel

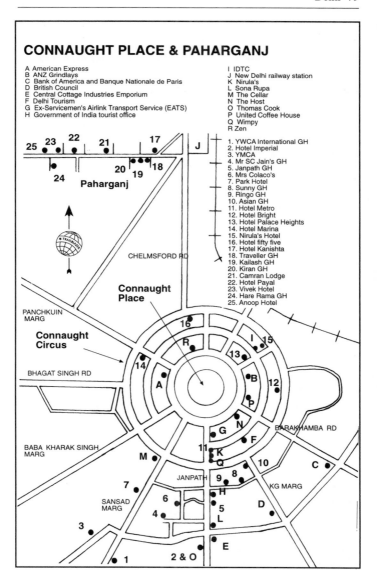

at 3/4 Punchkuin Road (Radial Road No.3). It's at the western end of this road, down a small residential side street. This also has well-furnished, clean double rooms for Rs450 (com), Rs650 (att), or Rs750 (att, AC). Both of these places get booked up quickly; it's advisable to phone ahead to check vacancies.

Expensive hotels (more than £20/US$30)

Delhi's smarter hotels are mainly found around Connaught Place and spread out to the south. The **Hotel Marina** [14] (☎ 332 4658, fax 332 8600) at 59 G Block, Connaught Circus, contains a restaurant, coffee shop, travel agency and laundry facilities in its plush surroundings. The comfortable rooms are Rs1190 and Rs1320 for a single and between Rs1600-2100 for doubles. On the opposite side of Connaught Place is **Nirula's Hotel** [15] (☎ 332 2419, fax 335 3957) in L Block, which is surrounded by Nirula's various eateries, ranging from an ice cream bar to a Chinese restaurant. This popular four-star hotel has pleasant and well-equipped rooms costing Rs1175 for a single and between Rs1800-2395 for a double. Just a stone's throw from Connaught Circus is the modern and uninspiring **Park Hotel** [7] (☎ 373 2477, fax 373 2025) at 15 Sansad Marg. Single rooms in this five-star hotel are Rs3200 and doubles from Rs3500 to Rs5500.

Five minutes' walk to the west, at 37 Shaheed Bhagat Singh Marg, is **The Connaught** (☎ 34 4225, fax 334 0757) where single rooms are US$60 and doubles between US$70 and US$90. If you can afford a little more the **Hotel Imperial** [2] (☎ 332 5332, fax 332 4542) is centrally located on Janpath, sheltered from the traffic noise by its extensive grounds. Plush doubles range from Rs3750 to Rs10,000 and within its old-style facade you will find several restaurants, a swimming pool and all the usual five-star facilities. To the south of the city, half way between the airport and the centre is **Claridges** (☎ 301 0211, fax 301 0625, 12 Aurangzeb Road), one of Delhi's legends. This beautiful hotel has four restaurants and a swimming pool and prices start from Rs3350.

WHERE TO EAT

Connaught Place has a wide choice of good restaurants which cover all budgets and palates. Although the McDonald's empire has not reached Delhi yet, there are several similar fast food restaurants, such as **Wimpy** and **Nirula's** in N Block, both popular with young Delhi-ites and Western travellers alike. The **United Coffee House** in E Block has reasonably priced south Indian, Chinese and European food. For something more up-market try **The Host** in F Block, or the ritzy **Zen** restaurant in B Block, which serves high class and expensive Japanese and Chinese food. **The Cellar** on the corner of Sansad Marg and Connaught Circus is excellent if you want a good fry-up for breakfast and at 46 Janpath you will find the excellent and good value **Sona Rupa**, which serves south Indian food downstairs and alcohol and north Indian food upstairs. Paharganj has lots of cheap eateries along the main street and several of the guest houses have roof-top restaurants which are popular with travellers.

SERVICES

Airline offices

• **Domestic airlines**   **Archana Airways** (☎ 684 2001) 41A Friends Colony East, Mathura Road; **Indian Airlines** have 24 hour booking at their main office at Safdarjang Airport (☎ 141, ☎ 462 0566, fax 463 4322). More convenient offices are at the Malhotra Building (☎ 331 0517, F Block, Connaught Place), and at the PTI Building (☎ 371 9168, Sansad Marg) both of which are open daily, except Sunday, 10am -5pm; **Jagson Airlines** (☎ 371 1069) 12E Vandana Building, 11 Tolstoy Marg.

• **International Airlines**   **Aeroflot** (☎ 331 2843) BMC House, 1st floor, Middle Circle, 1 N Block, Connaught Place; **Air Canada** (☎ 372 0043) Suite 1421, New Delhi Hilton; **Air France** (☎ 331 0407) 7 Atma Ram Mansion, Scindia House, Connaught Place; **Air India** (☎ 331 1225) Himalaya House, 23 Kasturba Gandhi Marg; **British Airways** (☎ 332 7428) DLF Centre, Sansad Marg; **Gulf Air** (☎ 332 4293) 12 G Block, Hotel Marina Arcade, Connaught Place; **KLM** (☎ 565 2715) Indira Gandhi International Airport, Terminal 2; **Lufthansa** (☎ 332 7268) 56 Janpath; **Quantas** (☎ 332 1434) Mohan Dev Bldg, 13 Tolstoy Marg; **Royal Jordanian** (☎ 332 7418) Jet Air, 56 G Block, Connaught Place; **SAS** (☎ 335 2299) 1st floor, Ambadeep Bldg, Kasturba Gandhi Marg; **Singapore Airlines** (☎ 332 0145) 11 G Block, Connaught Place; **Swissair** (☎ 332 5511) DLF Centre, Sansad Marg; **Thai** (☎ 332 3608) Ambadeep Bldg, Kasturba Gandhi Marg.

Banks

Among the many banks for foreign exchange are: **American Express**, A Block, Connaught Place; **ANZ Grindlays**, E Block, Connaught Place; **Bank of America** and **Banque Nationale de Paris**, Barakhamba Rd; **Thomas Cook**, (open 9.30am-8pm Monday to Saturday) Imperial Hotel, Janpath. There are 24 hour foreign exchange services at the State Bank of India and Thomas Cook at the airport and also at the Ashoka Hotel in Chanakyapuri.

Bookshops and libraries

There are many good bookshops and stalls around Connaught Circus; books are often cheaper than in the West. Good places to browse are the Bookworm, Radial Road 4, Connaught Place, and New Book Depot, B Block, Connaught Place. If you want a good read of the foreign newspapers, visit the British Council Library, 17 Kasturba Gandhi Marg.

Communications
• **Telephone and fax** You can make direct dial calls from any of the many STD/ISD booths around the city. Some will allow incoming calls and many have a fax service as well.
• **Post** Have your poste restante letters addressed to 'GPO New Delhi', as letters addressed to 'GPO Delhi' may end up in the Old Delhi post office. The poste restante is at the Foreign Post Office on Bhai Vir Singh Marg (Market Rd) to the west of Connaught Place.

Indian Mountaineering Foundation
The IMF (☎ 67 1211, Benito Juarez Road) is the official mountaineering body in India and it is necessary to get a permit from them if you intend to climb any peaks in the country (see p251). Their offices are in a smart building about a 30-minute auto-rickshaw ride from Connaught Place. Well known landmarks nearby are South Delhi University Campus and Dhaula Kaun.

It's a good place to come if you're a frustrated climber with a few days in Delhi to kill. The IMF have an excellent library full of expedition reports, books and magazines and also a tiny crag (in a hollow to the right of the main entrance) where you can practice your bouldering. They are also in the process of building a climbing wall but nobody knows when it's going to be ready – it was supposed to be completed in 1986! They can also provide you with information on climbing at local crags.

Medical clinics
The East West Medical Centre (☎ 69 9229, 38 Golf Links Rd) is a highly recommended private clinic, and failing that, you can try the All India Institute of Medical Sciences (☎ 66 1123, Ansari Nagar). There are several **pharmacies** in Connaught Place and in most other main shopping areas. An **ambulance** service is available by dialling ☎ 102.

Shopping
The best place to start looking for souvenirs is at the Central Cottage Industries Emporium on Janpath. This huge government run centre has high quality goods from all over India and is a good place to get an idea of what's available. The prices are fixed and are generally slightly more expensive than in the bazaars. Small boutiques continue all the way down Janpath to the Imperial Hotel, finishing with the Tibetan Market. There are more shops, emporiums and pavement traders all around Connaught Place and if you prefer shopping in a more authentic environment, try the small alleys around Chandni Chowk in Old Delhi.

Tourist information
While you are in Delhi, you will be approached by many people offering tourist information. These people are touts for tourist agents and are only after your money. There is only one main Government of India tourist

office in Delhi and that is at 88 Janpath (☎ 332 0005, open Monday to Friday 9am-6pm and 9am-2pm on Saturday). This is an excellent place to find out any information and to pick up a free map of the city.

State Government tourist offices can provide more relevant information for their regions: Himachal Pradesh (☎ 332 5320) have their offices at Chandralok Building, 36 Janpath; Jammu and Kashmir (☎ 332 5373) are at Kanishka Shopping Plaza, 19 Ashok Rd.

Most news stalls sell the excellent weekly *Delhi Diary* (Rs7.50) which gives listings of all the current films, exhibitions, plays and lectures, while also providing an invaluable city directory and map.

WHAT TO SEE

If you are short of time join an organised tour of the city. These are very good value for money and avoid the hassle of using the public transport system. Many companies will offer to guide you around Delhi; the two official companies, IDTC (☎ 332 2336, L Block, Connaught Place)and Delhi Tourism (☎ 331 4229, 36 N Block, Middle Circle, Connaught Place), are generally thought to be the best. Both offer morning tours of New Delhi and afternoon tours of Old Delhi (Rs50-80 each or Rs90-140 if booked together), and also run day tours to Agra (Rs300-440).

Red Fort

This was the centre piece of Shahjehanabad (Old Delhi), the great city built in under ten years by the Mughal emperor Shah Jehan in the seventeenth century. The whole city was surrounded by an 8.8km wall in which there were fourteen gates, five of which survive today: Delhi Gate, Kashmiri Gate, Turkman Gate, Ajmeri Gate, and Lahori Gate. On the eastern edge of the city was the huge Red Fort (Lal Qila), so named because of its massive red sandstone walls. The building of this impressive palace took place between 1638 and 1649, and the design is similar to the Agra Fort, where Shah Jehan's original capital was based. The modern visitor enters through the Lahori Gate which takes you into Chatta Chowk.There would once have been gold and silver for sale here; now it's full of souvenir sellers. Some of the important buildings within the fort are: the **Diwan-i-Am** (the hall of public audience) where the emperor would settle judicial matters of the general public; the **Rang Mahal**, or Palace of Colour; the **Khas Mahal**, which was the emperor's personal palace; and the **Moti Masjid**, Aurangzeb's personal mosque. The most impressive of the buildings is the **Diwan-i-Khas** (hall of private audiences) where the emperor would meet his nobles and ministers. In its former glory visitors were in no doubt that it was an attempt to create a copy of paradise as it is described in the Koran. There was once a ceiling of silver and gold; a 'Stream of Paradise' that cooled the air as it trickled through the building; a Peacock Throne made of gold and marble and inlaid with precious gems; still remaining are columns inlaid with semi-precious stones and the inscription on the north and south walls which translates as, 'If there is paradise on earth, it is here, it is here, it is here.'

The Red Fort is open daily from sunrise to sunset, Rs0.50. There's an excellent hour-long sound and light show each night (Rs20, ☎ 600121). The English commentary starts at 8.30pm September to October, 7.30pm November to January, 8.30pm February to April, 9pm May to August.

Jama Masjid

India's largest mosque is another of Shah Jehan's triumphs. It reportedly took 5000 masons six years to construct, starting in 1650 and costing Rs1,000,000. It was designed to hold the whole population at prayer and today has a capacity of 25,000 which is sometimes reached on Fridays and other holy days. It's worth climbing the southern minaret for the excellent views you get over Delhi (Rs5).

Entrance costs Rs15. You must remove your shoes and if you are wearing shorts, hire a robe to wrap around your legs.

Raj Ghat

In this green park, just south of the Red Fort and by the River Yamuna, is a black marble plinth where Mahatma Gandhi was cremated after his assassination in 1948. Prayers take place here every Friday evening.

India Gate

This majestic 42m high arch is a memorial to the Indian soldiers killed in WWI. It stands at the eastern end of Rajpath and provides the best views of Rashtrapati Bhavan and the symmetrical buildings of the Secretariat.

Rashtrapati Bhavan and Sansad Bhavan

Originally designed as a symbol of British colonial power by the ambitious English architect, Edwin Lutyens, **Rashtrapati Bhavan** was the former residency of the viceroy and is now the home of India's President. The building was erected between 1921 and 1929 and is a blend of European and Eastern styles. The huge gardens, however, are strictly Mughal in style and are open to the public once a year, in February.

Parliament House, or **Sansad Bhavan**, at the end of Sansad Marg is another of Lutyens' vast creations, although Sir Herbert Baker actually supervised the construction. The circular building now houses a library, chambers for the Council of State, an assembly chamber and a chamber for the Council of Princes. Today the two Houses of Parliament, the Lok Sabha and the Rajya Sabha, meet here.

Museums

The large **National Museum** gives an excellent overview of Indian culture with exhibits dating from Neolithic times to the twentieth century. It is located a little over halfway down Janpath. It's open Tuesday to

Sunday, 10am to 5pm, Rs0.50, ☎ 301 9538. The **Rail Transport Museum** is a must for all railway enthusiasts. India still has many working steam engines in use around the country; the best are kept off the rails in this museum. Among the wonderfully restored engines and carriages is the oldest engine in India, built in 1855. The museum is in Chanakyapuri, behind the Bhutanese Embassy. It's open Tuesday to Sunday 9.30am to 5pm, Rs2, ☎ 60 1816.

Tibet House

Discussion groups, lectures and retreats are held at the Tibet House (☎ 61 1515), 1 Institutional Area, Lodi Road, on the south side of Delhi. There's also a small museum (free) with a collection of Tibetan art and artefacts, and a handicraft shop. It's open Monday to Saturday 10am-1pm, 2-5pm.

Purana Qila

The 'Old Fort' is said to have been built on the legendary site of Indraprastha, the capital of the Aryans of 1000BC. In the sixteenth century it was part of the Emperor Humayun's capital and known as the sixth city of Delhi. The building was completed during the brief rule of the Afghan ruler Sher Shah (1538-45). Humayun came back to power after defeating Sher Shah's weak successor; but died in 1556 as a result of falling down the steep steps of the Sher Mandal which you can climb today for good views of the city. The fort is on Mathura Road, not far to the south-east of India Gate.

Nizamuddin

This small village, just south of the Purana Qila, has grown up around the shrine of the 14th century Islamic Sufi saint, Sheikh Nizam-ud-Din Auliya. Try to visit on a Thursday evening when *qawwali* singers gather to perform religious songs. There are several other important monuments in the area including the Jana-at-Khana mosque, west of the shrine.

Humayun's Tomb

It was usual for the Mughal rulers to build their tombs before they died. Humayun's accidental death prevented this tradition from being followed, so his widow, Haji Begum, built it in the 1560s. Its grand architectural style has led many to suggest that it was the forerunner of the Taj Mahal in Agra. The tomb is in Nizamuddin, just south of the Purana Qila.

Qutab Minar Complex

Fifteen km to the south of Connaught Place is a group of buildings which date from India's first Islamic rulers. The most well known of these is the Qutab Minar, a 72.5m high, red sandstone tower topped in marble, that dates back to 1199 when Qutab-ud-din started building the tower as a symbol of Islamic victory over Delhi. Next to the tower is the first mosque founded in India, the Quwwat-ul-Islam Masjid, which was built at a similar period out of the remains of 27 Hindu and Jain temples which the Muslims destroyed. Also in the complex is a fourth century iron pillar of the Gupta period, which has mysteriously remained virtually rust free despite its age. There is a local belief that if your arms can encircle the pillar with your back to it, then your wishes will be granted.

It's open daily from sunrise to sunset (Rs3). You can get there on bus No 505 from Ajmeri Gate.

Taj Mahal, Agra
India's most famous building is 200km from Delhi, close enough for a day trip. No matter how many times you've seen its image in print, nothing can prepare you for the visual impact of seeing the mausoleum in reality. It is perhaps the greatest monument ever built for love, standing in memory of Shah Jehan's wife of 17 years, Mumtaz-i-Mahal, after she died in childbirth in 1631. Work started on the building in the same year, but it took 20,000 workmen 22 years to complete this masterpiece of white marble symmetry. It's open daily from sunrise to sunset, and costs Rs10.50 8.30am-4pm, or Rs100 for entry before 8am or after 5pm.

Getting there There are several trains each day to Agra; the most convenient is the fully air-conditioned Shatabdi Express (2002) which departs New Delhi railway station at 06.15 (1 hour 55 minutes) and returns from Agra at 20.15. There are also regular buses (5 hours) which leave from the new bus terminal in south Delhi, called Sarai Kale Khan.

GETTING TO LADAKH
By air
The regular Indian Airlines flights into and out of Leh get heavily booked in the tourist season, so book as far in advance as possible. Whichever way you're flying, try to book your tickets in Delhi, as the Indian Airlines office in Leh invariably has long queues and the computers are frequently down. Delays and cancellations are common because the high mountains that surround Leh airport make the approach difficult if there is any cloud cover. For this reason, flights will leave Delhi only if they can be assured clear weather on arrival in Leh. If you can't get a seat on a direct flight, you could go via Jammu or Srinagar instead (see below).

It's also possible to fly to Kullu, 40km south of Manali, with either Archana Airways or Jagson Airlines most days of the week. These two operators have a habit of changing their services, so check their current flights with their offices in Delhi (see p81).

Indian Airlines flights from Delhi to Leh
• **Direct** (US$86, $1^1/_4$ hours) Indian Airlines fly direct from Delhi to Leh daily at 05.50 between 15 May and 15 September. There are flights throughout the year on Monday, Thursday and Friday at 06.40.

• **Via Jammu** On Saturday there is a flight via Jammu to Leh at 06.40 (US$86, 3 hours). Otherwise, there are flights to Jammu every day except Saturday, leaving at 10.15 (US$84, 70 minutes). Onward flights to Leh depart Jammu on Monday and Friday at 10.15 and on Saturday at 08.40 (US$50, 1 hour).

• **Via Srinagar** There are direct flights from Delhi to Srinagar on Tuesday, Thursday and Sunday leaving at 10.30 (US$92, $1^1/_4$ hours). Flights from Delhi to Srinagar via Jammu depart every day at 10.15 except Saturday (2 hours 35 minutes). Flights from Delhi to Srinagar via Amritsar depart on Monday, Wednesday and Saturday at 11.20 ($2^1/_2$ hours). There's only one onward flight a week to Leh which flies on Thursday at 10.25 (US$43, 45 minutes).

Srinagar

Continuing militant activity in Kashmir has meant that this beautiful part of India is now considered unsafe for travellers to visit (see the warnings on p50). The basic information below is given in case the situation changes for the better, or if you have no other option but to go via Srinagar.

Although there are hotels in the city, most are now closed and visitors stay on the famous houseboats on Dal Lake; not only more enchanting but also safer. The official rate for a deluxe boat is Rs750, A-class are Rs450, B-class Rs350, C-class Rs250 and D-class Rs120 inclusive of all meals, but you can expect to get a discount of at least 50% now that most of them are lying empty. Have a look at several boats to get an idea of what's available and make sure you know what's included in the price. There are also boats on Nagin Lake which is quieter and you are less likely to get hassled by endless vendors paddling over to you.

There is usually a curfew in place between dusk and dawn and you should get back to your houseboat well before this time, otherwise the *shikara* (water taxi) man will charge you an exorbitant rate which you can't refuse. Lastly, if you don't want to die prematurely, stay away from the old city where most of the fighting occurs.

By bus

Getting to Manali or Srinagar from Delhi is possible all year round but the two roads on to Leh from there are free of snow only during the summer. If you are entering Ladakh from Srinagar, the main obstacle is the Zoji La which is usually snow-free from the beginning of June to the end of October, but bad weather can significantly shorten this season. The Rohtang La and the Taglang La, between Manali and Leh, usually remain snowbound for longer. In a good year they will be open from late June to the middle of October, but after heavy snows they will only be passable from mid-July to mid-September. There are no through buses from Delhi to Leh, so whichever route you choose, you will need to spend at least one night in Manali or Srinagar before booking a second bus on to Leh.

• **Via Manali** Buses from Delhi to Manali take about 16 hours. See p92 for onward buses to Leh. Himachal Tourism (HPTDC) have comfortable buses to Manali leaving from their office at 36 Janpath at 06.00 and 18.00 daily. Luxury coaches cost Rs400, or Rs600 if you want air-conditioning. There are also several state-run buses to Manali every day which leave from the Inter State Bus Terminus (ISBT) near Kashmiri Gate. Prices vary between Rs180 and Rs350 depending on what class of bus you choose. Make sure you give yourself plenty of time, as you've got to book a seat at the relevant counter before you can board the bus.

• **Via Srinagar** Because of militant activity, bus travel in the Kashmir Valley is **not recommended**, particularly the Jammu-Srinagar service. Deluxe buses from Delhi to Srinagar take 24 hours, leave from the ISBT and cost Rs350. Buses depart from Srinagar each morning for Leh (Rs200-350) at about 08.30 and reach Kargil by 20.00, where you must spend the night. They then depart from Kargil at 04.30 next morning, arriving in Leh at about 15.00.

By train

If the political situation has improved you could use the railways to get to Jammu and take a bus on to Srinagar. Make reservations at New Delhi railway station (at the eastern end of Paharganj) at the excellent tourists' booking office on the 1st floor (7.30am-5pm). The best train is the overnight Shalimar Express (4645) which departs New Delhi station daily at 16.10 and arrives in Jammu at 06.30. The fare is Rs 165 for 2nd class and Rs450 in 1st. This connects with buses to Srinagar (Rs100-200, 12 hrs).

Manali

It takes sixteen hours to travel the 840km from Delhi to Himachal Pradesh's alpine playground of Manali. Situated at an altitude of 2050m (6730ft) on the west bank of the Beas River, it makes an idyllic stop before heading on over the Rohtang Pass to the barren mountain landscapes beyond. This rapidly expanding resort caters for both Western and Indian tourists with its many and varied hotels and restaurants. Although the town itself is not particularly attractive, it is surrounded by the lush orchards and dark forests, typical of the fertile Kullu Valley, and has enticing views to the north, of snow-capped 6000m peaks.

ORIENTATION

The bus stand is on the main street called the Mall, south of the tourist office. Most of the town's restaurants line the western side of the Mall and behind them is the area known as Model Town, where many of Manali's less interesting but conveniently-placed hotels are situated.

Three km north is the attractive village of Old Manali. Its peaceful surroundings, good views and budget guest houses have made it a popular place to stay. There's also some accommodation at Vashisht, 3km north-east of Manali although the main reason for visiting is to soak in the hot springs. There are public baths in the centre but the HPTDC baths (run by the tourism department), by the road into Vashisht, are better.

WHERE TO STAY

Prices below are for single/double rooms with common (com) or attached (att) bathrooms. Most of these places do not reduce their prices much outside the high season of April to June and September to November. You can, however, expect discounts of up to 50% in July or August from hotels which cater primarily to Indian tourists.

Budget guest houses and hotels

For 'Homely, Airy & Sanitary Accommodation' there's the **Sukiran Guest House** (☎ 2178), just off the Mall. This very basic place is convenient for the main bus stand; beds in the dormitory cost Rs20 and doubles are Rs130 (com). Cheap accommodation should also be available at the **Yatri Niwas**, opening soon by the tourist office.

The best budget guest houses are found in Old Manali. The **Veer Paying Guest House** (☎ 2410) costing Rs50/80 (att) is an excellent place. Back on the road into Old Manali is the **Hotel Krishna** (☎ 3071).

There are 12 rooms here; doubles for Rs50 (com). Down towards the river, the **Hotel New Bridge View** is rather more basic, but nonetheless atmospheric, with singles from Rs35 (com) and doubles from Rs45 (com). On cold nights you get a little stove in your room. Further down and on the other side of the road is **Hotel Dream River** with doubles from Rs180, triples from Rs350, all with bathroom attached.

The other accommodation area that's popular with travellers is the village of Vashisht, 3km from the bus station. Although the guest houses here are generally not quite as pleasant as those in Old Manali, Vashisht does have an added attraction in the hot springs here. There are about half a dozen cheap guest houses; the **Dharma Guest House** is one of the better places, with doubles from Rs80.

Moderately priced guest houses and hotels

Most hotels in Manali are aimed at the quantities of Indian tourists that the town attracts. You'll find the central area, Model Town, packed with places that charge about Rs350 for a double (att).

The most pleasant mid-range hotels are along the road between the new town and Old Manali. **Sunshine Guest House** (☎ 2464) dates from 1944. The proprietor and family are very hospitable and doubles cost from Rs300. They also have some modern cottages that sleep six. Nearby is a similar Raj-style guest house that's recommended, **John Banon's Guest House**. It's a little more expensive with doubles from Rs400. They've also opened a ritzy new resort next door.

More expensive hotels

At the bottom of the main town is the **Hotel Piccadily** (☎ 2149) which has rooms for Rs600/1300 (att). On the other side of the River Beas, about 1km downstream from the bridge is the **Manali Ashok Hotel** (☎ 2331) with doubles from Rs750 (att). Two km south is the **Holi-day Inn** (☎ 2262), which has doubles from Rs3000 (American plan – ie with all meals). Off season, there are good discounts at all these hotels.

WHERE TO EAT

If you're staying in Old Manali most of the guest houses offer basic meals for reasonable prices. The potato dishes at the Veer are heavenly. There are also several small travellers' cafés; above the river, the **Ish Café** offers pizzas. Near the New Bridge View Hotel is the **German Bakery** which sells brown bread and rolls.

Back in the main town there are numerous places to choose from. Some, such as the **Mayur**, **Mount View** and **Mona Lisa**, are deservedly popular and packed with Westerners. **MOC Restaurant** is an atmospheric place with good Tibetan and Chinese food, as well as some Japanese dishes such as tempura. For fast food visit **Kemps Corner** (pizzas, ice cream etc), or the **Madras Café** (vegetarian Indian – thalis from Rs30). For slow food there's **Peter's Restaurant**, a hippy hangover from the 70s which sells home-made bread and pots of jam.

GETTING AWAY

By air
The nearest airport is at Bhuntar, 10 km south of Kullu (40km south of Manali). Archana Airways and Jagson Airlines have regular daily flights to Delhi but changeable schedules. Contact travel agents in Manali for information. There are lots of buses between Kullu and Manali.

By bus
• **Leh** The journey to Leh is only possible during the summer months. For a description of the route see p135. The least painful bus on this bumpy two-day ride is that operated by Himachal Tourism (HPTDC). Tickets for the daily service cost Rs700, from the tourist office. For an extra Rs300 you have the dubious privilege of a bed in HPTDC's overpriced tented accommodation and an insipid evening meal. The only alternative is to bring your own food and sleep on the bus. The buses get heavily booked in July and August; buy your ticket as early as possible. There are also a few travel agents who operate similar private services.

Local HPSRTC and J&KSRTC buses also run on this route. Although not as comfortable they're much cheaper (Rs350-475) and stop overnight in Keylong (6 hours) where decent hotel accommodation is available. If you want to cut down the next day's 15-hour journey by an hour or two, you can carry on to Darcha where tents can be rented for the night.
• **Delhi** HPTDC have daily buses to Delhi costing Rs600 for air-conditioned luxury coaches and Rs400 for non-AC. The day bus leaves at 06.00 and arrives in Delhi at 20.00; the night bus departs at 17.00 and arrives at 10.00 the next morning. Tickets are available from the tourist office. There are also various state-run buses to Delhi from the bus stand.

By taxi
A taxi, into which you can squeeze up to six people, will cost Rs10,200 to Leh, although this price is sometimes negotiable.

Trekking to Ladakh
The 21-day trail from Darcha takes you across Zanskar right into the heart of Ladakh (see p32). Trekking agencies in Manali will separate you from your cash by organising everything for you but it is relatively simple to arrange the trek yourself. The Mountaineering Institute on the east bank of the River Beas and the tourist office in town are both good sources of information, and pony-men can be found below the bus stand. The ponies will take two days to get from Manali to Darcha and you can go by bus. Buy all your supplies in Manali as little is available in Darcha.

Cycling from Manali to Leh

Every year sees more and more cyclists attempting this high altitude cycle ride which must rate as one of the most spectacular in the world. If you don't feel up to going it alone then there are several adventure travel companies who run fully supported tours along the route (see p13).

The 485km journey through desolate and remote country involves climbing four major passes up to a height of 5328m (17,480ft), so both you and your bike must be in good condition. The route is slightly easier from north to south, but most cyclists find the objective of going to Leh more appealing and this direction is far better for acclimatisation. The right machine for the journey is really a question of preference. Mountain bikes with knobbly tyres seem to be the most popular, but plenty of people have completed the trip on touring bikes, or mountain bikes fitted with 26x1.5 tyres which will have you speeding along on the paved sections (about 50% of the road is sealed). Come prepared for every possible weather imaginable from scorching sunshine to freezing blizzards, even in mid-summer. There are several dhabas along the way where you can sleep and eat some awful food; to be on the safe side, you need to bring camping equipment and several day's supplies. Water is not generally a problem, except on the dry and barren More Plains between Pang and the southern base of the Taglang La.

A possible nine-day itinerary: Manali-Rohtang La-Koksar; Koksar-Keylong; Keylong-Patseo; Patseo-Baralacha La-Bharatpur City; B-City-Brandy Nullah; B-Nullah-Lachalang La-Pang; Pang-Taglang La-Rumtse; Rumtse-Tikse; Tikse-Leh (see p133 and p135). If it all gets too much, jump on the next passing bus or truck.

PART 4: LADAKH

Facts about the region

GEOGRAPHICAL BACKGROUND

Ladakh lies in the eastern half of Jammu and Kashmir State in the far north of India. It shares its much disputed north-western border with Pakistan, while to the north lies the Chinese province of Sinkiang, and to the east, Chinese-occupied Tibet.

Covering an area of about 60,000 sq km and ranging in elevation from 2600m to 7670m (8500ft to 25,165ft), it is the largest and highest district in India. A further 37,000 sq km of north-east Ladakh, an area called the Aksai Chin is presently illegally occupied by China.

Ladakh is sandwiched between two vast mountain systems – the Himalaya to the south and the Karakoram to the north. It is the latter range which provides the region with its highest peak, Saser Kangri (7670m/25,165ft). Between the two ranges are the Ladakh and Zanskar Mountains, north and south of the Indus Valley respectively. These run north-west to south-east, almost as far as Nepal in the case of the Zanskar Mountains and have peaks mainly between 5000m and 6000m.

Ladakh can be divided up into several geographic regions:
• **Central Ladakh** Ladakh's heartland is the central Indus Valley. This runs from Khalsi in the west to Upshi in the east, bounded by the Ladakh Mountains to the north and the Zanskar Mountains to the south.
• **Nubra** This region of deep valleys and high mountains, to the north of the Ladakh Range, encompasses the Nubra and Shyok river valleys and the eastern end of the Karakoram Mountains. It can be reached by road from Leh over the 5602m (18,380ft) Khardung La, reputedly the highest motorable road in the world.

The making of mountains
Ladakh is in the Trans-Himalayan region – the impact zone where the Indian continental plate collided with the rest of Asia. This monumental geological occurrence happened some 50 million years ago, creating mountain ranges from west to east across Asia. The Karakoram extend from the Pamirs in the west for 450km and include K2 (8611m/28,250ft), the world's second highest mountain; while the Himalaya, the highest mountain range in the world, continue east for 2400km reaching 8848m/29,028ft at Mount Everest. One effect of this collision is Ladakh's extraordinary variety of coloured rocks caused by the drawing up of deep marine deposits.

• **The Rupshu** This dry, high altitude plateau (4000-5500m) is in the south-east of Ladakh. If you're travelling up from Manali by bus, it's the first region you see. It's part of the much larger area of Chang Tang, which spreads east into Tibet for about 1500km, and whose landscape is characterised by vast plains, rolling mountains and blue, brackish lakes.

• **Zanskar** Between the Great Himalayan Range and the jagged mountains of the Zanskar Range is the 300km long valley of Zanskar. Access can be gained only by crossing high passes which effectively cut the valley off from the rest of the world during winter. With an average valley bottom altitude of 4000m (13,000ft), it's one of the highest inhabited regions of the world. The two major rivers are the Stod and the Tsarap which join to form the mighty Zanskar. This eventually merges with the Indus having cut an impressive gorge through the Zanskar Mountains.

• **Western Ladakh** The area around the town of Kargil is sometimes referred to as Lower Ladakh. It comprises a number of river valleys, principally the Suru, Drass, Wakha and the Indus downstream of Khalsi. The altitude here is lower than the rest of Ladakh and so vegetation is much more varied. Further to the west is the Zoji La, Ladakh's western gateway, which takes you over the Great Himalayan Range into Kashmir.

CLIMATE

Extremes of temperature

There's a saying that a person who has their head in the sun and their feet in the shade in Ladakh will endure both heat stroke and frostbite at the same time. While this is something of an exaggeration, in summer the sun is incredibly powerful but step into the shade and you may need an extra layer of clothing. Night temperatures are comfortably cool. Altitude also plays a strong role in regulating the temperature. One day you can be trekking at 3000m in the stifling heat, the next you can be battling over a 5000m pass in a blizzard. Generally, summer days are a warm 20°- 25°C.

Winter is a different matter. Even in Leh the thermometer rarely rises above freezing and has been known to drop as low as -40°C. In Zanskar temperatures as low as this are common.

Rain and snow

One of the great advantages of Ladakh to the trekker is that when the rest of the Himalaya are being saturated by the annual monsoon, Ladakh stays mainly dry. This is because the Great Himalayan Range forms an impenetrable barrier for the summer rain clouds that sweep up from the south.

Ladakh is dry in the extreme; a typical year sees under 100mm of rain fall. This gives Ladakh its characteristically barren landscape. Zanskar and the far west of Ladakh around Drass gets slightly more precipitation than the rest of the region; but this usually falls in winter as snow. Over the last few summers, however, there's been a lot more rain than usual.

HISTORICAL OUTLINE

The first mention of the country seems to have been made by Herodotus, who describes a land of wonderful ants, who in burrowing out their homes in the earth threw up gold. These ants were said to be nearly as large as dogs, and still more ferocious, with a keen sense of smell and great fleetness of foot. This made it very difficult for the Indians who wanted the gold to obtain it, and the only method found possible was to fetch the gold day by day when the ants slept, and bear it away on swift horses.
A Reeve Heber and Kathleen Heber *Himalayan Tibet and Ladakh*

Prehistory
Neolithic rock carvings have been found in many parts of Ladakh, from Zanskar to Nubra, showing that the area has been inhabited from the earliest of times. In keeping with many Himalayan regions, these carvings are often of Ibex, an animal that was given divine status throughout the Himalaya by the early inhabitants.

Tribal herdsmen from the west and east slowly settled in Ladakh over the centuries. Traces of these early influxes are still evident in the people in parts of Ladakh today. The Aryan Dards, who came to Ladakh from Kashmir and northern Pakistan, preserve their unique culture in the Dha-Hanu area, while the Rupshu region is largely populated by Tibetan herdsmen, whose semi-nomadic way of life has changed little in the intervening centuries. Other races also trickled into the region, notably from central Asia and Baltistan. Gradually this ethnic hotchpotch integrated into the more unified culture you see today.

The emergence of a nation
From the 6th to the 9th century, the area now known as Ladakh was influenced by the greater powers that surrounded it. Kashmir, Tibet and China were all keen to increase their territory and it seems likely that they all invaded the region at one time or another. Eventually Tibet won the struggle but only held a loose claim on the area. A more direct interest wasn't shown until the collapse of the Tibetan dynasty in 842. This resulted in a power struggle among the ruling classes, which led to some members of the ousted royalty, notably Nyimagon, travelling to western Tibet in search of new dominions. They took control of Ladakh, Guge, Perang, Zanskar and Spiti. Ladakh was allocated to Pelgigon, Nyimagon's eldest son, who installed himself as the first king in the mid-10th century.

Buddhist influences
Buddhism was flourishing in western Ladakh well before the Tibetans arrived, possibly taking root as early as the second century while much of eastern Ladakh and western Tibet was still practising the ancient Bon religion, an animistic belief presided over by shaman priests. The Buddhist influence came via India and, in particular, Kashmir. The rapid rise of Hinduism throughout India forced Indian Buddhist monks to seek sym-

pathetic areas to which they could migrate. Many travelled to Ladakh bringing with them their artistic skills and religious beliefs. The eighth century rock carving of the Maitreya, or future Buddha, at Mulbekh is a fine example of Buddhist art in the Indian tradition, prior to the Tibetans.

Nyimagon's dynasty was keen to nurture Buddhism and help encourage its revival in Tibet, a move which became known as the **second spreading**.

By the 12th and 13th centuries Buddhism was flourishing in Tibet but had been replaced by Hinduism in India and Islam in Kashmir. Ladakh, unable to rely on its traditional religious and cultural guides, turned instead to Tibet. A strong bond developed between their monasteries with young Ladakhi monks being sent to Tibet to be trained in the finer points of monastic life. This tradition continued for over 700 years until the Chinese occupation of Tibet put a stop to it.

> ### The second spreading
> The protagonist of this movement was a scholar named Rinchen Zangpo, sometimes referred to as 'the great translator', who had the onerous task of making Indian Buddhism accessible to the Ladakhi and Tibetan people.
>
> Modern day visitors to Ladakh will see his name again and again in connection with various monasteries. While many claim to have been founded by him, it's unlikely that he was as productive as they would like you to believe. It's true that many monasteries were built at this time, and although Rinchen Zangpo was not personally responsible for all of them, he was probably the inspiration behind this building frenzy. Unfortunately, only a handful of gompas, of which Alchi is the finest, remain intact from this era.

The Namgyal dynasty

Continuous raids on Ladakh by the plundering Muslim forces of central Asia and Kashmir were a feature of the fifteenth and sixteenth centuries. The more accessible western part of Ladakh took the full brunt of this aggression and was partially converted to Islam. Ladakh, as a result, was divided and weakened, with Lower Ladakh ruled by King Takpabum from Basgo and Temisgam, and Upper Ladakh by King Takbumde from Leh and Shey. It took Bhagan, the grandson of the Basgo King, to unite Ladakh by overthrowing the king of Leh. He took on the surname of Namgyal (meaning victorious) and founded a new dynasty which still survives today. This new lineage was not immune from Islamic attack either: during the 1530's and 40's Ladakh was constantly besieged by central Asian forces under the intrepid warrior, Mirza Haidar.

The strong rule of the brutal King Tashi Namgyal (1555-1575) strengthened a flagging and low-spirited country and managed to repel most of the central Asian raiders. He is best remembered for the imposing royal fort he built on top of Namgyal Peak and the Gonkhang just

---

(Opposite) Top: The imposing 17th century Palace overlooking Leh was the home of Ladakh's Royal Family until they moved to Stok after the Dogra invasion in the mid-19th century. **Bottom:** Balti-style polo is played in Leh as it has been for hundreds of years; the only change being a shift of venue from the main bazaar to this purpose-built ground.

below. The fortunes of Ladakh continued to flourish under his nephew, Tsewang Namgyal, an eminent soldier who temporarily increased his kingdom as far as Nepal.

The Muslim invasion

It was at the beginning of the seventeenth century, during the reign of Jamyang Namgyal (Tsewang's brother), that the proponents of Islam made the most concerted effort to convert Ladakh once and for all. The Baltistan army under Ali Mir stormed through the country destroying all Buddhist artefacts that they came across and thwarting the Ladakhi's attempts to stop them. Today there are few gompas that date from before this catastrophic episode as most were razed to the ground. Alchi and a few hill gompas are the exception.

Jamyang Namgyal was forced to marry Ali Mir's daughter, Gyal Katun, and to promise that any offspring from this union would be first in line for the throne, thereby ensuring future Islamic kings. However, in an ironic twist of fate, her subjects saw the new queen not as a Muslim but rather as the manifestation of a Buddhist goddess! Buddhism was resurrected with increased vigour.

Sengge Namgyal

The son of Jamyang and Gyal Katun, Sengge Namgyal, the 'lion' king (1616-1642), is perhaps the best remembered of Ladakh's kings. In an effort to bring Ladakh back to its former glory he embarked on an ambitious and energetic building programme which produced several gompas, the most famous of which is Hemis, many mani walls, the huge statue of Buddha at Shey and the skyscraping palace overlooking Leh. He was also a courageous soldier, expanding the kingdom into Zanskar, Spiti and the west Tibetan province of Guge. He had less success in the west, being badly defeated by the Mughal army that had already taken Kashmir and Baltistan. Peace was restored only by his agreeing to pay the Mughals a regular tribute; a promise that he never honoured. Although he is constantly praised in the chronicles, his extravagant and overambitious reign had negative consequences for the future of Ladakh.

The loss of independence

His son and heir, Deldan Namgyal (1642-1694), had to pay for his father's defiance by building a mosque in Leh in order to placate the powerful Mughal emperor, Aurangzeb. He was also supposed to pay the tribute but like his father, either paid infrequently or not at all. He led a successful campaign against the Baltis in the west and defeated a Mughal army that came to their aid. However, he made a grave mistake with his

(**Opposite**) **Top:** Preparing a brew of butter tea over a yak dung fire after a long day's trek; Pogmar (see p220). **Bottom:** The large houses of Temisgam reflect its important past; in the 15th century the village was one of the capitals of Lower Ladakh.

allies on the eastern border by going against the Dalai Lama, siding instead with Bhutan in a religious dispute. A combined Tibetan and Mongol force descended on the impudent king and forced him to take refuge in the fortress at Basgo, where he was held for three years. The Tibetans were finally forced to withdraw by an advancing Kashmiri army but this help from Deldan's former enemies did not come cheap.

While Ladakh remained internally autonomous, the Kashmiris now assumed overall power. The king was made to convert to Islam, all Ladakh's valuable *pashmina* wool had to go to Kashmir, and the long ignored tribute had to be paid. As with the other attempts to convert Ladakh to Islam it was the people who were impossible to win over, remaining true to their Buddhist roots.

The Treaty of Temisgam in 1684 settled the dispute between Ladakh and Tibet but by means of various trade and religious agreements it ensured that Ladakh became partially controlled by its eastern neighbour as well. Sandwiched between Kashmir and Tibet and answerable to both, Ladakh was severely restricted in what it could do beyond its borders.

The Dogra invasion

By the beginning of the nineteenth century the Mughal empire had collapsed and Sikh rule had been established in Kashmir. Meanwhile, Ladakh had been weakened by a series of poor kings and seemed an obvious target for the expansionist ambitions of the Sikh ruler, Ranjit Singh. His commander in chief, Zorawar Singh, invaded Ladakh with 5000 men in 1834, meeting little resistance from the poorly equipped and trained Ladakhi army. King Tshespal Namgyal was dethroned and the royal family exiled to Stok, where they still live. Ladakh came under Dogra rule and it was incorporated into the state of Jammu and Kashmir in 1846. However, Ladakh was allowed to maintain a large amount of autonomy and to keep its links with Tibet.

Partition and the Indo-Pakistan wars

The tragic events that swept over India in the run up to partition in 1947 mercifully avoided Ladakh. Buddhists and Muslims continued living side by side, without any major incidents, as they had done for centuries. Partition left Ladakh as part of the Indian state of Jammu and Kashmir with the result that it would be administered from Srinagar.

In 1948, just after partition, Ladakh was invaded yet again. This time by Pakistani raiders who managed to take Kargil, occupy Zanskar and get to within 30km of Leh. The capital was badly defended and volunteers were hastily sought and trained. Fortunately, reinforcement troops were sent in by air and a battalion of Gurkhas made its way slowly to Leh on foot from the south. Both reached Leh in time to expel the raiders and return Ladakh to India. Kargil was the scene of fighting again in 1965 and 1971 during the two Indo-Pakistan wars, when both nations challenged the position of the cease-fire line. This ran extremely close to Kargil thus involving it in the skirmishes. The Indian army managed to push it back to 12km from the town in 1971, where it still remains.

Chinese aggression

The events that took place on Ladakh's northern and eastern borders had much wider repercussions for the region than the series of Indo-Pakistan wars. The first blow to Ladakh was the Chinese closure of the border between Nubra and Sinkiang Province in 1949. This effectively stopped the traditional trade route between India and central Asia, and starved Ladakh of the 1000 year old business that had been generated from the caravans.

In 1950 the Chinese authorities invaded Tibet. For a decade the Tibetans were assaulted with violence and propaganda which culminated in the brutal suppression of the Lhasa uprising in 1959. The Dalai Lama sought refuge in India and has since been followed there by thousands of refugees. The Chinese then continued their expansionist programme into Ladakh by occupying 28,500 sq km of the Aksai Chin, a high desolate plain in the north-east of the region, where they promptly built roads connecting Tibet with Sinkiang. In 1962 the Chinese launched a massive attack on the borders of Ladakh but were repelled by Ladakhi and Indian troops. The loss of the worthless land of the Aksai Chin was not an important issue but the proximity of the Chinese, who by now were working closely with the Pakistanis, posed a real threat to India. This was demonstrated by the joint construction of the Karakoram Highway.

Suddenly, the strategic importance of Ladakh was recognised by the rest of the subcontinent. The region's isolation was swiftly brought to a close by the rapid completion of the 434km Srinagar to Leh highway, cutting the journey from 16 days to 2, and enabling a massive military build up to ensue. Simultaneously, China closed the Tibetan border and brought to an end the 700 year old paternal link between the gompas of Ladakh and Tibet.

Siachen Glacier war

The most constant and least talked about conflict between India and Pakistan has been going on for over ten years at the head of the Nubra Valley. This extraordinary war on the longest glacier in the Karakoram, is the highest in the world with fighting at up to 6500m (21,000ft). The exact position of the cease-fire line in this remote part of the Karakoram has never been fully agreed. When rumours started circulating that Pakistan might try to stake a claim on the Siachen Glacier and the surrounding peaks, Indian troops swiftly occupied the area in 1984. Fighting soon broke out and skirmishes have continued ever since. The severe cold restricts the fighting to the summer but this hasn't limited the casualties. Far more people have died as a result of the environmental conditions (altitude, crevasses, avalanches and exposure) than have from the actual fighting.

Towards autonomy

Since partition, Ladakh has been governed by the State Government based in Srinagar. This has never been a wholly satisfactory arrangement and Ladakhis feel that they have often been neglected by the politicians in Kashmir. Calls for a Union Territory, separate from Jammu and Kashmir State and directly governed from New Delhi, have circulated since the early 1970s but have met with little success. Among the few efforts designed to help develop the region was the opening up of Ladakh to foreign tourists in 1974. In 1979 Ladakh was split in two, allegedly for the convenience of administration, into the supposedly 'Buddhist' Leh District and 'Muslim' Kargil District, of which Zanskar was a sub-division. This upset many people, not least the Zanskaris, who were justifiably concerned about who was going to represent their Buddhist interests. This unnecessary division started to rock the centuries' old cohesiveness between Buddhists and Muslims.

In the early 1980s the State Government mishandled several simple, localised problems, sparking off demonstrations throughout Ladakh. Continued apathy, corruption and Muslim bias from the State Government throughout the decade provided the catalyst for violent riots in Leh in 1989 between Buddhists and Muslims. This culminated in the police opening fire on a peaceful demonstration, killing three innocent people. More subtle agitation ensued, provoking the Ladakh Buddhist Association (LBA) to call for a social and economic boycott of Muslims.

In 1989 there were further demands for a Union Territory which were soon toned down to a more realistic demand for autonomous status within the state. Pressure from within Ladakh increased and the process gathered pace. The LBA lifted the boycott against the Muslims in 1992 and since then there has been greater co-operation between the two religions.

Ladakh Autonomous Hill Development Council

In October 1993 the Central Indian Government and the State Government agreed that Autonomous Hill Council Status would be granted for Ladakh. Under this proposal, only control over law and order would remain with the Kashmir government. Responsibility for almost everything else, including development, education, culture, the staffing of government posts and the collection of local taxes, would be placed in the hands of the Ladakhis. In September 1995 the decentralised and democratic Ladakh Autonomous Hill Development Council became reality, and a new era for Ladakh began.

ECONOMY

For centuries Ladakh has enjoyed a stable economy based on self-reliance. But over the last 50 years, the region has shifted away from this sustainable economy towards one based on dependence on outside forces, and is slowly being drawn into a much wider economic sphere, over which it has little control. Misguided policies to 'help' this 'deprived and backward' region, along with the build up of a large population of Indian troops and the influx of foreign tourists, have all contributed to encouraging a money economy. A materialistic culture where the notion of having a job and buying what you need, rather than producing it yourself, is now becoming more widespread. While change is inevitable, it doesn't have to take the form of rapid Western-style modernisation.

Fortunately Ladakh is the home of several forward-thinking indigenous organisations who are swimming against this tide of inappropriate change (see p119). By encouraging ecological and sustainable development which preserves and builds on traditional practices, it is hoped Ladakh will avoid the pitfalls which so many other blindly modernising, developing countries have suffered.

> **Pashmina**
> This incredibly fine wool from the underbelly of the Chang Tang goat is the basis for Srinagar's cashmere shawl weaving industry. This industry has been vital to Srinagar's economy since the 17th century and goes some way towards explaining Kashmir's obsession for control of Ladakh. Cashmere fabric is notoriously expensive because each goat produces only small quantities of this soft hair and its processing is incredibly time consuming. Cheaper wool is available from Mongolia and Iran, but is thought to be of inferior quality.
>
> Since the 1684 Treaty of Temisgam, Ladakh has had a monopoly on the purchasing of this valuable product from the nomads of Rupshu and Chang Tang, although the agreement also stipulated that it could be sold only to Kashmiri traders. The monopoly still exists today, and although it has kept the price of pashmina artificially low, it has supported a unique way of life on the Chang Tang plateau.

Agriculture

Ladakh has traditionally been an agricultural subsistence economy based on growing barley, wheat and peas and the keeping of yak, *dzos* (yak-cow crossbreeds), cows, sheep and goats. At lower elevations fruit is grown successfully, while the high altitude Rupshu region is the preserve of nomadic herders. Surplus produce is traded for tea, sugar, salt and various luxuries such as the semi-precious stones that adorn women's head-dresses, or peraks.

There is little that can be exported for economic gain. Two exceptions, however, are apricots from western Ladakh and pashmina, the goats' wool from the Chang Tang plateau which is used for the production of cashmere shawls.

Sustainable agriculture

In many ways it's amazing that the harsh environment of Ladakh can support any agriculture, and yet a highly productive subsistence system has provided the population with most of their needs for centuries. In fact, when average crop yields are compared, they are almost as high as those of intensive, high input farms in Europe. The success of this system is due to the refinement of techniques to suit the environment and a social structure that supports agriculture. For example:

• The lack of water is overcome by diverting melt water from mountain streams along sophisticated irrigation channels.

• The shortage of fuel wood is overcome by using dried animal dung. The hardy local breeds of livestock also provide farmers with power for ploughing and threshing while producing useful by-products such as milk, cheese and wool.

• As the animal dung is used mainly for fuel and not for fertiliser, human 'nightsoil' is collected in dry latrines and spread on the fields instead.

• An extensive system of sharing resources throughout a village, called *langde*, evolved so that the labour intensive activities, such as sowing and harvesting, can be completed without having to hire labourers.

• Another system called *rares* means that each family has to take it in turn to herd all the animals in the village for a day.

• Both the tradition of passing on land only to the eldest son and the practice of polyandrous marriages (whereby brothers share a common wife) prevent the fragmentation of family land.

In recent years, several trends have started to undermine this integrated agricultural system and destroy the fragile environment on which farming depends: more people are leaving the villages to seek employment in Leh; those that remain are moving towards growing single cash-crops; polyandry and other social structures are becoming relics of the past; people are beginning to perceive farming as a lowly occupation; and the government is promoting highly subsidised hybrid seeds, chemical fertilisers and pesticides, while distributing subsidised food at half its actual price to the markets of Leh.

There is a realisation that if these trends go unchecked agriculture will suffer a demise, there will be a decline in soil and water quality and Ladakh will become dependent on imported food. Within the last decade or so, efforts have been made by various non-governmental organisations (NGO's), in particular LEDeG (Ladakh Ecological Development Group), to raise awareness of the dangers of 'modern' methods, to increase the status of farmers and to harness the benefits of the sustainable and productive traditional system. There is now growing evidence that the farmers' initial excitement with the new techniques is gradually being replaced by a return to their faith in traditional agriculture.

Trade

In the past, Ladakh's geographical position at the cross-roads of some of the most important trade routes in Asia was exploited to the full. Ladakh's kings happily collected tax on the goods that crossed their kingdom from Turkistan, Tibet, the Punjab, Kashmir and Baltistan, while a minority of Ladakhi people were profitably employed as merchants and caravan traders. However, since the Chinese authorities closed the borders into Tibet and central Asia, this trade has completely dried up. Business is now reliant on the more fickle market of the Indian army and summer tourists.

Tourism

Since 1974, when Ladakh was opened to tourists, the industry has expanded rapidly. On average it now receives 16,000 tourists a year. Although in Ladakh as a whole, tourism only employs 4% of workers, in Leh it employs 15%. It also accounts for almost 50% of the region's GNP. See p139 for information on how to limit your impact on Ladakh.

EDUCATION

For almost 50 years the education system in Ladakh has been in chaos. It is based on the Indian education system which is a poor copy of the British system. Schools are now well distributed throughout Ladakh but 75% of them are primary only (5-11 years). These are attended by about 65% of the children, but there is a high level of absenteeism, especially in the busy agricultural seasons when the children's help is needed on the farms. As there are fewer middle and high schools, study beyond the age of 11 often involves leaving home and living in rented accommodation.

Low salaries (Rs1500-3500 per month) attract poor quality teachers, most of whom have to be recruited from outside Ladakh. Teacher absenteeism is also a problem and it is not unheard of for teachers to charge for private tuition on subjects that they themselves failed to teach in school.

As if this were not enough, the Western-biased curriculum teaches the pupils nothing of their own land or history and they aren't even taught in Ladakhi. Until the age of 14 they learn in Urdu and after that in English. They then have only two years to master this new language before taking the all important matriculation exam, in English. This is their passport to jobs and further education: 95% fail it. It seems that for the vast majority, schooling has served only to alienate them from their native culture.

The long term outlook is a little more promising. In 1993 SECMOL (Students' Educational and Cultural Movement of Ladakh) launched a campaign called 'Operation New Hope' aiming to provide 'culturally appropriate and locally relevant education' by a number of means which include producing Ladakhi textbooks, adopting one language for the teaching of maths and science at all ages, and the regular training of teachers. A government degree college has been opened in Leh, thus providing further education students with the option of staying in Ladakh, rather than having to move to Delhi or Kashmir.

THE PEOPLE

The 160,000 strong population of Ladakh is a result of the blending of many different races, in particular the Tibetans and the Dards.

Tibetans

The nomadic and semi-nomadic **Changpa** people of the Rupshu plateau are pure Tibetans and it is probably herders like them who first populated Ladakh. Through centuries of experience they have mastered the art of not only living but thriving in one of the most hostile environments on earth. Since the early 1960's their numbers have increased as Chang Tang nomads from across the Tibetan border flee the occupation of their homeland by the Chinese. Leh has also provided a home from home for about 3500 **refugees** who live in the various camps around the city.

The looks and the way of life of both the **Ladakhis** of central Ladakh and, perhaps even more so, the **Zanskaris**, reflect a strong influence from central Tibet. Moving east, this influence diminishes and is replaced by that of the Dards. The one exception to this is the **Baltis** who live around Kargil and the Suru Valley. They have Tibetan origins, speak a language that has Tibetan links and were once Buddhists, though today they are devout Shiite Muslims.

Population control

Living in a landscape where resources are severely limited encouraged the Ladakhis to adopt customs which kept the population stable and prevented the fragmentation of family land. Central to this was the right of primogeniture, whereby all the land was inherited by the eldest son and could never be split or sold. Naturally, this left the remaining sons without an inheritance. It was therefore the custom that at least one son would become a monk, while the others were free to seek their fortune in any way that they saw fit without the support of the family, or alternatively, to enter into a polyandrous marriage with their eldest brother's wife. In this way, the celibate monks would require only minimum support from the community in return for religious duties, while one family could live off the same land for centuries without increasing the size of the population, a polyandrous family is unlikely to produce any more offspring than one husband and one wife.

Fraternal polyandry was a remarkably effective solution which, perhaps surprisingly, resulted in few problems. The younger brother or brothers accepted their eldest brother's authority, and the question of who was the genetic father of the children was thought irrelevant. The children called the head of the household, 'big father' and the other brothers, 'little father'.

If there were no sons, then the land would go to the eldest daughter and the exact opposite arrangement would occur. She would bring in a husband, who would have no rights over her land, and her sisters would either become nuns, would marry into another family or would join their eldest sister in a polygamous marriage. The guiding principle throughout was that the land never got divided.

Although these customs of polyandry and of primogeniture are still occasionally practised, it has been to a much lesser degree since they were made illegal in the early 1940's. Whilst this was done with the intention of protecting the rights of the individual, it has completely changed rural society. Now the population is increasing and the village land can no longer sustain the communities.

Dards

These people originate from Gilgit in Pakistan. They now live in Drass and the Dha-Hanu area. Although originally Buddhist, the Dards around Drass have embraced Islam and have been strongly influenced by their Kashmiri neighbours. Those in the Dha-Hanu area, known as **Brokpa**, have preserved their Buddhist faith and hold on to many of their original customs and traditions.

In most villages in Ladakh you'll find another group of Dards, the **Mons**, descendants of Ladakh's early settlers. Whilst these people represent Ladakh's lower class the segregation is nothing like as severe as that found in the Indian caste system. Their traditional roles as musicians, blacksmiths and carpenters are highly valued in the community.

Health
Infant mortality in Ladakh is 85-90 deaths per 1000 births which is fairly typical of Asian countries but unacceptably high compared to the rate of 6-8 per 1000 in the West. Life expectancy of 67 years is slightly higher than the Asian average of 62 but lower than the West at 75.

Others
Some of the constant visitors to Ladakh over the centuries have inevitably settled here. This is particularly true of Leh, where you can find small communities of Kashmiris and central Asians whose forefathers came when it was an important city on the great trade routes across Asia. Thousands of Indian military personnel are the most recent incomers.

RELIGION
Tibetan Buddhism
Ladakh is one of the few places where you can see this branch of Mahayana Buddhism (see p55), sometimes also called **lamaism**, being practised as it would have been in Tibet before the brutal Chinese suppression. Buddhism has permeated Ladakhi and Tibetan culture since the 7th century AD.

Tibetan Buddhism is a mystical religion which absorbed many of the magical and superstitious features of Tibet's previous shamanistic Bon religion, along with elements of Hindu Tantrism (hence Tantric Buddhism, which in emphasising that there are two forms of every deity, male and female, encouraged the total fulfilment of sexual desires as a means of overcoming these urges, rather than the more usual recommendation of abstinence). With an array of deities, beliefs, rituals and symbols it's incredibly complex, but to most Ladakhis, who don't concern themselves too much with these difficulties, it becomes a practical and down-to-earth philosophy which emphasises one thing – compassion.

Lamas It is usual for most families to have at least one son who is a lama (monk). At an early age he will be sent to the **gompa** (monastery) to which his village is attached where he will be educated in the religious teachings. Monks are highly respected in the community and spend a lot of their time away from the gompa performing religious ceremonies in the villages. The heads of gompas are called *kushoks* and are reincarnations of previous venerated lamas. The head of Tibetan Buddhism and the traditional political ruler of Tibet is the **Dalai Lama**, an incarnation of

Avalokiteshvara, the bodhisattva of compassion. The current Dalai Lama is the 14th in a succession that originated in the 14th century and is now living in exile in Dharamsala, Himachal Pradesh.

The lamas of Tibetan Buddhism are divided into four main sects. The oldest is the **Nyingmapa** (the Ancient Order or Red Hat sect) and was founded by the great sage Padmasambhava in the 8th century. Next came the **Sakyapa** sect, followed by the last of the Red Hat schools, the **Kagyupa**. The most recent order is the **Gelukpa**, more commonly known as the Yellow Hat sect, who came from a reform movement in the 1400's and who are led by the Dalai Lama. All of these sects are represented in Ladakh, but the most common are the Kagyupa and Gelukpa.

Om mani padme hum

This is the great mantra of Avalokiteshvara, the bodhisattva of compassion. Its loose meaning is 'Hail to the Jewel in the Lotus', the jewel being the Buddha. However, it is believed to contain far deeper magical properties that are released when it is recited, the more times the better. So, as well as continuously chanting the mantra, it's also printed on **prayer flags** which release the magic formula into the winds with each flutter, or is written on lengths of paper which, when placed inside **prayer wheels**, are released with each revolution. These vary in size from the small pocket versions which revolve with the flick of a wrist to the huge cylindrical drums needing all your weight to set them in motion. These must only be turned in a clockwise direction.

Mani walls are made up of mani stones which have the mantra carved on them. Those who commission and carve the stones gain merit and these walls are so situated that the maximum number of living beings will also benefit, by passing in a clockwise direction. They are a relatively new concept, being first introduced in the fifteenth century to honour the death of a king. The building of mani walls soon became popular, particularly as a way of punishing criminals, and they can now be found even in the remotest parts of Ladakh, ranging in size from a pile of stones to massive structures over a kilometre long.

Islam

Although Ladakh is usually described as a Buddhist region, there is also a large minority of Muslims (about 45%). Constant invasion by Islamic forces in the west of Ladakh gradually led to the conversion of the previously Buddhist people. Most Ladakhi Muslims still live in Kargil District where they account for 85% of the population. Here they are particularly puritanical Shiites. Leh also supports a small population of Muslims, mainly Sunnis, who are descended from immigrant Kashmiri and central Asian traders.

Christianity

There is a very small community of Ladakhi Christians in Leh. Most belong to the top rungs of Ladakhi society and were converted by the Moravian missionaries who first came to Ladakh in 1885. They built two churches, one in Leh and one in Shey.

PART 5: LEH & BEYOND

Leh

There is nothing whatever to do. That is Leh's charm...nothing to do but to slow down, relax, laze, to become one vast transparent eye. **Andrew Harvey** *A Journey in Ladakh*

Leh, the capital of Ladakh, lies nestled among low hills on the north side of the Indus Valley, between the Stok Mountains to the south and the Ladakh Range to the north. For centuries it has been a place where travellers of different nationalities have rested, before continuing over the mountains along the ancient trade routes that radiate from the city. Today, Leh is popular with a different kind of mountain wanderer and makes an ideal base for treks in the region.

The town's activities still centre on the bustling main bazaar. Indian soldiers, Kashmiri souvenir sellers and Western tourists have now replaced the exotic traders from Turkistan, Afganistan and Tibet, while the load-bearing camels and horses have given way to diesel-belching Tata trucks. There have been many recent changes as a result of wider contact with the rest of world but much goes on as it always has: Ladakhi women sell vegetables along the shady side of the main bazaar; old men and women spin hand-held prayer wheels in the narrow side streets; Muslims congregate in animated conversation around the mosque; and every shop in town closes early when the final polo match of the season is played.

It's worth spending a few days in Leh before embarking on your trek not only to acclimatise to the rarefied air but to give yourself time to explore the fascinating villages nearby. If you've just come up from the south, then the dry, hot days and cool nights will come as a welcome relief after the summer humidity of the Indian plains. The town is brimming with excellent guest houses

> **Beware of the altitude**
> Most people who ascend rapidly to Leh by plane or bus will feel some effects of the altitude. At 3500m (11,500ft) it is vital to take it easy for the first few days: don't overexert yourself; drink lots of water, soup or tea; avoid alcohol at least until you're acclimatised; and look out for any symptoms of altitude illness (see p238). If you are in any doubt about symptoms, assume that it is AMS and act quickly and appropriately. Twenty-four hour medical help is available by phoning ☎ 560.
>
> Being at such high altitude is not all bad news. What could be nicer for the first few days of your holiday than having to submit to lethargy and self-indulgent laziness?

run by welcoming Ladakhi families and the only difficulty with eating out, is deciding which of the many good restaurants to choose.

Leh is a small town with a population of about 25,000. Because of this it's easy to escape from the vibrant chaos of the centre by walking out into the surrounding fields along poplar and willow lined paths. Peace is readily found in the cool dark of a nearby gompa.

HISTORY

In the fifteenth century both Leh and the village of Shey shared the responsibility of being the capitals of Upper Ladakh. Shey was the more fortified of the two, while Leh was in a prime position for trade. The town's growth in importance is reflected by the building of the first royal residency on top of Namgyal Peak by Tashi Namgyal in the sixteenth century and then the building of the majestic Royal Palace by Sengge Namgyal a century later. Since then Leh has remained the administrative and commercial capital of Ladakh.

Leh's prosperity derived from its location at the foot of the Khardung La, the gateway of the infamous trade route to Yarkand in Turkistan (see p208). The trade involved the people of Leh at all levels: a few undergoing the rigorous journeys over the mountains themselves, some merely setting up as merchants, while others profited indirectly by providing services to the constant stream of visitors.

Since the Chinese closure of the trade routes in 1949, Leh's economic base has shifted. It now concentrates on providing services to the new incomers, notably the thousands of Indian troops who have moved into the area since the 1960s and the influx of foreign tourists since 1974. Leh has come face to face with a world with which it had little previous contact, a world in which technological advances and economic gain are the driving forces. Leh is gradually adopting this inappropriate model of development and is beginning to suffer from corresponding environmental and social problems. However, all is not bleak. The changes that have been brought about are relatively recent and are not irreversible. What's more, Leh is the home of several excellent grass routes organisations who are striving to stem this tide, and adopt a more sustainable and appropriate way forward for this fascinating city.

ARRIVAL

• **By air** Leh's small airport is 3km to the south of the town. There is a tourist information desk in the arrivals hall, and you are required to fill in a registration form while waiting for your luggage to arrive. By far the easiest way into Leh is by taxi (Rs70). There is supposed to be an airport bus to meet new arrivals but this rarely materialises. If you want to catch a bus, then wait by the main gates and stop any that are heading uphill.

• **By bus** Most buses will drop you at the main bus stand, a ten- minute walk from the centre of town. Himachal Tourism buses are far more obliging and will drop you by their centrally located office on Fort Road.

ORIENTATION

Everything is within walking distance. The central focus is the main bazaar, a wide and straight street with the Royal Palace above it at one end. The majority of shops are found along this road at ground level and popular restaurants take up the first floor space. The old town, a fascinating network of rabbit-warren streets, is immediately beneath the Palace, while the rest of Leh sprawls away downhill from here.

The main bus stand, hospital, Tourist Reception Centre and post office are all outside the centre along the road leading south to the airport.

WHERE TO STAY

Hotel areas

• **Leh** There is a vast range of accommodation in Leh from cheap guest houses (Rs30) to expensive hotels (Rs1500). Restaurants, shops, trekking agencies, buses and taxis are all nearby making it the most convenient place to stay. Guest houses and hotels are dotted all around the town.

• **Chanspa** (Changspa) This village lies on the west side of Leh along the road to the Shanti Stupa. There are places to stay for all budgets and tastes, the majority are at the cheaper end. It's a good 10-15 minute walk from the town centre and well away from the noise and crowds but there are few places to eat out and it's not ideal if you've got a lot to organise.

• **Sankar** is a quiet village 10-15 minutes walk to the north of Leh. There are only a few guest houses here and no other facilities. It's the perfect place to stay when you want to get away from it all.

Prices and seasons

Prices vary enormously depending on the time of year. The high season of July and August is when the hotels are at their most expensive. These are the prices given below. They are for single and double rooms with attached (att) or common (com) bathrooms. The 'budget', 'moderate', and 'more expensive' categories are based on the price of the cheapest double room. Prices for the more expensive hotels often include some meals and where this is the case the cheapest option is shown.

Discounts of 25% are often available at the beginning and end of the season, particularly in the hotels (rather than guest houses), and it's sometimes possible to get a slight reduction if you're staying in the same room for a long time. Many places are closed between November and May. Two or three of the big hotels stay open all year round and many of the guest houses will let you stay even though they're not officially open. Hotels are [keyed] to the map overleaf.

Leh Accommodation Prices given are for singles/doubles with common (c) or attached (a) bathroom. Listed in ascending order by price for double rooms. Phone numbers are shown in brackets.

1 **Zen Garden Restaurant cum Camping Site**
Rs40 per tent
2 **Palace View GH**, Kiddar Rs30/60 (c)
3 **Phuntsogling GH** dbl: Rs60-100 (c) Rs120 (a)
4 **Namgyal GH** dbl: Rs60-100 (c) Rs150-200 (a)
5 **Ichamshenpa** dbl: Rs80 (c)
6 **Shanti GH** dbl: Rs80-100 (c)
7 **Oriental GH** dbl: Rs80-150 (c), Rs200 (a)
8 **Eagle GH** dbl: Rs80-200 (c)
9 **Tak GH** Rs60/90 (c)
10 **Greenland GH** Rs50/100 (c)
11 **Shangrila GH** Rs50/100 (c)
12 **Yaksha GH** (3799) Rs70/100 (c)
13 **Rainbow GH** Rs80/100 (c)
14 **Khan Manzil GH** (3781) dbl: Rs100 (c)
15 **Lyon GH** dbl: Rs100 (c)
16 **Karzoo GH** dbl: Rs100,120 (c)
17 **Hotel Hills View** (2258) dbl: Rs100,125 (c),
Rs150(a)
18 **Hotel Kang-La** (3670) dbl: Rs100,150 (a)
19 **Palace View Hotel** dbl: Rs100 (c), Rs160 (a)
20 **Broad View GH** dbl Rs100 (c) Rs150,200 (a)
21 **Otsal GH** Rs50/120 (c)
22 **Sabila GH** Rs60/ 120 (c)
23 **Dehlex GH** (3855)dbl: Rs120 (c)
24 **Jigmet GH** Rs60/120,150 (c), dbl: Rs250 (a)
25 **Old Ladakh GH** dbl: Rs120 (c), Rs180 (a)
26 **Ti-sei GH** dbl: Rs120-160 (c), Rs200-250 (a)
27 **Padma GH** (3730) dbl: Rs120-200 (c)
Rs200 (a)
28 **Two Star GH** Rs70/130 (c)
29 **Antelope GH** (2286) dbl: Rs130 (c), Rs170,
200 (a)
30 **Changlo Chan** (3674) Rs75/150 (c)
31 **Larchang GH** Rs150 (c)
32 **Maryul GH** dbl: Rs150 (c)
33 **Asia GH** Rs80/150,200 (c)
34 **Hotel Choskor** (3626) dbl: Rs150-200 (a)
35 **Paul GH** (3750) dbl: Rs150 (c), Rs 250 (a)
36 **Warilla GH** dbl: Rs150 (c), Rs300 (a)
37 **Bimla GH** (3854) dbl Rs180 (c) Rs300-400(a)
38 **Hotel Himalaya** dbl: Rs200 (a)
39 **Hotel Zambalha** (2333) dbl: Rs200 (a)
40 **Hotel T-Suru** dbl: Rs200-300 (a)
41 **Hotel Yasmin** (3731) dbl: Rs200-300 (a)
42 **Indus GH** Rs120/200-300 (c), dbl: Rs300-
400 (a)
43 **Pangong Hotel** (2500) dbl: Rs200-350 (a)
44 **Hotel Horizon** (3702) dbl: Rs250 (a)
45 **Hotel Tso-Kar** dbl: Rs250 (a)
46 **Dreamland Hotel** dbl: Rs250,300 (a)
47 **Hotel Ibex** dbl: Rs250-350 (a)
48 **Lung-Se-Jung Hotel** (2393) Rs250/300 (a)
49 **Kailash GH** (3653) dbl: Rs300 (c), Rs750 (a)
50 **Hotel Ri-Rab** (3693) dbl: Rs400 (a)
51 **Hotel Khayul** (2521) dbl: Rs400-500 (a)

52 **Hotel Rockland** (3689) dbl: Rs400-550 (a)
53 **Hotel Chonjor** (2575) Rs450/500 (a)
54 **Khangri Hotel** (2251) Rs450-700/550-800 (a)
55 **New Lasermo** (2513) Rs400/600(a)
56 **Hotel Snow View** dbl: Rs650 (a)
57 **Hotel Bijoo** (2331) Rs600/700 (a)
58 **Hotel Yak Tail** (2318) Rs725/750-925 (a)
59 **Hotel Spic and Span** (3865) Rs700/800 (a)
60 **Hotel Rafica** (2458) Rs425/850 (a)
61 **Tsemo-La Hotel** (3890) Rs675/900 (a)
62 **Hotel Tsomo-Ri** (2471) Rs675/900 (a)
63 **Hotel Horzey** (3618) Rs800/950 (a)
64 **Hotel Omasila** (2319) Rs900/1000 (a)
65 **Hotel Singge Palace** (2422) dbl: Rs1000 (a)
66 **Hotel Ga-ldan Continental** (2373) Rs1000/
1200 (a)
67 **Hotel Thong Sal** (2427) dbl: Rs1500 (a)
68 **Hotel Lingzi** (2220) Rs1100/1500 (a)
69 **Hotel Lha-Ri-Mo** (2301) Rs1200/1500 (a)
70 **Hotel Peerless K-Sar Palace** (2548) Rs1200/
1500 (a)
71 **Hotel Sun and Sand** (3632) Rs1120/1505 (a)
72 **Hotel Kang Lha Chhen** Rs1320/1650 (a)

Restaurants
1* **Amdo Cafe 2**
2* **Amdo Cafe No.1**
3* **Budshah Inn Restaurant**
4* **Burman Restaurant**
5* **Dreamland Restaurant**
6* **German Bakery Coffee House**
7* **Guru Chat**
8* **Hotel Ibex**
9* **Hotel Yak Tail**
10* **Instyle Cafe and Penguin Bar**
11* **Kokonor Restaurant**
12* **Kyishong Restaurant**
13* **La Montassori Restaurant**
14* **Lhasa Restaurant**
15* **Mentokling Restaurant**
16* **Mona Lisa Garden Restaurant and Bar**
17* **Monalisa German Bakery**
18* **Mughal Darbar Restaurant**
19* **Nepal Restaurant**
20* **Pumpernickel German Bakery**
21* **Snowland Restaurant**
22* **Summer Harvest Restaurant**
23* **Tibetan Friends Corner Restaurant**
24* **Tibetan Kitchen**
25* **Tibetan Restaurant (Devi)**
26* **Wok Tibetan Kitchen**
27* **Zen Garden Restaurant cum**
Camping Site

Sankar

NOTE: RESTAURANTS INDICATED BY ASTERISK *

TO SHANTI STUPA

SANKAR GOMPA

Palace

Namgyal Peak

LEDeG

38 & LEHO

SYED ALI SHAH POSTCARD SHOP

Chanspa

JAMA MASJID

MORAVIAN CHURCH

Old Town

Stream

BANK

GOMPA

DELITE CINEMA

MEDITATION SUB-CENTRE

CATS

PO

MANI WALL

HIMACHAL PRADESH TOURISM OFFICE

TAXI

TOURIST OFFICE

Polo Ground

DISTRICT COMMISSIONER

INDIAN AIRLINES

LEDeG CRAFT SHOP

KUNSOI MEDICAL HALL

SUPERINTENDENT OF POLICE

Stream

SECMOL

OLD BUS STAND

TO NUBRA

GOMPA

MAIN BUS STAND

LEH

MANI WALL

SNM HOSPITAL

ALL INDIA RADIO STATION

TIBETAN CHILDREN'S VILLAGE HANDICRAFT CENTRE

PETROL STATION

TRAILBLAZER

TOURIST RECEPTION CENTRE

GPO

TO AIRPORT & SRINAGAR

TO MANALI

0   800 metres

Camping

Although there are two campsites in Leh, the only one worth using is the **Zen Garden Restaurant cum Camping Site** [1] in Chanspa. It costs Rs40 per tent and is quite secluded among trees by the river. The only facilities are a Ladakhi toilet. The other site is opposite the Antelope Guest House [29]; it seems to be used more as a public toilet than a campsite. It may also be possible to camp at one of the farms around Leh; you will have to ask permission and have patience with the local children, who will be fascinated by your antics.

If there are no vacancies anywhere when you first arrive, it's sometimes possible to pitch your tent on the roof of a guest house until a room becomes available.

Budget guest houses (£4/US$6 or less)

Private guest houses are the most popular places to stay in Leh. Not only are they the best value for money, but also the most interesting and ecologically sound. Most are run by Ladakhi families who convert their homes into guest houses for the summer and back into their homes for the winter. Although the accommodation may be simple, it's almost always comfortable and clean. You will need to have your own sleeping bag or bedding. Hot water is by the bucketful (Rs5) and most of the cheaper places have Ladakhi toilets, increasingly now being replaced by flush systems, a worrying trend in a town with no proper sewage infrastructure.

Just below the polo ground is the cheapest guest house in town – the **Palace View Guest House, Kiddar** [2] (not to be confused with the Palace View Hotel). It has single rooms for Rs30 and doubles at Rs60, all with common bathrooms. It's a bit dirty but what do you expect at these bargain prices? You'll only see the view of the Palace if you're particularly tall and standing on the roof! Above the polo ground, by a group of chortens, is the **Namgyal Guest House** [4]. This is run by a friendly Ladakhi family who go out of their way to make you feel at home. It is superb value for money with comfortable and clean double rooms for Rs60-100 (com) and Rs150-200 (att). They are always willing to have people in the winter.

The **Old Ladakh Guest House** [25], in the old town below the Palace, has nice double rooms for Rs120 (com) and Rs180 (att), while the attractive **Antelope Guest House** [29] (☎ 2286), on the road to Sankar, has double rooms for Rs130 (com) and rooms with attached bathrooms for Rs170/200.

On the other side of town up a small alley by the Instyle Cafe is the **Dehlex Guest House** [23] (☎ 3855), a beautiful house with a colourful garden. There are double rooms for Rs120, all with shared bathrooms.

Another well-decorated place is the **Padma Guest House** [27] (☎ 3730). This has rooms for Rs120-200 (double, com) and Rs200 (double, att). There's one particularly nice room upstairs with great views to the mountains.

If you want somewhere peaceful then the hard to find **Warilla Guest House** [36] is a good choice. It's on the south side of Leh and is surrounded by fields. Double rooms are Rs150 (com), or Rs300 (att). Just as secluded but not so far out of town is the new **Maryul Guest House** [32] above the Ecology Centre. All rooms are double with shared bathroom and cost Rs150. There's a lovely garden that you can sit in.

There's a wide choice of places in Chanspa village. One of the first you reach is the **Yaksha Guest House** [12] (☎ 3799). This is very much a working farm with cows in the yard and surrounded by barley fields. All rooms share a bathroom, singles cost Rs70 and doubles Rs100. The **Otsal Guest House** [21], just after the bridge, has rooms overlooking the river that cost Rs50 for a single (com) and Rs120 for a double (com).

If you don't mind a long walk, or have some form of transport, then the **Oriental Guest House** [7], below the Shanti Stupa, is a wonderful place to stay. This large traditional house has views to the Palace and to Leh and Tsemo gompas. The rooms are Rs80-150 for a double (com) and Rs200 (att). In the evenings you can eat with the family and are always made to feel at home.

The best views in Leh are without a doubt from the **guest house** (no name) just below the Shanti Stupa. The rooms for Rs100 (com) look out over the town and the Indus Valley to the Stok Mountains.

Moderately priced guest houses and hotels (£4-8/US$6-12)

Many of the places to stay in this price range still retain the charm of the budget guest houses while providing a few extra comforts. Most of the rooms have attached bathrooms. The **Hotel Himalaya** [38] is a balconied hotel in a peaceful willow grove on the road to Sankar. The rooms are reasonably priced at Rs200 for a double (att).

If you follow the path to Sankar gompa you eventually reach the beautiful **Kailash Guest House** [49] (☎ 3653). Although it seems expensive at Rs300 for a double (com) or Rs750 for a double (att), it's an extremely comfortable and peaceful place to stay. The rooms are immaculately clean, there are wonderful views to the mountains and the walled garden is a riot of colour.

If you want to be more central the **Dreamland Hotel** [46],which has doubles for Rs250/300 (att), is very convenient yet quiet, being set back from the road.

Further down the same road is the **Hotel Tso-kar** [45] which shares the same flower-filled courtyard as the Tibetan Kitchen. All rooms are Rs250 (double, att). Just to the north is the very homely **Bimla Guest**

House [37] (☎ 3854). Double rooms cost Rs180 (com) and Rs300-400 (att). There is a cosy sitting room, with TV, that can be used by the guests.

Down the track almost opposite the Instyle Cafe, the **Pangong Hotel** [43] (☎ 2500) has large doubles (att) with good mountain views for Rs200-350. There's a path leading west off this track that takes you past a few hotels and guest houses, one of which is the modern and efficient **Hotel Yasmin** [41] (☎ 3731, fax 01982-3731). This costs Rs200-300 for a double with attached bathroom. Hot water is an extra Rs5 per bucket.

More expensive hotels (above £8/US$12)
There are plenty of hotels at the upper end of the market that are still cheap by Western standards. Almost all of them have a restaurant on the premises and the prices often include breakfast. All rooms have attached bathrooms with running hot water. The very central **Hotel Yak Tail** [58] (☎ 2318, fax 3825) is popular with tour groups and is one of the few hotels open all year. Rooms cost Rs750-925 for a double (att) and Rs725 for a single (att). Some of the big rooms in the new block have nice balconies.

The **Tsemo-La Hotel** [61] (☎ 3890) which is next to the Ecology Centre, is a very attractive building set in a mature garden. Room prices include breakfast and are Rs675 for a single (att) or Rs900 double (att).

To the south of the town centre is the efficiently run and very clean **Hotel Singge Palace** [65] (☎ 2422, fax 3987) which has doubles for Rs1000 (att). Its Ladakhi style dining hall and garden lawn with tables and chairs make it a pleasant place to stay. Further down the same road is the cheaper **Hotel Spic-n-Span** [59] (☎ 3865, fax 3615). Despite its naff name this is a nice hotel with single rooms for Rs700 (att) and doubles Rs800 (att). Prices include breakfast.

The secluded **Hotel Thong Sal** [67] (☎ 2427) is on the outskirts of Chanspa, beneath the Shanti Stupa. Rooms with amazing views to Stok and the mountains are Rs1500 for a double (att) with full board. The friendly owner will ferry you to and from Leh or arrange a taxi.

Probably the most impressive looking hotel and also one of the most expensive in Leh is the **Hotel Lha-Ri-Mo** [69] (☎ 2301). Bedecked with prayer flags, it looks more like a gompa than a hotel. Rooms cost Rs1200 single (att) and Rs1500 for a double (att) with breakfast. The complex even has its own gift shop.

The most exotic place to stay in Ladakh is the **Ladakh Sarai** (☎ 214 through exchange ☎ 180, or Delhi ☎ 011-7533483) at the village of Stok (14km from Leh). This is a collection of 15 luxurious *yurts* (round tents) in a willow grove overlooking the Indus Valley. Prices are from $45 per person.

The Leh area code is 01982. If phoning from outside India dial +91-1982.

WHERE TO EAT

Breakfast

Most guest houses and hotels can provide you with a simple breakfast of bread and jam with tea or coffee. If you are getting up early this is definitely the best option as restaurants don't begin to open until about 8.30am. Ladakhi bread with locally produced apricot jam (Rs5) is highly recommended. You can get this at **The Wok Tibetan Kitchen** [26] and **Dreamland Restaurant** [5], among others. Porridge, made either with tsampa or oats, is on almost everyone's menu as are omelettes. Brown rolls, cinnamon rolls and croissant (more like white bread in a crescent shape) can be had at **Instyle Cafe** [10] and also at the **German Bakery Coffee House** [6]. The latter also does a set breakfast of toast, eggs, hash brown, tea or coffee for Rs40. Muesli with curd and honey is Rs35.

Lunch and dinner

• **Ladakhi, Tibetan and Chinese** The majority of restaurants in Leh fit into this wide ranging category. Prices don't vary enormously wherever you go and are generally between Rs20 and Rs40 for a main meal. Standard dishes on the menus include soups, chop-suey, chow mein, momos and all manner of rice dishes, all of which can be ordered with meat or vegetables. Most will also have a go at some easy Western dishes in an attempt to satisfy everyone's palates.

There are a number of such places along the main bazaar, all of which are above street level. **The Wok Tibetan Kitchen** [26] is always popular as is the nicely decorated **Amdo Cafe No.1** [2], both of which overlook the main bazaar. The entrance to the latter is off a small side alley with a couple of butcher shops on it. If the sight of dismembered carcasses hasn't killed your appetite then you should enjoy the good food here. Its sister restaurant, with the inspired name of **Amdo Cafe 2** [1], is on the other side of the road. Their cheese fried momos are highly recommended. ('Amdo' is the eastern province of Tibet. There is a legend that the people of this remote region, over 5000km away, were originally from Ladakh). Further along the street is **La Montessori Restaurant** [13] which has a similar menu. Their large bowls of soup are excellent.

If you're on a tight budget try some of the smaller Tibetan restaurants where the food is superb and the prices low. The atmospheric **Kyishong Restaurant** [12] is very popular with Tibetan locals and its extensive menu is one of the few that includes tsampa among more usual dishes of fuyong, sweet and sour spring rolls and bamboo shoots. It's very good value and the prices include unlimited cups of black tea. The **Tibetan Restaurant (Devi)** [25] is a simple place sandwiched between the two German Bakeries and the very friendly owners, who make a wonderful cup of cinnamon and cardamom tea (Rs4), have made it popular with travellers and locals alike. Another small and popular place is the **Tibetan**

Friends Corner Restaurant [23]. This again serves Tibetan and Chinese food and is good value. For desert, try the spectacular 'chocolate custer with fire' (Rs30) – it's sure to turn a few heads.

For really good and authentic Tibetan cooking **The Tibetan Kitchen** [24] is hard to beat. How about a Ruchotse, 'Dumplings of mincemeat or vegetables with vegetable stock, garnished and served in bowls' (Rs35), or perhaps Tingmo and Fingsha, 'a velvet soft steamed bread served with meat or vegetable curry' (Rs35). It's closed between 4 and 6pm.

The **Dreamland Restaurant** [5] also has good Chinese and Tibetan food. If you want a feast order gacok (Rs700 for six people) six hours in advance. This selection of mutton, egg, carrots, peas, cauliflower, black mushroom, rice, steamed momo, vegetable salad, sweet dishes and fruit should satisfy most appetites. There is a useful noticeboard on the back of the door which you can use for contacting trekking partners.

The outdoor restaurants are always popular with travellers. **Instyle Cafe** [10] cook most types of food with reasonable success and there's a well used noticeboard to leave messages on. **Hotel Yak Tail** [58] (☎ 2318, fax 01982-3825) is a good place for well-cooked Chinese, Tibetan, Indian and Western dishes, whilst relaxing in their beautiful courtyard.

• **Indian** Good Indian cuisine is surprisingly hard to find in Leh. The smart **Summer Harvest Restaurant** [22] specialises in Indian and Kashmiri dishes and has Tibetan and Chinese food as well. The **Budshah Inn Restaurant** [3] (☎ 3913), on a top floor to the left of the mosque, makes up for its lack of atmosphere with a wide selection of Indian, Kashmiri and Tandoori dishes and is particularly popular with Indians working in Leh.

• **Western** Most places have a few easy-cook Western meals on their menus. Fried egg and chips to satisfy the most homesick Brit are available almost everywhere, as are other travellers' favourites such as banana and honey pancakes, mashed potato and cheese and various styles of spaghetti (thinly disguised noodles!). If you are really craving some Western food then the dark and intimate **German Bakery Coffee House** [6] has lasagne (Rs45-50), pizza (Rs45-50) and burgers (Rs35/40). However the food at this German-owned restaurant sometimes leaves a little to be desired and is expensive for what you get. The **Mentokling Restaurant and Bar** [15], with tables and chairs set under trees in its big walled garden, also offers pizzas and snacks. Its claims of 'making your visit to this beautiful land simply mind boggling' and that its 'over hospitable staff...give you the warmth of a family' are a little exaggerated.

• **Israeli** Only one restaurant goes out of its way to cater to the large number of Israeli travellers. **Mona Lisa Garden Restaurant and Bar** [16] has falafel and humus on its menu along with the usual Chinese dishes.

• **Bakeries** The two most popular bakeries, the **Pumpernickel German Bakery** [20] and the **Monalisa German Bakery** [17], are almost next door to each other and sell very similar fare. They both seem quite expensive considering you could get a full meal for the price of a slice of cake, but the mouth watering choices such as 'choco banana cake' (Rs22) or plum crumble (Rs40) are hard to resist, especially if you've been away trekking for a few days. The former has a good selection of second-hand books for sale and a noticeboard for finding trekking partners or selling gear. If someone you know has a birthday then they will also make and decorate a cake to order.

If you are just off on a trek stock up on 'six grain trekking bread' (Rs25) which lasts for up to 10 days (wrap it in some cloth and don't let it get wet), a few 'farmers loaves' which last for up to 6 days, muesli (1kg for Rs250) and lots of energy-giving muesli biscuits (Rs5 each).

• **Vegetarian** Almost every restaurant in Leh serves vegetarian food and most have as wide and as varied a menu as the non-vegetarian choice.

• **Snacks** Every evening between 7pm and 8pm the main bazaar becomes a hive of activity. It's at this time that you will find roadside vendors selling charcoal grilled sweetcorn and fried spicy nibbles.

Delicious dried apricots are available everywhere and try the Ladakh Dry Fruits Store (next to the LEDeG Craft Shop) for other healthy snacks such as dried blackberries, roasted barley and nuts.

SERVICES

• **Airline Offices** Indian Airlines has an office a long way down Fort Rd. There's a computerised booking system but it's regularly out of action. If you're booking a flight then make sure you have enough foreign currency or travellers' cheques to pay for it – they don't accept credit cards.

• **Banks** The State Bank of India has a foreign exchange counter at the Tourist Office in town (open 10.30am-1.30pm Mon to Fri, 10.30am-12pm Sat). In July-August turn up early or you'll have to queue for an hour or more.

You can avoid this long wait by changing money at some of the large hotels or at the Ladakh Art Palace, on the backstreet leading to the north end of the polo ground, but you won't get such a good rate of exchange. There is nowhere in Leh where you can get a cash advance on a credit card, so make sure you have plenty of travellers' cheques or cash.

• **Barber** A haircut will set you back all of Rs20 and with it you'll receive a complimentary scalp massage. A shave with a cut-throat razor is Rs10, but make sure they use a fresh blade: Aids is on the increase in India. There are barbers on Naw Shar and also near the bus stand.

• **Bookshops, newsagents and libraries** There are only two book-shops in Leh and both are owned by the same people. Artou Bookshop and Lost Horizon Bookshop have a good selection of books on Ladakh, the Himalaya and a wide range of other titles. If you've just finished your novel you can trade it in for another at one of the many shops that sell second-hand books as a sideline. Newspapers are in hot demand in Leh and their arrival is dependent on flights. The only newsagent is the small shop below the Pumpernickel German Bakery [20].

The town library has a very limited selection of books and will glad-ly accept any books you wish to donate. A few books on the Himalaya and Buddhism may be of interest. The Ecology Centre has an excellent library which is open to anyone (10am-4.30pm). It has a vast range of books and journals on sustainable development, ecology, philosophy, religion, Himalayan history and culture, and Himalayan travelogues.

• **Dentist** There's a dental clinic below the Budshah Inn [3] open 8-10am, 4-7pm.

• **Horse riding** Ladakhi horses are used more as beasts of burden than for riding but most have also been schooled for riders. Ask at the trekking agencies and expect to pay about Rs300 per day. You may find it hard to get a horse in July and August because they'll all be out on treks.

• **Laundry** There are lots of places that will wash and iron your clothes for a few rupees per item but don't expect the *dhobi-wallah* to read the care label. Hang on to your synthetic-fibre trekking clothes as they won't take kindly to a hot iron!

• **Left luggage** You can safely store the things you don't want to lug into the mountains at your guest house or hotel. There's rarely a charge.

• **Liquor store** The small shop opposite the main taxi stand sells beer, rum and whiskey.

• **Medical clinics** Medical help phone numbers: ☎ 560 (24 hours), or ☎ 212/313/214 (10am-4pm). For serious medical and altitude related problems go to the Sonam Narbu Memorial (SNM) hospital. Treatment is free, but the hospital will soon be introducing private rooms for tourists who want and can afford more personal treatment. Consultations are from 10am to 2pm. Otherwise see Dr Tsering Narboo at the Kunsoi Medical Hall (☎ 3899, open 9-10am and 4-7pm). Consultations cost Rs31. If you've got a stomach complaint get a stool test (Rs30) from either the hospital or from the Ladakh Clinical Laboratory which is below the Budshah Inn [3], (open 8.30 to 10am and 4.15 to 7pm).

The army has a hospital equipped with a pressure chamber for those suffering from AMS, but as it runs off the unreliable mains electricity, you are safer going to the SNM hospital which has supplies of oxygen.

• **Meditation** Mahabodhi International Meditation Centre (☎ 2591), Devachan (near Choglamsar) runs residential courses and meditation cum trekking camps (Rs6000 for 10 days) for those who want to improve their spiritual as well as their physical well-being. They also run daily group meditation classes at their sub-centre in Chanspa from 5-7pm, except Sundays. Both centres are open Monday to Saturday, 10am-5pm.

NGOs (non governmental organisations)

Leh is the base for several indigenous organisations doing extremely worthwhile work in the development field. They are not tourist attractions but if you have something to offer, they may welcome your support.

• **Ladakh Ecological Development Group** (LEDeG, Leh, Ladakh, 194101. ☎/fax 2484) LEDeG, probably the most well known of Ladakh's indigenous NGOs, aims to promote 'ecological and sustainable development which harmonises with and builds on the traditional culture'. This is achieved by regular campaigns on environmental matters; encouraging local education; improving and raising the status of traditional organic agriculture; spreading the use of appropriate technologies, including solar ovens, micro-hydro plants and Trombe wall solar space heaters; and by nurturing local, small scale handicraft production in rural areas. Volunteers are always welcome and there are often informal study groups on development and ecology for visitors. Their headquarters is at the Centre for Ecological Development.

• **Ladakh Environment and Health Organisation** (LEHO, Himalaya Hotel Complex, Leh, Ladakh, 194101. ☎/fax 3680). Set up in 1991 to raise awareness in ecological and social issues. They run a variety of projects which include preventative health care, the promotion of sustainable agriculture, pashmina wool development, and job training.

• **Students' Educational and Cultural Movement of Ladakh** (SECMOL, PO Box 4, Leh, Ladakh, 194101). SECMOL works to restore pride in Ladakh's unique culture and to improve the chaotic education system by promoting culturally appropriate and locally relevant education. It welcomes visitors who are genuinely interested in real cultural exchange between 2pm and 5pm, Monday to Friday.

• **Photography** It's best to wait until you get home to have your films developed although there are a few places in Leh that will process print film. The nearest processing place for slides is in Delhi. Both N. Bijoo and Sons, on the main bazaar, and Syed Ali Shah & Sons Postcard Shop, usually have a reasonable stock of print and transparency film. However, it's more expensive than in the West and you won't know how long the film sat in the sun on its way up to Leh. The latter shop also sells excellent pictures of Ladakh and Ladakhis that the owner has taken himself. They're very good value for money at Rs100 to Rs200 for a large print, especially when you consider the cost of enlarging a print in the West.

• **Post and telecommunications** There is a **post office** on the main bazaar open 10am-4.30pm, but there is no Poste Restante facility here. Your letters will have inconveniently been kept at the Poste Restante at the main post office (next to the Tourist Reception Centre) on the road to the airport. The address is: Poste Restante, GPO, Leh, Ladakh, 194101, India. Alternatively you can have your mail sent to one of the communications agencies which will charge you a small commission.

There are lots of communication agencies in Leh (look for the yellow signs) where you can make national and international **phone calls** and send and receive **faxes**. An international phone call will typically cost you Rs80 per minute or Rs98 to the USA. Most places operate a call back system which is Rs10 per minute. Sending an international fax costs Rs3 per second and Rs20 to receive. Gypsy's World, ☎ (+91)-1982-3835, on Fort Road is a reliable place to have faxes sent.

Leh only has twelve outgoing lines and six incoming ones which inevitably leads to problems. You'll have more success at getting through if you try ringing late at night when fewer lines are in use.

• **Rafting** Several companies offer rafting on both the Indus and the Zanskar. There are sections to suit all abilities from a gentle, grade two float, up to a white-knuckle ride on a grade five rapid. Day trips are available (from Rs750 per person) but the best way to see the river is to make a three- or four-day excursion, camping on the beaches and visiting a few sights along the way. Perhaps the ultimate trip for those trekking to Zanskar is to arrange for the rafts to meet you at Padum, and then ride the river back down to Nimu (Rs2200 per person per day) – surely preferable to the long and dusty road journey.

Protected area permits
Visitors need a permit to get into any of the recently opened areas in Ladakh. These are Nubra, Pangong Lake, Dha-Hanu, Tsomoriri and Tsokar. This allows you to stay in the area for a maximum of seven days. Officially you must travel in a group of at least four people and follow one of the several identified tour circuits (unofficially the regulations seem to be fairly flexible). You can either apply directly in person to the District Commissioner's office or go through one of the many travel agencies who will charge you about Rs100 per person for the privilege. The latter is by far the easiest option. You will usually need to take along photocopies of your passport and visa.

If you are less than four people, do not worry. Many of the travel agencies will tag your names onto the bottom of another group's application and get round the regulations that way. Alternatively, if you can produce photocopies of four people's passports you will be issued with a permit, whether the owners of the other passports are coming with you or not. It will be assumed that you are travelling by bus or jeep. While it's perfectly legal to get there by other means, the authorities are understandably suspicious of independent trekkers, cyclists or motorcyclists wandering around their sensitive border areas. So if you are planning an alternative way in, it's best to keep your plans quiet unless specifically asked. If you are trekking then get your permit dated from the day you are entering the protected area, not the day you are leaving Leh. This will give you an extra day or two to explore the region.

You should be aware that the travel agent who issues you with a permit is responsible for your safe return to Leh. You owe it to them not to overstay your seven days and not to go missing! Occasionally the regulations tighten up, so find out the latest situation when you arrive in Leh.

• **Shopping** If you are buying souvenirs you can make sure your money goes towards a good cause at the Tibetan Children's Village Handicraft Centre. Open 8am-5pm Monday to Saturday, it's just below the hospital on the road to the airport and has a large selection of clothes, thankas, Tibetan carpets, jewellery and trinkets, all at reasonable prices. Much of what's on sale is made at the centre and all the profits go back to helping the children at SOS TCV in Choglamsar.

There are two LEDeG Craft Shops, one at the Ecology Centre and the other just off the main bazaar. They sell the handicrafts produced from their various projects as well as books, T-shirts and postcards.

Other good buys in Leh are traditional clothes which you are unlikely to find elsewhere, such as the stovepipe hats or *tibi*; the long coats that are worn by men and women called *kos* or *gonchas*; the elegant Tibetan pinafore dresses favoured by younger Ladakhi women known as *pumet* in Ladakhi, or *chuba* in Tibetan; a *stodtund*, the short jacket worn by Leh's taxi drivers; or the traditional pointed shoes called *thigma pabu*. These can all be found in Ladakhi shops in and around the main bazaar.

• **Tourist information** There's a tiny and poorly stocked tourist information office in town and also the Tourist Reception Centre (☎ 2497) on the road to the airport. They can give you a free map and a vaguely useful tourist directory. The Tourist Reception Centre also hires trekking equipment (see below). They are both open 10am to 4pm, Monday to Saturday.

• **Trekking agencies** Leh's many trekking agencies should be able to help you organise anything from a single pony-man to a full-blown luxury trek. Many also have a certain amount of equipment for hire. The standard of the agencies varies enormously, so it's well worth visiting several to get an idea of what you'll get for your money.

• **Trekking equipment rental** While most trekking equipment can be hired in Leh, the quality leaves a lot to be desired. The Tourist Reception Centre stock the basics such as sleeping bags (Rs20 per day), rucksacks (Rs12) and tents (Rs40) while the helpful Footprints Adventure Company (at Hotel Ibex) can also provide you with trekking poles (Rs30) and ice axes (Rs50). Another useful place to try is The Travellers' Shop on Fort Rd which can provide almost everything you may need including insulating pads (Rs15), stoves (Rs15), crampons (Rs20), and rope (Rs20). They occasionally have plastic mountaineering boots and dehydrated food as well, but don't count on it. If you suddenly feel like some impromptu climbing Cozy Homes tailor's, below the LEDeG Craft Shop, has odd bits of gear such as ice screws, axes and crampons for hire. It's also worth asking trekking agencies, as they have equipment that they're often willing to hire out.

• **Visa extensions** You can extend your visa for only up to 15 days in Leh and the length of stay granted seems to depend on the mood of the official you see. On a bad day he may well give less than 15 days. If you need longer you'll have to go to Delhi (see p56). The office is in the Superintendent of Police's building, open from 10am to 4pm.

NIGHTLIFE

Bars

Leh begins to quieten down once it gets dark. You can get a drink at a few of the garden restaurants: the **Penguin Bar** [10] at Instyle Cafe has a variety of bottled beers, (Rs40-50) while the popular **Mona Lisa Garden Restaurant and Bar** [16] has a more extensive bar; the **Mentokling Restaurant and Bar** [15] has an all day Happy Hour from 9am to 6pm and serves cocktails and spirits as well as beer.

Cinema

The latest releases from Bollywood (as Bombay's huge film industry is known) are screened at the Delite Cinema near the old town. Showings are at 2pm and at 7.15pm and cost Rs7 for upstairs and Rs5 for down.

Other entertainment

There are two cultural shows most evenings. One given by the Cultural and Traditional Society (CATS) near the Instyle Cafe, while the other is up by the Palace and is performed by the Ladakh Artists Society of Leh (LASOL). Both last an hour and costs Rs50. The programmes include folk music and dances, an explanation of traditional dress and the serving of chang and salt butter tea. They're very professionally performed and well worth seeing.

LOCAL TRANSPORT

There are few better ways of seeing the nearby sites and getting your body used to the altitude, than hiring a **bicycle**. Lost Horizons opposite Hotel Yak Tail hire out reasonable quality mountain bikes for Rs200 per day, but check the brakes, especially if you're thinking of free-wheeling down from the Khardung La. If you really want to pose then you could hire a **motorbike**. The most popular is the 350cc Enfield Bullet (Rs500-800 per day); smaller 100cc Yamahas are also available (Rs400-600). Travel agents should be able to find one for you. As with bicycles, you will be required to leave some kind of deposit behind, usually your passport or air ticket. This is an ideal way to get around Ladakh and gives you incomparable freedom. The roads are generally good and relatively free of traffic although you should ride very defensively as nobody will give way to you. Take plenty of petrol if you're venturing far; there are few petrol stations outside Leh.

You can pick up a **taxi** from the Taxi Operators' Union rank (open 7am-6pm) on Fort Road in the centre of town. While most places in Leh, apart from the airport, are within easy walking distance, taxis provide a convenient if expensive way to get around the Indus Valley. None of the taxis are metered but this shouldn't cause any problems as there are official rates to most places in Ladakh. Most drivers should have a rate list on them, or you can check the rates at the Union office. These rates are for the peak tourist season only; ask for a discount at other times of year. If you're catching a plane early in the morning then be sure to book a taxi the night before, as there is never much activity at the taxi rank first thing.

Buses are the cheapest means of transport but they can be overcrowded; although the main Indus Valley is well served, remoter villages can be very difficult to get to. (See 'Beyond Leh', p127, for details). Both the J&KSRTC buses and the privately operated buses leave from the main bus stand. The private buses have their destinations written on the front, but finding out destinations and departure times of the others is usually a matter of asking as many people as you can find. The information office is rarely staffed.

WHAT TO SEE

Leh Palace

The Palace stands majestically overlooking the town which allowed the king to survey his subjects at all times. Today it stands empty, as it has since the mid-nineteenth century when the royal family moved to Stok Palace after they were besieged by Kashmiri forces. It was built by King Sengge Namgyal in the seventeenth century in the same style as the Potala Palace of Lhasa. Although not on quite the same scale, it still stands nine storeys high. At the time it must have been one of the highest buildings in the world. The upper floors were used by royalty, while the store rooms and stables took up the lower floors, hence the larger windows at the top.

There is very little to see in the Palace today as the whole building is in a poor state of repair but there are good views across Leh and it's a fascinating walk through the alleys of the old town to get there. The old town is full of traditional architecture and many households have retained some of their rural values, keeping livestock in their backyards and drying fodder on the roofs. The alternative way up is to take the gentle track that begins above the polo ground.

Namgyal Peak

Namgyal Peak is crowned by the now ruined fort of Tashi Namgyal that sits high above the Palace along with the Gonkhang and the Maitreya temple. Some of the best views of the locality are from this vantage point. The red Gonkhang was built in the sixteenth century by Tashi Namgyal and is where he offered the bodies of the defeated Mongols to the deities. There's a portrait of the king here, in which he's seen drinking chang. Just below this building is the temple of the Maitreya which may date from the first king of Leh, King Takbumde. There are various ways up to the peak; the most straightforward is to follow the steep path that can be seen snaking down from underneath the buildings. Visit early in the morning to avoid the heat and to be certain that you'll find a monk there who can show you around.

Jama Masjid
This Sunni mosque is at the end of the main bazaar. The muezzin's call to prayer soon becomes a familiar sound as it drifts out across the town. The threat of military action by the Mughal Emperor Aurangzeb prompted King Deldan Namgyal to build the mosque in about 1661. The building, which is in the Ladakhi style of architecture, can accommodate more than 500 people. It's open throughout the day but try to avoid visiting during prayer times. Shoes must be removed and women should cover their arms, legs and hair. Women are not allowed into the central section.

Sankar Gompa
This colourful gompa belongs to Spituk and is the residency of their kushok. Entry is permitted only early in the morning or late in the afternoon but there is nothing to stop you wandering around the peaceful courtyard at other times in the day. You get to the gompa by taking the stream-side path just before the Antelope Guest House. This is a pretty 2km walk through fields which takes you past some interesting ornate chortens.

Shanti Stupa
Visible from most of the town, this new stupa was officially opened in 1985. The peace pagoda is part of the legacy of the Japanese Fujii Guruji who, as part of his mission to promote world peace through Buddhism, built pagodas and temples all over the world. It stands above Chanspa overlooking Leh and the Indus Valley. It's possible to take a taxi all the way to the top but a good test of your acclimatisation is to walk up the 542 steps. The stupa may be a bit garish but the views are spectacular.

Centre for Ecological Development
When you first arrive in Leh and the altitude is making you feel lethargic, go up to the Ecology Centre one afternoon to watch the excellent one-hour video, *Ancient Futures*. It's shown every afternoon at 4.30pm and is free. The film provides a valuable insight into the culture of Ladakh and the problems that the region faces today as it struggles to come to terms with recent changes. It should be compulsory viewing for every visitor.

The centre is the headquarters of LEDeG (see p119) and has an excellent library, a shop selling locally produced handicrafts and demonstrations of various appropriate technologies such as solar ovens, Trombe wall solar space heating units (on the side of the library), and solar water heating systems. It's open 10am-4.30pm, daily.

Dzomsa

This black and white photo exhibition with its thought-provoking text is well worth a visit. Above Mona Lisa German Bakery, it's open Monday to Saturday 2pm-6pm. Dzomsa means 'meeting place'.

Polo

There are lots of matches throughout the summer on the highest polo ground in the world. Keep an eye out for posters advertising the next game. They attract a huge crowd, are very exciting and free.

MOVING ON

By air

The high mountains, altitude and strong winds around Leh airport mean that departing planes are restricted to carrying 75% of their total capacity. The other problem here is that flights may have to be cancelled owing to bad weather, a not infrequent occurrence. As a result getting a confirmed flight during the summer can be very difficult so book as far in advance as possible even if you're not 100% sure you'll be leaving by plane. You can always get your money back as long as you ask for a refund before your flight date; make sure you get your refund in Leh: you enter a bureaucratic minefield if you wait until you reach your destination. If you're on the waiting list for a flight, it's still worth turning up at the airport in time, as the number of passengers that can be carried varies with the weather.

Security is comfortingly tight at Leh airport. You and your bags will be thoroughly searched as you leave; this is partly to stop the export of antiques, (it's illegal to leave Ladakh with anything over 100 years old), but mainly to stop terrorist attacks.

Indian Airlines flights from Leh to Delhi

• **Direct** (US$86, 1 hr 15 mins) Indian Airlines fly direct from Leh to Delhi daily at 07.55 between 15 May and 15 September. There are also flights throughout the year on Monday, Thursday and Friday at 11.55.

• **via Jammu** On Saturday there is a flight via Jammu to Delhi at 10.30 (US$86, 3 hours). Otherwise, there are flights to Jammu every Monday and Friday at 08.35 and on Saturday at 10.30 (US$50, 1 hour). Onward flights to Delhi depart Jammu every day at 15.05, except Saturday when they fly at 12.20 (US$84, 70 minutes).

• **via Srinagar** There is only one flight a week to Srinagar, which leaves on Thursday at 08.40 (US$43, 45 minutes). Direct flights from Srinagar to Delhi leave at 14.40 on Monday, Wednesday and Saturday; and at 12.45 on Tuesday, Thursday, and Sunday (US$92, 11/4 hours). Flights from Srinagar to Delhi via Jammu depart at 13.40 every day except Saturday (2 hours 35 minutes).

By bus

The Leh-Manali road can be open from as early as the end of June to as late as mid-October, you'll have the highest chance of getting through from mid-July to mid-September. The road to Srinagar is open from about the beginning of June to the end of October, depending on the weather.

• **To Manali** The most popular and comfortable bus is that run by Himachal Tourism (HPTDC). The tickets cost Rs700 and are available from the Himachal Tourism office (open everyday from 9am to 7pm) in Leh. It's recommended that you buy your ticket three or four days in advance. The bus leaves from outside the office at 06.00 daily and it takes two days of about 10 hours each day to reach Manali. The overnight stop is at Sarchu where tented accommodation is available. As there are no alternative places for you to stay, Himachal Tourism gets away with charging the exorbitant rate of Rs300 per person for a shared tent, supper of dal and rice and a packed breakfast. Several travellers have succeeded in sleeping on the bus for free; a sleeping bag is needed as it gets very cold. A few tour operators in Leh run similar buses for Rs600, also with tented accommodation.

The other possibility is to take a local bus all the way. Although these leave extremely early in the morning, (04.30 daily from the main bus stand), they go all the way to Keylong, which they reach at 19.00. The advantage of this is that there are some good places to stay in this interesting small town for far less than you'd pay for a grotty tent in Sarchu. The bus departs Keylong for Manali at 04.30 the following morning and reaches its destination at 11.00. These buses are cheaper; A class is Rs475 and B class Rs350. Tickets just to Keylong are Rs400 (A class) and Rs300 (B class). See p92 for details of onward transport from Manali to Delhi.

• **To Srinagar** Far fewer Westerners now travel this way because of the unrest in Kashmir (see p50). The journey takes two days, with an overnight stop at Kargil. J&KSRTC buses leave Leh's main bus stand daily at 05.30 and reach Kargil at 15.00. Leaving Kargil the next morning at 04.30 they arrive in Srinagar between 18.00 and 19.00. Fares are Rs333 for a supercoach and Rs222 for A class (there's no B class on this route). Some of the travel agencies in Leh occasionally run private tourist buses to Srinagar for about Rs250.

Because of militant activity, bus travel in the Kashmir Valley is **not recommended**, particularly the Srinagar-Jammu section. There are daily buses onward from Srinagar to Delhi (Rs350, 24 hours) or you can catch one of the frequent buses to Jammu (Rs100-200, 12 hours), many of which connect with the daily Delhi-bound trains.

By taxi

If you can't get a flight out of Leh and you can't bear the thought of another bus journey, taking a taxi to Manali or Srinagar may be the

answer. When the road has been damaged by landslides jeeps are sometimes the only vehicles that can get past. On the route to Srinagar taxis
have the added advantage that you can stop off at some of the interesting
sites along the way. A one-way trip costs Rs10,200 to Manali and Rs5980
to Srinagar. You can squeeze up to six people in a jeep.

Beyond Leh

Scattered along the Indus Valley, both east and west of Leh, are other fascinating towns, villages, monasteries and palaces. Some are visited by
almost every traveller who comes to Ladakh while others remain the preserve of the dedicated few.

A tour of the gompas is high on most peoples' lists. Whether you
decide to see as many as possible or to spend more time at one or two is
up to you. Buses connect most of the principal villages and provide a
cheap means of transport. If your time is limited it may be more convenient to hire a taxi for a day between three or four people. A round trip
taking in Shey, Tikse, Hemis and Stok will cost Rs905, or if you've got
the energy you could add Chemre, Tak Tok, Matho and Stakna to the
above list for Rs1500. A tour to the west stopping at Basgo, Likir, Alchi
and Lamayuru is Rs1900 one way or Rs2350 return. Go to the taxi office
for other alternatives. You can usually visit gompas between 8am and
5pm and most now charge an entrance fee of Rs10-20.

Interesting places further afield include the Suru Valley and Zanskar,
and now that entry has been allowed into the former restricted areas (now
called 'protected areas') the choice is wider than it has been for decades.
The government is trying to develop the tourism potential of these areas
but at the moment the infrastructure is minimal and permits are still
required. Check in Leh to find out what facilities you can expect. Nubra
and Dha-Hanu are the easiest to visit as they can be reached by public
transport. The simplest way to get to Pangong Lake, Tso Moriri and Tso
Kar is with an organised tour.

The Indus River

At 2900km long, the river that gives India its name is one of the longest in the world.
By the time it enters Ladakh it has already come 700km from its source in south-west
Tibet. From here it continues through Kashmir and then across Pakistan, collecting
the combined waters of the Jhelum, Chenab, Ravi, Beas, and Sutlej from its largest
tributary, the Panjnad. It disgorges its contents, now heavily laden with sediment, into
the Arabian sea near Karachi. The Ladakhis call the river, Sengge Kabab, meaning the
Lion River, after the legend that it springs from the mouth of a lion.

West of Leh

Spituk
This was the first Gelukpa (Yellow Hat) monastery to be established in Ladakh. Rinchen Zangpo predicted that a monastery would be founded here that would set an example to other monasteries in the land. The monastery you see today was built in the 15th century on the site of an 11th century temple. As it's situated on top of a small hill there are good views over the Indus Valley. There are buses to Spituk (20 minutes) every 15 minutes throughout the day, or alternatively you could get a taxi for the short journey; Rs130 one way or Rs185 return. (**Festivals**: 7-8 Jan 1997; 26-27 Jan 1998; 15-16 Jan 1999).

Phyang
The building of this 16th century gompa was ordered by the king, Tashi Namgyal. It's thought that he was trying to seek forgiveness for blinding his elder brother, a devious act that made him heir to the throne and soon after, king. The gompa sits on a small hill above the attractive village and like Lamayuru belongs to the Kagyupa (Red Hat) order of monks.

There are three buses a day (45 minutes) from Leh at 08.00, 14.00 and 17.00. Taxis cost Rs335 one way or Rs450 return. (**Festivals**: 17-18 July 1996; 5-6 Aug 1997; 25-26 July 1998; 14-15 July 1999).

Likir
This impressive monastery dates back to the 12th century but the original structure was destroyed by fire so the buildings you see today are about 200 years old. The monks are of the Gelukpa order, and the kushok is the Dalai Lama's younger brother. As well as looking after this monastery, the monks also take responsibility for Alchi Gompa and several of the smaller gompas in the area. For information about Likir village see p178.

There's a privately-operated bus everyday to Likir (Rs30, two hours) which leaves from the main bus stand sometime between 15.00 and 16.00, or you could take a taxi; Rs760 one way or Rs850 return. (**Festival**s: 5-6 Feb 1997; 24-25 Feb 1998; 14-15 Feb 1999).

Alchi
The *Choskor*, or religious enclave, is one of the most important cultural sites in Ladakh. Built in the eleventh century, it is a treasure trove of early Buddhist art in the Kashmiri tradition, a style quite different from the Tibetan art found in Ladakh's other monasteries. Also unlike other gompas, it is hidden down by the river rather than in the more usual elevated

---

(**Opposite**) Sankar Gompa is a gentle 2km walk from Leh and makes a worthwhile excursion.

position. This may explain why it wasn't destroyed by the various invaders who have passed by throughout the centuries. It was constructed under the supervision of Kaldan Shesrab, a follower of Rinchen Zangpo, the man responsible for reviving an interest in Buddhism at that time. Alchi is one of the few remaining examples of that era.

The village and gompa are reached by crossing the Indus just beyond Saspol and doubling back on yourself for about 2km. There are daily buses from Leh at 15.00 (Rs25, 3 hours). They return to Leh the following morning, leaving Alchi at 07.30. Taxis cost Rs805 one way or Rs990 return. (See p196 for further information on the village).

Rizong

The solitary Gelukpa monastery at Rizong lies up a side valley to the north of the main road between Nurla and Saspol and is accessible only on foot. For an hour you walk up the narrow winding valley; first you reaching the nunnery and then about a kilometre further on you see the monastery towering up above you.

Gelukpa monasteries are known for their strict discipline but Rizong is reputed to be the strictest of them all. The 30 or so monks own nothing more than the robes they are wearing and all eat the same food from the monastery kitchen. The gompa, just over 160 years old, contains little of historical interest but its location in this quiet valley is worth the tiring walk.

Lamayuru

The gompa at Lamayuru is one of the most immediately striking in Ladakh. Its position on top of a beautifully eroded crag, complete with rock pinnacles and caves, gives it an almost fairy tale quality as it stands over the small village below. There is a local legend that the whole valley was under a deep lake until the holy man, Nimagou, prayed for a monastery to be founded here. With that, the lake drained away. The site of the monastery is probably the oldest in Ladakh with the first temple, like so many others, being built at the time of Rinchen Zangpo.

The monastery is officially called Yung-dung Tharpa Ling, or 'place of freedom', after it was declared a holy site in the 16th century. In such places even criminals could be safe from persecution if within one square mile. It now belongs to the Kagyupa sect. For information about the village see p184.

To get there take any bus that is going to Kargil or Srinagar (see p126). The journey takes about six hours. A taxi one way will cost Rs1690 or Rs2050 return. (**Festivals**: 2-3 July 1996; 21-22 July 1997; 12-13 July 1998; 30 June, 1 July 1999).

(**Opposite**) **Top:** Lamayuru Gompa perched high above the village fields. **Bottom:** Large families will often send their youngest son to the local monastery to be educated a monk. These young monks are from Chemre Gompa.

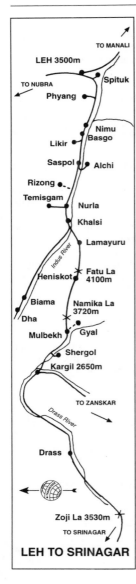

TO MANALI

LEH 3500m

Spituk

TO NUBRA

Phyang

Nimu
Basgo

Likir

Saspol   Alchi

Rizong

Temisgam

Nurla

Khalsi

Lamayuru

Indus River

Heniskot   Fatu La
            4100m

Biama   Namika La
            3720m

Dha

Mulbekh   Gyal

Shergol

Kargil 2650m

TO ZANSKAR

Drass River

Drass

Zoji La 3530m

TO SRINAGAR

LEH TO SRINAGAR

The Leh- Srinagar Highway

This 434km highway leaves Leh passing the airport and **Spituk** gompa. After the army camps the road rises up to a plateau and passes the turning to **Phyang**. The gompa lies a couple of km north of the road. Just before Nimu (36km) the Indus and Zanskar rivers meet at an impressive confluence.

The next 60km are a culture vulture's dream, passing the temples and derelict fort at Basgo (6km); the large monastery at **Likir** (10km); painted caves at Saspol (10km); the historic gompa at **Alchi** (2km); if you take a track heading north off the main road in 7km you will reach the gompa at **Rizong**; or get off at Nurla (15km) and walk the 4km north to the ruined castle and temples at Temisgam (p183).

Just beyond Khalsi (11km) the road crosses the Indus and slowly winds its way up to the beautiful gompa at **Lamayuru** (27km). On the left, just before reaching the village, there are great views of the 'moonlands'. You continue climbing for 15km to the highest pass on the route, the Fatu La (4100m/13,450ft). After crossing another pass, the Namika La (3720m/12,210ft) (36km), the road descends to the village of Mulbekh (15km) where there is a gompa. Just before the village, at the side of the road, there's an ancient nine-metre sculpture of the Maitreya, or future Buddha, carved into the rock. If you leave the highway and follow the Wakha River upstream from here you can visit the tiny cliff face gompa at Gyal. Beyond Mulbekh there is a turning on the left that takes you to the small cave gompa at Shergol (7km).

The formerly important town of **Kargil** (34km) marks the transition to a predominantly Muslim area and from here you can either continue west to Kashmir or take the rough road south, up the **Suru Valley** to **Zanskar**. 56km further along the main highway is Drass, the last major village in Ladakh, whose hardy Dard inhabitants have to put up with appalling winter weather of continuous heavy snowfall and temperatures as low as minus 40°C. In just under 40km the road crosses the Zoji La (3530m/11,580ft), leaving behind the arid mountains of Ladakh to descend through the lush, wooded Sind Valley to the Vale of Kashmir and Srinagar (110km).

Distances given above are from the place last mentioned; and are approximate. Places in bold print are covered in more detail in this section.

Kargil (2650m/8700ft)

This uninspiring Muslim town is the overnight halt for all buses travelling between Leh and Srinagar or on to Padum. Most trekking supplies can be bought here, the Tourist Reception Centre rents out trekking equipment and there is a State Bank of India if you need to change money. It makes most sense to stay close to the bus stand if you are just passing through, as the buses leave early in the morning.

The two closest hotels are the International and the Crown. Both have double rooms for Rs100, but the former is better value as the price includes an attached bathroom.

Buses leave Leh daily at 05.30 reaching Kargil at 15.00. Prices are Rs111 for an A class bus and Rs88 for B class. Buses from Kargil to Leh leave at about 05.00 (Rs88). Taxis to Kargil cost Rs2890.

Zanskar

Most visitors to this remote Buddhist region are trekkers, the main town of Padum being a convenient starting point for several strenuous but spectacular treks across the convoluted Zanskar Mountains. Padum and the main Zanskar Valley can now be reached from Kargil by a road that stays open from around mid-July to the end of October. This is a beautiful, though somewhat uncomfortable, journey and you should be prepared for delays as the road conditions are often appalling.

From Kargil, the road runs south up the predominantly Muslim Suru Valley for 67km to Panikhar. The Balti settlements along this valley are surrounded by lush fields growing a wide variety of crops and fruits; the villages themselves are rather untidy and in disrepair. As you gain height the mighty snow-capped peaks of Nun (7135m/23,410ft) and Kun (7077m/23,220ft) gradually become visible and soon dominate the view.

The road swings around to the east, past the last Muslim settlement of Parkachik, to the Buddhist Gelukpa monastery at Rangdum (63km), sitting astride a small hill in the middle of a wide plain. The Pensi La (4400m/14,440ft) and the entrance to Zanskar are only 20km on from here. The road descends to the Stod River which it then follows, past the well cared-for Zanskari villages, to Padum (90km). See p229 for further details on Padum.

During the main trekking season, there are usually buses every other day from Kargil to Padum (Rs100, 16-18 hours) and it's also possible to hitch a ride on a truck. If the road across the Pensi La is closed, there are daily buses as far as Panikhar (3 hours) and from there it's a week's trek along the vehicle-free road to Padum.

South-east of Leh

Choglamsar
This is a Tibetan refugee village where the Dalai Lama has his beautiful temporary residence (not open to tourists) and where the Central Institute of Buddhist Studies is based. There are lots of buses going east from Leh, all of which pass through Choglamsar. Alternatively a one-way taxi ride will cost Rs95;Rs130 return.

Shey
This was the old capital and the home of the kings of Ladakh before the new capital became established in Leh.

The palace sits in a strategic position on a spur jutting out into the Indus Valley. The main temple contains a large Buddha statue sculpted by Nepalese craftsmen. It is believed that after its completion they settled in the area of Chiling and started the now famous metal working industry there. In the courtyard there's an impressive gold topped stupa best viewed from above. The top of the palace is reached by some very dilapidated steps and from here there are wonderful views across to Stok and Spituk, and also of the hundreds of stupas on the desert to the north-east.

It is possible to stay in Shey at the Hotel Shilkhar below the palace. They have double rooms for Rs150 (att). There are buses to Shey every hour from Leh.

Tikse
If you're going to see only one monastery, make it Tikse (Thiksay/ Thekse). This large gompa is an impressive sight, situated on top of a craggy hill while the rest of the complex sprawls down beneath it. It was founded in the fifteenth century by Gelukpa monks. The temple on the right of the courtyard houses a 15 metre statue of the Maitreya, or future Buddha, which was finished in 1981, while at the back of the Dukhang there is a 565 year old Buddha. The monks here are helpful and friendly and the whole gompa is well cared for. There are buses from Leh every hour, or you can get a taxi (30 minutes). (**Festivals**: 29-30 Oct 1996; 17-18 Nov 1997; 6-7 Nov 1998; 27-28 Oct 1999).

Stok
This has been the royal palace since the king was dethroned by the Dogras and is now the home of the last king's widow. There's an interesting museum that contains an odd collection of exhibits including the king's teacup holder, the queen's turquoise head-dress, some armour and

a stuffed yak. It is open from 8am to 7pm and costs Rs20. There are buses to Stok at 07.30, 14.00 and 17.00. A taxi will cost you Rs245 one way or Rs365 return.(**Festival**s: 15-16 Feb 1997; 6-7 Mar 1998; 24-25 Feb 1999).

Matho

This is the only Sakyapa gompa in Ladakh and has become famous for its annual festival, during which specially chosen monks become the vehicle for an oracle. For several days they answer people's questions and predict the following year's events while in a trance. Occasionally their superhuman powers are put to the test. They have been known to sprint along the thin outer wall of the gompa and over the roofs without falling, and have been seen to cut their mouths and hands with knives until they bleed profusely; the next morning there are no scars to be found.

The main temple isn't particularly interesting but there is a tiny museum on the left side of the courtyard which is worth seeing. It contains a stuffed yak, old masks, skulls and costumes that are used at the festival. Right at the top of the gompa there's the highly revered Room of the Oracles. Women are not allowed into this tiny room and photographs must not be taken. The floor is covered in grain,

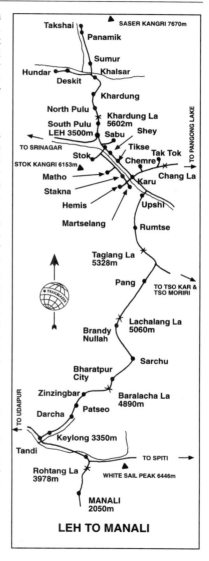

LEH TO MANALI

taken from every field in the village to ensure a harvest for the next year. It's almost pitch dark inside but you can just make out the walls which are covered in grotesque and frightening masks. It's not a place for the easily scared. The monastery is situated at the foot of the Stok Mountains midway between Hemis and Stok. (**Festivals**: 21-22 Feb 1997; 12-13 Mar 1998; 1-2 Mar 1999).

Stakna

This Kagyupa gompa is sited in a commanding position on its own plug of rock in the centre of the Indus Valley. It was repainted in 1982 and is now one of the most bright and colourful gompas in Ladakh. It lies between Hemis and Matho and is reached by taking the bumpy road that runs along the left (W) bank of the Indus.

Hemis

This monastery has become famous because of its spectacular annual festival. It's even more special if you can coincide your visit with the unfurling of the monasteries' vast thanka, thought to be the biggest in the world. However, as this is only displayed at every twelfth festival you'll have to wait until 2004 for the next showing. Although it is the largest and richest of Ladakh's monasteries, it is not the most beautiful and much of the gompa looks run down and in need of restoration. Unfortunately the gompa's wealth is held mainly in land and not in cash.

The gompa was founded in the 17th century and is sometimes called Chang Chub Sang Ling, 'the solitary place of the compassionate ones'. It belongs to the Kagyupa sect. Try to see the impressive image of Guru Padmasambhava which is in a temple behind the Dukhang (the temple on the right).This huge statue is 12 metres high and was completed in 1984.

The village and gompa lie tucked up a little side valley south-west of Karu. As you drive up to it you pass two enormous mani walls. There are various places where you can eat in the village and also a campground.

Buses leave Leh at 09.00 daily and sometimes at 15.00 as well (2 hours). Check when these return to Leh because you may find you'll need to spend the night in the village. You shouldn't have any difficulty finding a room if this is necessary. Taxis cost Rs680 one way and Rs748 return (1 hour 15 minutes). (**Festivals**: 26-27 June 1996; 15-16 July 1997; 4-5 July 1998; 23-24 June 1999).

Chemre

This gompa looks more impressive from afar than close up, sitting astride a hill high above the village. It's situated about half-way along the quiet road from Karu to Tak Tok and worth a visit if you are passing. The Kagyupa monastery was built in 1645 in honour of Sengge Namgyal after his death. (**Festivals**: 9-10 Nov 1996; 27-28 Nov 1997; 17-18 Nov 1998; 5-6 Nov 1999).

Tak Tok

Tak Tok (Thak Thak/Trakthok/Tak Thog) means 'rock roof' and this interesting little monastery is built around a cave where it is believed Padmasambhava lived and meditated for a while. The cave is now a cool dark temple. This is the only gompa in Ladakh of the Nyingmapa sect, the oldest Tibetan order. It's 20km up a side valley north-east of Karu. (**Festivals**: 25-26 July 1996; 13-14 Aug 1997; 3-4 Aug 1998; 23-24 July 1999).

The Leh-Manali Highway (see map p133)

This 485km highway descends from Leh to the village of **Choglamsar** and then follows the River Indus in a south-easterly direction passing the historic sites of **Shey** and **Tikse** (17km from Leh). The royal palace at **Stok** is reached by branching off at Choglamsar and taking the road over the Indus up to the village at the foot of the mountains. There's an alternative and little-travelled route on this side of the Indus which takes you past the gompas at **Matho**, **Stakna** and **Hemis** before rejoining the main highway. At Karu (18km from Tikse), it's worth making a short diversion up the quiet side valley to the north-east, to see the less tourist visited gompas of **Chemre** and **Tak Tok**. The road leaves the Indus Valley at the truck-stop village of Upshi (14km from Karu) to head south along the west bank of the tumbling Kyammar Lungpa to the military camp at Rumtse (30km), before climbing to the Taglang La (30km). The concrete urinals and tea stall rather detract from the experience of standing at 5328m (17,480ft) on top of the highest pass on the route, but the road sign prompts you into the correct frame of mind by exclaiming 'Unbelievable! Is it not'.

Twenty km of unpaved hairpins takes you down to the wide and windswept More Plains, the summer grazing grounds for the sheep, yak and goats of the Changpa nomads. The 48km plateau comes to an abrupt end when the road descends for 7km into a wide gorge at the army and road builders' depot at Pang (see p222) and a few km further on, there is a collection of dhabas and tents for benighted travellers. There are 25km of truly awe-inspiring scenery between Pang and the double pass called the Lachalang La (5060m/16,600ft), on the southern side of which you'll find the road workers' camp called Brandy Nullah (34km). It's a further 20km or so to the tented camp at Sarchu, where most of the tourist buses pull in for the night.

There's another small collection of dhabas at the incongruously named Bharatpur City (26km), which you pass before climbing to the bleak summit of the Baralacha La (10km, 4890m/16,040ft). The road continues south-west past Zingzingbar and the police post at Patseo (25km), to Darcha (16km), where there are some dhabas and a campsite. The small town of Keylong (32km) is a convenient place to break your journey as there are several small hotels.

The road crosses the Bhaga River at Tandi (6km), just before it joins with the Chandra to form the Chandra-Bhaga River, or Chenab, and this same water eventually flows into the Indus in Pakistan. The route veers round to the east, passing through prosperous Lahauli villages along the Chandra Valley, until it reaches the ramshackle collection of dhabas and a police checkpoint at Koksar (36km). As you climb the looping road towards the Rohtang La (20km, 3978m/13,052ft) there are wonderful views to White Sail Peak (6446m/21,149ft) and its smaller neighbours. The road improves dramatically as you hurtle down from the pass towards Manali (51km), and the abundance of greenery and trees makes a dramatic change to the arid mountains that you've left behind.

Approximate distances given above are from the last place mentioned. Places in bold print are covered in greater detail elsewhere in this section.

Protected areas

All travellers visiting these areas must get a **permit** in Leh (see p120).

Nubra

After years of speculation, the sensitive border region of Nubra was finally opened to foreigners in 1994. Although it lies just north of Leh, access is only possible from mid to late summer, when the road over the Khardung La is free of snow.

The district is characterised by deep, sheer-sided valleys, high mountains and long glaciers. It is here that you will find the highest peak in Ladakh, Saser Kangri, (7670m/25,165ft) which was first climbed in 1973, and also one of the longest glaciers in the region, the 70km Siachen Glacier, which is still the scene of fighting between India and Pakistan. Sandwiched between the Karakoram Mountains to the north and the Ladakh Range to the south lie the Shyok and Nubra rivers. The fertile villages are scattered along these two valley floors.

Because of the lower altitude a wide diversity of fruits, vegetables and grains are grown, creating the impression of abundance. Yet this is one of the poorest areas of Ladakh and facilities for the traveller are few and far between. Although accommodation and food can usually be found, you should bring anything else you need with you. Don't forget to pack your Ladakhi phrase book as few people speak English.

Deskit There's a beautiful gompa perched on a rocky spur high above the village with friendly monks and breathtaking views. A good 7km walk from here leads to Hundar (Hundat) where there's a ruined gompa.

The world's highest motorable road

It's a hair-raising ride over the Khardung La with no shortage of heart-stopping moments. You feel your fears are justified as you pass the mangled wrecks of vehicles that have plummeted over the edge. However, the stunning views help to divert your attention. It takes three hours from Leh to the top, with one stop at the checkpoint at South Pulu. Between here and North Pulu the road is unpaved and very rough. You are invited to take a free cup of tea when you reach the Khardung La (5602m/18,380ft). It is not clear whether this is designed to help you cope with the altitude or to soothe frayed nerves!

The views over the Zanskar Mountains are fantastic and if the altitude measurements are to be believed, you are now 100 metres higher than Mount Everest base camp and 795m above Mont Blanc, not bad for a local bus journey! You descend to North Pulu where there's another checkpoint and then through the pretty village of Khardung to the Shyok Valley floor and Khalsar, where you can get a simple meal.

Deskit's idyllic setting is marred by an ugly housing project in the village. You can either stay at the pleasant campsite just past the bridge or at the overpriced and unfriendly Olthang Guest House (Rs150).

Panamik The famed hot springs are nothing to get excited about. They are in an ugly building on the hillside and the smell and high temperature of the water doesn't entice you to bathe. There are some nice walks down by the river and a good five-hour excursion across the valley to a beautiful gompa, visible from Panamik, and a waterfall. Go upstream for 4km towards Takshai, cross the Nubra River on a bridge and then double back for 4km on the other bank. It is possible to ford the river below here and return to Panamik via Sumur but the river crossing can be very difficult.

There is a campsite and a couple of friendly but modern guest houses in the village (Rs150 for a basic double). It's also often possible to stay with families if you ask around.

Sumur This pretty village with its gompa is worth visiting if you have the time. There is a guest house and campsite here.

Getting to Nubra There are two buses a week to Panamik, which also stop at Khalsar and Sumur. They leave the main bus stand at 05.00 on Mondays and Wednesdays (Rs60, 8 hours). The return journey is made on Tuesdays and Thursdays, again departing at 05.00. You can also catch a bus to Deskit from Leh, every Friday at 05.00 (Rs55, 7 hours). A Jeep taxi will cost you Rs5000 for 2 days.

Hitching is far easier out of Nubra than the other way round. But if you want to try, the trucks usually leave Leh in a convoy early in the morning. The hippest way to Nubra is on a bicycle and the number of people who have cycled over the highest road in the world is still relatively small. If you're not a hard-core hill climber then put your bike on the roof of a bus and enjoy the longest free-wheel of your life.

Pangong Lake

This vast lake, 150km long and 4km wide, stretches from the north-east of Ladakh across the border into Tibet. The lake has no outlet so the water has a high salt and mineral content. Because of this the lake cannot support aquatic life, hence its distinctive and beautiful shades of blue, described by Gypsy Davy and Lady Ba in their *Himalayan Letters* as an 'azure sheen of turkis blew'. There are some interesting birds around the lake shore including a few pairs of the very rare and endangered black-necked crane. You can reach the lake only by jeep which is easily arranged in Leh (Rs5000 for two days).

Tso Moriri and Tso Kar

These high altitude lakes are situated in the Rupshu region of eastern Ladakh. Tso Moriri is surrounded by mountains and is formed by a tributary of the Spiti River. This rare habitat attracts the barheaded goose which breeds here during the summer around the inlets of the lake. Tso Kar is another brackish lake and this whole region has supported a vital salt industry that allowed the nomadic inhabitants, the Changpas, to trade with merchants from the rest of Ladakh.

Travel by jeep is really the only feasible way of getting here. This will cost Rs15,700 for three days.

Minimum impact

Pangong Lake, Tsomoriri and Tsokar all have extremely fragile ecosystems and provide habitats for some rare species of birds. Since 1994, when foreign tourists were first allowed to visit these areas, there has been a marked decline in the sighting of many birds and other wildlife. As Ladakh has no tourism management scheme it is up to the tourists themselves to make sure they do not destroy the very things that they have come to see. If certain simple practices are followed then the damage inflicted on these unique areas can be reduced:

• Set up camp 2-3km away from the lake shore to make sure that the lakes are not polluted and that the wildlife is not disturbed.

• Do not go to the toilet, wash your body, brush your teeth or wash your pots and pans near the lake shore. The lakes have no outlet and therefore any chemicals introduced to the water will remain there.

• Take all garbage away with you. It's not good enough simply to bury it.

• Don't allow your guide to drive to the shore of the lake. Get out and walk instead. The increase in vehicles close to the water's edge is doing untold damage.

• Encourage others to do likewise, particularly your guide and other Ladakhi helpers.

Dha-Hanu

Downstream from Khalsi, along the lower Indus, live a unique group of Dard people known as Brokpa. In most other areas the Dards have been strongly influenced by either the Tibetans or by the Muslims but here in the area of Dha-Hanu they have retained much of their original culture. They are the only ones to have preserved their unique form of Buddhism which is mixed with the pre-Buddhist animistic religion, Bon. They are a fascinating people who are very different from other Ladakhis, with their strong Aryan looks, language and clothing (they wear colourful flowers in their head-dresses).

Tourists are allowed to visit two villages in the area, Dha and Biama. There are daily buses to Dha from Leh at 09.00. A taxi there and back will cost Rs2805.

Tsestalulu Juice

This healthy, environmentally friendly drink is made from the berries of the thorny sea buckthorn plant which grows naturally in many parts of Ladakh. The small scale, local production of this high vitamin C drink by the Indus Tsestalulu Society aims to provide a source of income for previously unemployed, uneducated and economically deprived rural people on the back of an all Ladakhi product. It is hoped that this will help prevent country to town migration, while providing a delicious and healthy drink for Ladakhis and thirsty trekkers. It costs about Rs22 for a 650ml bottle.

PART 6: MINIMUM IMPACT TREKKING

Minimum impact trekking

Take only memories. Leave nothing but footprints. **Chief Seattle**

Ladakh's unique culture and amazing natural environment is why travellers have been drawn to this remote region for centuries. Despite the harsh climatic conditions, the people have created a prosperous and harmonious way of life that reflects the Buddhist principle of the interdependence of all things. Not only do the Ladakhis demonstrate respect for one another, as demonstrated by the stability and fairness inherent in family and community relations, but also for the natural environment, something that many in the 'modernised' West are now trying to rediscover.

However, the last fifty years of being part of India, and in particular the last twenty or so years of having foreign tourists, has had more effect on Ladakh's culture, environment and economy than several centuries of foreign merchants and traders. The changes have been most apparent in and around Leh, where there has been a steady erosion of the traditional values in favour of Western style materialism and an increase in environmental problems but the effects have also been felt in the remote mountains. Short-sighted development policies of the 1950s and 60s helped to create the notion that the Ladakhis were a backward and primitive people and that the only way to modernise was to follow the Western model of economic and technological growth. This is reinforced by cinema, television and advertising which portrays a biased picture of the West with all its glamour and wealth, while nothing even approximate to the Ladakhi lifestyle is ever shown, making them seem absurd. Then the arrival of foreign tourists further propagated the myth that West is best. Here are people who seem to have almost limitless amounts of money, who can travel whenever and wherever they like and who never seem to work. It is not surprising that impressionable teenagers are influenced by this alluring new culture.

Ladakh is now part of the 'developing' world, the process of change has permeated too far into Ladakhi society for this not to be so, and no matter how attractive a traditional rural society like Ladakh may seem, it is wrong and extremely damaging to make the land into some kind of museum. The Ladakhis now have a choice over how their region develops and Western tourists must be aware that they play an important role in determining what this future will be. By taking some simple and practical steps, all visitors can minimise their impact on, and in some cases be of benefit to, Ladakh's culture, environment and economy.

CULTURAL IMPACT

Interacting with Ladakhis

It is unavoidable that you won't leave some impression of your culture by visiting Ladakh; instead of just consuming the country like another product, try to give something back. Tourists are in a powerful position to present a more balanced picture of life in the West and you are the ones who should actively speak out when you see something being done for the benefit of tourists which is obviously harmful or degrading to the local environment or culture. However, unless you make an effort to communicate, all that the Ladakhis will see is yet another rich tourist on holiday – an inaccurate picture of someone not particularly well off by Western standards, who has worked extremely hard to pay for a trip out to Ladakh and who cares for and admires the country and its people.

You will get the most out of your visit if you travel in small groups, allow lots of time and try to be constantly aware. Although many Ladakhis speak good English, do try to learn a few words of Ladakhi as this will be greatly appreciated and will underline the importance of their language. When telling somebody about your home country talk about the problems as well as the good things. Explain about the environmental and social costs of living in a 'developed' country, or how lots of people will now pay more money to buy local, organic food and to use methods of natural health care, rather than relying on the so-called 'modern' techniques. If you are asked how much you earn, put it in context by explaining that almost half of your income goes on paying for somewhere to live, say how much a week's supply of groceries will cost or how much it would cost to travel a short distance on a local bus. Interaction with the Ladakhis should be a two-way process and a holiday is the perfect excuse to spend time learning from them.

• **Encourage local pride** Express an interest in all things Ladakhi and explain why you've come all this way and spent all that money to come to their country. Try to eat local food, adapt to local practices and use local services so that you can experience the culture at first hand. Make a point of letting the people know what you like about it: if you have chosen your guest house because it has a Ladakhi toilet or solar heated hot water, then tell the owners.

• **Dress and behave modestly** Too many trekkers insult the Ladakhis by the way they are dressed, although complaints are never heard because the Ladakhis are too polite. It's very easy to respect local customs by not revealing legs, shoulders or backs. Men should always wear a shirt and trousers; if you must wear shorts while trekking, make sure they are cut long. Women should wear loose trousers or skirts that come to below the knee and tops that cover shoulders and back. Bright colours and body-revealing lycra are not appreciated. Never bathe in the nude.

• **Respect local etiquette** Ladakhis have different ways of doing things and by following these simple guidelines you will avoid causing offence. The most useful word to learn is *Julay* which can be used at any time of the day to greet people, say goodbye or to thank someone. As you trek through villages you will be greeted by everyone in this manner and it is polite to do likewise.

When offered something it is polite to decline several times before accepting. Use both hands to receive things. If you are pointing at something then use your whole hand rather than just your finger. The feet are considered unclean, so don't point them at people or step over anything such as people, food, tables or religious articles. Similarly, if you have your legs outstretched Ladakhis will be loathe to step over them, so move them out of the way or preferably, keep them folded under you if you're seated on the floor. Religious objects, including anything that contains pictures of religious objects (postcards or books), should be kept high off the floor.

When in public do not display your affection for others by holding hands, hugging or kissing. This can easily offend or embarrass Ladakhis. Don't share utensils when eating or drinking – learn how to drink from a water bottle without your lips touching it.

• **Respect religious customs** When visiting monasteries it is particularly important that you wear appropriate clothes, take off your shoes or boots before entering the temple, don't smoke, don't touch any religious objects and always remember to give a small donation. The larger monasteries now charge an entrance fee to make sure you don't forget. If you want to photograph the frescoes inside monasteries bring a tripod or some fast film; don't use a flash as this can damage the paint work.

Religious festivals are sacred occasions and you will upset many local people if you wander around taking photographs while the dances are going on. Recently, masked dances have been performed outside of monasteries as a tourist attraction, especially during the Ladakh Festival. This is considered deeply sacrilegious and you should express your disapproval by not supporting such an exploitation of religion and by complaining to the relevant organisers.

Always walk to the left of Buddhist monuments (chortens, mani walls, prayer wheels) by keeping them on your right. Prayer wheels should be turned in a clockwise direction. Don't sit or leave your pack on mani walls or chortens and never move mani stones.

• **Respect people's privacy** Ladakhis get just as annoyed by people peering into their lives as you do. Always put yourself in their position, especially before taking someone's photograph. It's a common courtesy to ask for permission before taking a shot and if they don't want their photo taken then please respect this. Don't pay people for posing for you. It is much better to take down their address and send them a copy instead. Pony-men, and others that you spend some time with, may also ask you to send them copies of the photos you've taken of them. It is a cardinal sin not to follow this obligation through, it costs you very little and means a great deal to those at the receiving end.

• **Be modest with your wealth** However poor you think you are at home, by Ladakhi standards you are very wealthy. Don't flaunt this wealth by showing off your hi-tech equipment. Leaving it lying around unattended is further proof that you could easily afford to replace it.

• **Discourage begging** Begging in Ladakh started as a children's game to see if they could get a 'bon-bon' or 'school pen' from the always obliging tourists. However, it has developed into a far more serious problem by fostering an attitude of dependency among the young. Don't give anything to people who ask for it, after all, giving sweets to children in a country which has few dentists is not an act of charity, and if you want to give money, it is best to ask the advice of one of the excellent NGO's (see p119) working in Ladakh to whom it should be given.

• **Don't play doctor** While trekking you may occasionally be asked by locals for medicines or to treat wounds. Unless it is simply a case of cleaning a cut and applying a plaster you should encourage them to go to the nearest health post. There is usually one in larger villages. If you try to treat something more complicated and your efforts do not work, you may begin to undermine the people's faith in Western medicine. This will encourage them to patronise the local shaman rather than the health post.

• **Keep your sense of humour** It is considered the height of bad manners to lose your temper and you will almost never see a Ladakhi losing theirs. Although things can sometimes be very difficult, always try to maintain some perspective on the situation. You are not at home but in a land where things are done differently and where concepts of time are simply different from your own. See the funny side of your predicament, there will always be one.

ENVIRONMENTAL IMPACT

Litter

Litter is a very recent problem in Ladakh. It is only since the arrival of non-biodegradable consumer items from India and the rest of the world that the concept of litter has begun to take hold. Before, everything was made from biodegradable materials or continuously recycled, there was no waste. However, today it is a serious problem both in Leh and on the major trekking routes and in the latter case it is only the trekkers who are to blame. The difference between trekking a popular route at the beginning of the season and at the end is phenomenal. In the first instance there is hardly a sign of people having passed by, but a couple of months later the route is littered with streamers of toilet paper, tin cans and plastic bags. The solution is simple and summed up in the often used phrase, 'pack it in, pack it out'.

The problem in Leh is immediately obvious to the visitor who can't avoid the litter that lies in the streets, but unfortunately there is no easy solution. Leh has no proper infrastructure to cope with litter. While there are litter bins situated around the town which many tourists diligently use, there are few appropriate places for it to be taken after that. The facilities that are available are hopelessly inadequate as litter left in heaps is soon scattered far and wide by scavenging dogs and the wind, while the incinerators pump toxic fumes into the atmosphere.

• **Don't leave litter** When trekking it is a simple matter to bring along a extra bag in which to put all non-organic litter. This applies equally to those trekking with ponies and to those backpacking. You can also significantly cut down on the amount of potential waste you bring into the mountains by repacking items to avoid unnecessary packaging. Picking up other peoples litter is very helpful and sets a good example to others. Burning litter is frequently claimed to solve the problem, but many items do not burn properly and the fire leaves unsightly scars on the ground. It is far better to get into the habit of taking all non-organic waste out with you. If you are trekking with an organised group it is your responsibility to ensure that the crew dispose of the litter properly and that it isn't simply buried or left. Don't just imagine that waste will biodegrade; although most organic material will break down quite quickly, other biodegradable waste can take years to break down in this cold, dry climate. Also, don't assume that you can leave litter in villages; while much of it may be recycled they don't have any facilities to deal with the rest.

Having advocated bringing all your litter back to Leh, you then have to decide what to do with it there. However, it is far better to have it concentrated in one place where there is a chance that it will be dealt with properly, than left in the mountains where it will remain for generations to come. More pressure is coming to bear on Leh's authorities and it is likely that proper litter disposal systems will be introduced soon. In the meantime all you can do is try to keep your consumption of packaged goods to a minimum, reuse as much as possible and dispose of any litter in the bins provided.

• **Burn used lavatory paper** On the trail, if you can't get used to the water-and-left-hand method then make sure you burn all the loo paper that you use. Keep a cigarette lighter or some matches in the same plastic bag as the loo paper specifically for this purpose. Tampons/sanitary towels should be disposed of in the same way or buried. Used loo paper burns easily and there is no excuse for the 'pink flowers' of paper that decorate the trails. Not only is it unsightly, but unhygienic as well, especially when it's blown around campsites and into water sources.

• **Avoid bottled mineral water** Mineral water is sold widely in India and Ladakh in non-returnable, non-biodegradable plastic bottles. As there are several other ways to make ordinary tap water safe to drink (see p236), it is unnecessary to add to the litter problem by buying mineral water. If you treat the water yourself you not only save money, (Rs15-20 a litre), but you can be absolutely sure that the water you are drinking is safe (the seals on plastic bottles are not 100% tamper-proof).

• **Dispose of used batteries outside India** Most places in India have no safe means of disposing of batteries, the contents of which are highly toxic. Discarded batteries end up polluting the soil and water, or even as children's playthings. Pack batteries out for disposal in the West.

Water
• **Don't pollute water sources** When defecating in the mountains always ensure that you are at least 20 metres away from any water source and bury your faeces. This is made easier if you are with an organised group as a hole will be dug, over which a toilet tent will be erected. Ensure that you sprinkle earth into the hole after each visit and that it is properly filled in when you break camp.

If you are bathing, washing clothes or washing up in a stream, make sure you do so downstream of any nearby houses. If you want to use soap or shampoo then fill a container (collapsible buckets available in outdoor shops are ideal) and wash away from the stream. The need to wash clothes with soap can be minimised by rinsing them in a stream daily. The hot sun will make sure that they dry rapidly, but modern synthetic fibres can quite comfortably be wrung out and worn damp if it's not too cold. There is never any need to use soap or washing up liquid for cleaning pots and pans, as a good wire scrubber, or failing that, a handful of small pebbles, will get any pan sparkling in no time.

• **Toilet habits** Ladakh's traditional composting toilets are ideally suited to the environment and their use should be encouraged. No water is used (or wasted), the smell is negligible because of the dry climate and the end product is one of the best fertilisers around for organic agriculture. In rural areas the process saves animal manure which when dry, can be used more efficiently for fuel, essential in a region with hardly any wood. When using a Ladakhi toilet, usually situated upstairs and on the north side of a Ladakhi house, don't use water and remember to shovel some earth or ash (there's normally a pile in a corner) down when you've finished, this stops the smell and discourages flies. Don't throw tampons or sanitary towels down the hole.

Unfortunately, many guest houses in Leh have introduced flush toilets purely to please visitors. These are having disastrous effects on the local environment. First, they are using up extremely valuable fresh water supplies and second, Leh has no sewage system to deal with the waste that is produced. Instead, the groundwater supplies and the streams are becoming heavily contaminated because of poorly constructed and poorly maintained drains and septic tanks. Even if sewage-treatment works could be built and there was enough water, polluting chemicals would have to be introduced into the systems and the toilets would still be useless in winter when they freeze over. Various local organisations have tried to make guest house owners aware of the problem, but have met with little success because the owners believe that Western toilets are essential to attract guests. Therefore it is up to travellers to make them aware that you would prefer traditional toilets rather than Western style ones. After all, most trekkers are quite happy without flush toilets in the mountains and surely you didn't come to Ladakh to be comforted by Western 'luxuries'.

Erosion and vegetation depletion

The lack of vegetation, the gradual growth of the Himalaya by several millimetres per year and the searing heat of summer and freezing conditions of winter all combine to give the mountains of Ladakh a high rate of denudation. Although your actions may seem minuscule in comparison to these natural processes, when they are multiplied by several thousand trekkers each year they become rather more significant.

• **Stay on the main trail** Avoid taking shortcuts on steep sections of trail, your footsteps will be followed by many others. If you happen to damage walls or irrigation channels make sure that you repair them as someone's livelihood may be a stake.

• **Travel light** By travelling light you can use fewer pack animals which minimises the amount of erosion you cause and reduces the amount of grazing that will take place on the valuable mountain pastures.

• **Don't damage plants** Leave plants alone so that they can be enjoyed by other passers-by. You won't get through customs with a rare Himalayan specimen so don't try. Take care where your boots tread so that you don't disrupt fragile high altitude ecosystems.

• **Don't light open fires** Wood is a scarce resource so don't use any for making fires. You should always bring a stove and enough kerosene to cook on and remember that a camp fire is a selfish luxury. Fires create ugly scars on the ground that take years to fade away. While locals may well use animal dung fires to cook on, trekkers should not copy them as the fuel is a valuable resource for other travellers and villagers.

• **No running hot water please!** Many of Leh's guest houses now have running hot water. A few heat the water by solar panels and this should be encouraged, but most use highly inefficient wood fuelled boilers. Very little of this wood comes from Ladakh but is instead transported at great environmental and financial cost from mostly unsustainable forests in Himachal Pradesh and Kashmir. The cheaper guest houses take a far more environmentally friendly approach by heating one bucket of water at a time, usually when the stove is being used for cooking anyway. A bucketful of water is ample for a good wash.

ECONOMIC IMPACT

There is no doubt that tourism is an important force in the economy of Ladakh. This is particularly valuable now that the traditional trade routes, which previously provided Ladakh with a stable economic base, have closed. Although tourists may spend a large amount of money in Ladakh, much of that goes straight into the pockets of non-Ladakhis only to be taken out of the region at the end of the tourist season. Thus the Ladakhis have to put up with the cultural and environmental problems that tourism brings without benefiting as much as they could from the profits.

• **Check out your trekking company** If you book an organised trek in your home country a proportion of what you pay stays in the West to cover the company's administrative costs. Try to find out how your company spends its money in Ladakh. Does it use local services, buy locally produced food and goods, or employ local staff? Some companies bring Nepalese staff over, as Ladakh's peak season coincides with Nepal's off season. If you use an agency in Leh, is the company run by Ladakhis or employing Ladakhi staff? If you trek independently you will contribute more to the local economy. For this reason you should try to find a pony-man close to the start of your trek so that the money directly benefits the local community.

• **Use local services** Be choosy about how and where you spend your money. Hotels, guest houses, restaurants, souvenir shops and trekking agencies are increasingly being run by outsiders. This means that all the profits that they make with your money disappear with them, back to Delhi and Kashmir at the end of September. One estimate was that only 10% of souvenir shops in Leh were run by Ladakhis. You should use local services to boost the local economy; you'll benefit as much as the Ladakhis. Trying out Ladakhi-run accommodation will soon prove to you that their guest houses give far better value and are much more interesting than the overpriced and uniform establishments that are part of national and international chains. They may have all mod cons but are you seeking a home from home? If so, why travel?

• **Buy local products** Handicrafts have always been important in a region that has traditionally provided for its own basic needs. However, the souvenir shops of Leh are flooded with goods imported from the rest of India; sold at a higher price than in Delhi. The potential for Ladakhi crafts is slowly being realised, especially as their manufacture can provide villagers with a supplementary income during the six to eight winter months when there is little agricultural work. This therefore diversifies and strengthens the rural economy. Ask for Ladakhi handicrafts and try to find out where they were made. Some of the state-run handicraft centres merely compound the problem by encouraging people (mainly women) away from the farms to work in small scale craft factories rather than their homes, thus further undermining the traditional agricultural economy.

It is illegal to buy any object that is more than 100 years old. Abiding by the law is not enough: don't buy anything which is obviously robbing Ladakh of its cultural heritage, such as old thankas, statues and other religious objects, or even personal jewellery or old traditional tools.

When buying supplies for a trek, make the most of locally produced food such as the organic vegetables sold along the main bazaar, or dried apricots and roasted barley. When eating in restaurants and hotels try to support the local economy by asking for traditional Ladakhi food.

• **Pay the right price** Try to get an informed idea of how much things are worth. Guest house owners, staff at the tourist information and other

---

Camping

In the main trekking areas there is almost no real wilderness as most land is subject to village or communal rights. In effect you are walking and camping in someone's backyard and should therefore behave appropriately. You are generally free to pitch your tent on any open ground, but if you want to camp in a village you should ask permission, unless there's an obvious campsite. Also be prepared to pay a nominal fee if the villagers ask for one. In popular trekking areas villagers will often walk a considerable distance to collect this fee before you leave in the morning. The typical rate of Rs20 per tent represents a considerable income for very little effort.

This is a perfectly fair deal, especially if you have pack animals which are grazing on their pastures. However, there is a common misconception among pony-men and guides that you pay this fee in lieu of the villagers clearing up your litter. This is not the case; they have no satisfactory way of disposing of metals and plastics and if this attitude prevails the villages will begin to look like rubbish tips. Please carry all your litter out with you and dispose of it properly in Leh.

If you are using pack animals the choice of camping spots will be determined by where the best fodder can be found. This isn't usually a problem, but it can occasionally lead to an early halt if your pony-man isn't sure of the availability of fodder or water further on.

travellers can all be helpful. If you pay too much you will encourage inflation but by not paying enough you will deprive people of their rightful earnings. It is not always appropriate to bless people with your money as it can enforce the idea of a monetary economy in an area where more appropriate economic systems are operating. Particularly in remote rural areas, giving money in exchange for food or accommodation may not be accepted, in which case you should always have some useful gifts (such as tea, penknives, lighters) which can be given instead.

Organising your trek

PONY-MEN AND PACK ANIMALS

One of the most enjoyable ways to trek in Ladakh, whether you are on your own or with a few friends, is to hire a few ponies or donkeys to carry your food and equipment. The pony-man (it's almost always a man) who accompanies you will do far more than just look after the animals. He can also be your guide, translator, tutor, cook and companion.

If you're travelling in a large group, you may prefer to hire an additional cook and even a guide as well. This can be done in exactly the same way as outlined below.

First, find your pony-man
• **Independently** The independent trekker in need of a pony-man/guide should have few problems in finding a competent local. For the well-known Markha Valley trek start by making enquiries in Leh and at the nearby villages of Stok, Spituk or Choglamsar where many of the pony-men live. If you are planning on doing routes such as Likir to Temisgam, Lamayuru to Alchi, or Across Zanskar which all begin a fair distance from Leh, you're better off waiting until you arrive at the trailhead village before making any arrangements. The villages of Likir, Alchi and Lamayuru, as well as Padum in Zanskar are all used to the needs of trekkers. The best people to ask are shop keepers and the owners of restaurants and guest houses; ask as many people as possible. The quicker the news spreads around the village the sooner a pony-man will materialise. If your requirements are simple you're unlikely to have to wait more than a couple of days.

• **Through an agency** The alternative is to use one of Leh's many trekking agencies. They come into their own if you can't spare the time to look yourself, want a fully organised trek, or if you are looking for someone to guide you on one of the less well-known treks. There aren't

many pony-men who are familiar with treks such as Leh to Nubra or from
the Indus Valley to the Rupshu, and the knowledge of a good agency can
save time. However, you'll be charged Rs50-100 more per day than if you
went direct to a pony-man (more if the trek begins a long way from Leh)
and you have no control over who the agency picks for you.

Pack animals
• **Ponies, donkeys or yaks?** The most common pack animals in
Ladakh are donkeys and ponies. Very occasionally you will see yaks
being used but this is rare. Donkeys can carry about 30kg each, while a
pony can take up to 60kg. You often won't have much choice over
whether you hire ponies or donkeys as it depends on which animals are
available. Your choice of pony-man is far more important than your
choice of animal. The one exception to this is on the trek from Padum to
Darcha which involves a deep river crossing. The water is often too high
for the tiny Ladakhi donkeys and so it's advisable to hire ponies.

• **How many?** One of the quirks of using pack animals is that no matter
how little gear you have, you will almost always have to hire a minimum
of two. Contrary to popular opinion, this is not just the pony-man's scam
for making more money. For a start it's not only your belongings that
need to be carried but also those of the pony-man plus fodder for the animals. It is also a matter of safety. If one of the animals got injured there's
still another to carry the load, and if you fell ill the pony-man has a way
of carrying you out of the mountains.

To work out how many animals you'll need for a trek you have to
decide how many large bags you are going to take ('large' being about
15kg, or the size of a full 60 or 70 litre backpacking rucksack). Count on
two bags of that size per animal plus an extra animal for your pony-man.
For example, two people taking the same amount of food and gear as they
would on a backpacking trip would find two animals suitable, one for
them and one for the pony-man. However, most people enjoy the luxury
of being able to take slightly more than you could backpacking, especially where food is concerned. In which case an animal each may be more
realistic. If you're in any doubt, show the pony-man how much gear
you've got and listen to his advice.

• **Packing** The pony-men are experts at loading up their animals and
have a seemingly endless range of methods for getting the distribution
right. This is especially important on steep sections of the trail where a
slipped load can send an animal to its death. To make life easier for them,
try to split your luggage into even numbers of equally weighted bags, for
instance, two rucksacks and two food bags. If you don't, you may find
your luggage being unpacked so that the best balance can be found.
Smaller items such as fuel bottles and day-packs are not such a problem

and can usually be tied on or put in the middle between the larger sacks. One word of warning: even if you aren't expecting any rain make sure your belongings are well packed in plastic bags as the pony-man's fuel containers and stove have a nasty habit of leaking all over your sleeping bag. The smell of kerosene is not conducive to a good night's sleep and is almost impossible to get rid of.

Payments and responsibilities

• **Costs** The cost of a pack animal varies between Rs150 and Rs300 per day and tends to be the same whether you hire a pony or a donkey. The pony-man doesn't charge any more for tending the animals and is usually willing to act as your guide for free. However, if you want him to be your cook as well, this will cost about Rs250 a day. Prices are at their highest during July and August but you should be able to negotiate a better rate before and after the peak season.

• **Negotiations** A diplomatic attitude is essential when negotiating with your pony-man. It's self-defeating to annoy him before you've even started your trek. You must first decide how long you want to hire him for. The pony-man is usually a good judge of how long a particular trek will take but most tend to be cautious with their estimate until they've seen how fast you walk. It is expected that you will also pay for each day of your pony-man's return journey at half the daily rate.

You need to make it clear from the outset the precise role you are employing him for. Is he literally just providing the animals to carry your bags, or would you like him to act as a guide and possibly a cook as well? If you would like him to guide you, ask him how many times he has walked the route before. There have been several instances of 'guides' getting lost, so you need to be confident that he knows the way before hiring him. If he is to cook for you, you need to establish what food to buy and who's going to buy it – his culinary skills may well be limited to chapatis, rice and dal. If you want to cook on your own, make sure that your pony-man brings his own stove and enough food for himself.

• **Your responsibilities** As the employer you must remember that you are ultimately responsible for his welfare. Before you set off make absolutely sure that he is suitably equipped for the conditions that you are expecting. If he isn't, then see that he either borrows or buys whatever he needs, or be prepared to lend him any of your spares, particularly at cold, high altitude camps.

After you've finalised the agreements, it's usual to give him enough money to cover any initial expenses such as buying food and equipment. The balance, along with an appropriate tip should be paid at the end of the trek (an extra day's wage for every seven days is about right). Any equipment or unused food and kerosene is always appreciated and can be given in lieu of a full tip.

Trekking alone

One or two routes, such as Likir to Temisgam, won't present the experienced lone trekker with any problems, but most routes in Ladakh are a much more serious undertaking, being less travelled, at higher altitude and with fewer villages. Every year a few hardy backpackers set off alone to trek these routes and have a very rewarding experience. However, in order to do so safely, you not only have to be extremely experienced in high-altitude wilderness travel, but also aware that if anything goes wrong it's very unlikely that anyone will be close enough to help you. The occasional tragic poster in Leh, appealing for any information on Westerners who have gone missing while trekking alone, serve as a sad warning of the inherent risks of such a venture. It's not advisable for women to trek alone.

However, there is no reason why you shouldn't travel to Leh on your own with the intention of trekking. It's generally easy to find trekking partners once you've arrived as there are noticeboards in the popular restaurants and at the tourist information office which are good places to look or advertise for fellow trekkers. Alternatively, organise your own trek with a pony-man. This is a wonderful way to walk and the best way to learn a lot about what you're seeing. Your companion will probably be able to speak enough English for both of you to get by, but you will obviously get the most out of the experience if you endeavour to learn a few words of Ladakhi.

LOCAL EQUIPMENT

If you can bring good quality trekking and camping gear with you from home, then do so. If you find you've forgotten something, or you arrive in Leh without any equipment then it's quite possible to make do with what's available there.

Hiring

The entrepreneurs of Leh have been quick to capitalise on Ladakh's growing trekking industry and it's now possible to hire most items of trekking equipment that you could need (see p121). While the quality may not be quite up to the standard you'd expect in the West, most of it is perfectly serviceable, although you should check everything thoroughly before hiring it.

Buying in the bazaar

An alternative to hiring is to buy local equipment from the bazaar. The advantage of this is that it can be resold or given to your pony-man as a tip at the end of the trek. Strong canvas **rucksacks** (Rs150) make ideal holdalls for your food or any other gear but are agony to have on your back for long. You will also see fake rucksacks bearing Karrimor, Lowe Alpine or Berghaus labels. While they will probably last for a trek or two, don't forget to pack a needle and thread. You won't have many problems finding **clothes** to keep you warm: thick woollen jumpers, hats, socks and gloves are widely available but finding decent waterproofs is much harder. Other clothes that you should be able to find are sun hats and trousers, which you can also get made up by a local tailor. Some trekkers find the army surplus stores close to the old bus stand in Leh useful for ex-army trousers, jackets, gloves, hats and sleeping bags (Rs350).

The kerosene **stoves** (Rs180) available in the bazaar are perfectly adequate if you are hiring ponies but are far too bulky and heavy for backpacking. **Kerosene** (Rs5 per litre) is the most widely used and obtainable fuel, although **petrol** (Rs17 per litre), while harder to find, is often preferable as it's easier to light. Filter the fuel through cloth or filter paper as both fuels are very dirty and will clog your stove in no time if you're not vigilant about cleaning them. Make sure you buy enough fuel for your stove as it's unlikely that you will be able to re-stock in the mountains.

The fuel and water **containers** (Rs25-35) from the bazaar invariably leak from the lid, but they are better than nothing. Buy lots of **matches** and keep them in various strategic places where they can't get wet and won't get lost. **Candles**, **torches** and **batteries** can all be bought in Leh, but the batteries are of appalling quality and in very few sizes. If you intend to cook rice or dal a **pressure-cooker** is essential. Other useful items are good metal **plates**, **mugs**, **pots**, **pans** and **cutlery**, **rope** for stream crossing and **plastic sheeting** for groundsheets or makeshift tents.

> **Pressure cookers**
> Water boils at a lower temperature at high altitude because of the lower atmospheric pressure – at 3050m it boils at 90°C while at 4575m it boils at 85°C. Therefore, cooking food by boiling takes much longer in Ladakh than it does at sea level. Rice and dal, in particular, can take forever. One of the ways around this problem is to buy a pressure cooker (Rs250 for a two-litre cooker, which is the right size for two people) in the main bazaar. Although they are heavy and bulky, you won't need to take nearly as much fuel because things cook more quickly.
>
> It takes a lot of faith to cook in a pressure cooker as you can't see how things are progressing inside and it's all too easy to end up with a burnt mess stuck to the bottom of your pan. From personal experience I highly recommend that you practise before you leave on your trek.

FOOD FOR TREKKING

A wide range of suitable trekking food is available in Leh so there's no need to bring mountains of specialised dehydrated food from home. As it's unlikely that you will be able to buy food on the trail, it is vital that you purchase enough to last for the whole trek, plus some emergency rations, just in case.

To cope with the physical demands of trekking you need a good balanced diet that provides about 4000 calories a day, or about double the amount you need for a more sedentary lifestyle. Fat provides twice the energy of other food groups but takes a long time to digest and fatty foods are hard to take trekking. It's far better to base your diet around lots of carbohydrates (rice, noodles, breads), which provide energy more quickly and will keep you going longer. Supplement this with fats and proteins (dal, nuts, cheese and meat). Sugars (sweets, chocolate, jams and honey) are also useful as they are absorbed and converted into energy even more quickly than carbohydrates but their effect soon wears off and won't keep you going for long. Eating enough, however, is not always as easy as it sounds, as high altitude can sometimes have the effect of suppressing your appetite. If this is the case, you'll really have to be determined to force enough food in.

What to eat

Listed below are some ideas for what to eat while trekking. If you are an imaginative cook you will be able to dream up far more interesting meals but at least this serves as an indication of what's available in the shops. The weights given are a very rough guide to how much will be needed per person per day. It's highly recommended that you try out your chosen menu before you leave on your trek. This way you'll know if you've got enough and whether your cooking arrangements work.

Leh is the best place to stock up with food. Some of the trailhead villages have shops (see the relevant entries in Part 7) in which you could probably buy enough for a trek if you

> **Ladakhi trekking diet**
> The only food the Ladakhis take with them on a journey into the mountains is a small bag of tsampa, a brick of tea, some butter, a little salt and sometimes some dried cheese. The tsampa and cheese can then be mixed with the salt butter tea to the consistency of porridge, or into a stiff dough. This is then rolled into balls and eaten either immediately, or saved for later in the day. It takes very little time or fuel to boil a pan of water and if a storm or lack of wood make it impossible to light a fire, then the tsampa can be eaten straight out of the bag with a little water. As with all good trekking food, it's versatile and simple.
>
> The Western palate takes a little time to get used to the nutty taste of tsampa along with the rancid cheese and salty tea. A more palatable alternative is to mix tsampa with dehydrated soup or sweet tea. Although it's highly nutritious, you do need to eat a fair amount before you feel full, so experiment a little before you commit yourself. Tsampa is rarely sold in general stores and finding it can sometimes be hard. Try asking the owner of your guest house or ask shop keepers if you can buy some of their personal supply.

had no other option, but there won't be much choice. Leh's general stores can provide almost all your requirements apart from vegetables, which are best bought from the local women who sit along the shady side of the main bazaar. These are usually organically grown and come from local farms. Guaranteed organic produce is sometimes sold at the LEDeG craft shop as well. In contrast, the vegetables and fruit from the main vegetable market are mostly imported and are unlikely to be organic. The Ladakh Dry Fruits Store (next to the LEDeG Craft Shop) has the best selection of dried fruits, roasted barley and nuts.

• **Breakfast** Tsampa or oat porridge (100g) made with powdered milk and sugar makes a simple and sustaining breakfast which will warm you up while the frost still hangs on the tent. Bread (see Bakeries on p117) with the locally produced apricot jam, or peanut butter is another good alternative, but it's bulky to store and can be difficult to keep dry and fresh. If you have any chapatis left over from the night before, these are also delicious with jam. Other possibilities are cornflakes, muesli, eggs (hard to keep intact but excellent for protein), dried fruit or biscuits. Wash this all down with a large mug of instant coffee, tea or hot chocolate.

• **Lunch and snacks** 'Lunch' tends to start a couple of hours after breakfast and goes on into mid-afternoon. Having a little bite to eat each time you stop to rest is a good way to keep your energy up throughout the day. Peanuts, roasted barley, dried fruits and chocolate bars are the easiest and quickest to eat, (reckon on 150-200g of nuts or grains a day per person). Other options are bread, chapatis or biscuits with tinned cheese, tuna, peanut butter or jam. Although quite bulky, cold potatoes (cooked at breakfast), on their own or with mayonnaise, make a delicious change.

• **Dinner** The key to a simple main meal is to be able to cook it all in one pot. For example, dried noodles (150g-200g) and vegetables can all be boiled in a pot to which you can add some spices, ginger and a packet of soup to add to the flavour, plus some peanuts or tinned cheese for protein. If you want to travel very light then only add onions and garlic to the above concoction, rather than lots of vegetables – you'll still have a tasty and nourishing meal. For the ultimate is convenience cooking, you can buy 'two-minute noodles', complete with a sachet of masala flavouring, but the ravenous trekker would easily be able to consume at one sitting two or three packets which, although light in weight, are very bulky.

Dal (80g-100g) with rice (150g-200g) or chapatis is a more traditional trekking meal, but one which requires a lot more effort and equipment. The orange *masur* dal is the quickest to cook. Chapatis are messy and time consuming to make, but if you're prepared to make the effort you can produce enough for breakfast and lunch as well.

Tinned tuna or eggs can add more variety to your meal. Don't forget to buy salt, pepper, spices, stock cubes or packet soups. Butter and oil can also be obtained if you want to fry anything, but as most food can be boiled this just makes washing up harder. The whole meal can be finished off with dried fruit, chocolate and a hot drink.

Small change
Rs100 notes are next to useless in the hills as people rarely have change. Stock up on lots of Rs2, Rs5 and Rs10 notes in Leh so that you can pay for camping charges and any food that may be for sale on the trail. As always, make sure that none are damaged as you won't be able to get rid of them if they are.

• **Emergency rations** Pack some food which the body can quickly and easily convert into energy: muesli, sweet biscuits, dried fruit, nuts, chocolate bars and hot drinks – just in case you get stranded.

How to pack it

Plastic bags are the best things to pack your food into but those available in India have a tendency to split, so double or triple pack everything. To save time on the trail and to make sure that you don't run out of food halfway through your trek, divide all your food into the right portions for each meal. If you are taking bread with you then wrap it in some plain material to keep it fresh. It may be hard to keep it dry if it rains, but wrapping it in plastic is a sure way to make it go off. The whole lot can then be put in one or two canvas bags or rucksacks ready to load onto your ponies.

Buying food on the trail

Occasionally you will come across a village with a shop or a seasonal tent restaurant but as you can never guarantee that they will be open or have anything in stock, they are really only useful for non-essentials like biscuits and chocolate.

PREPARING YOURSELF

Leh stands at an altitude of about 3500m/11,500ft. Most visitors will have flown in from altitudes barely above sea level. It is vital, therefore, to acclimatise to at least the altitude of Leh before you set off on your trek. Failure to do so will lessen your enjoyment and could, in extreme cases, be fatal.

It takes a minimum of three days to begin feeling at ease with the thinner air and about a week before you start feeling like doing anything energetic. The longer you spend acclimatising the more you'll enjoy the trek without constantly wondering why you left home in the first place.

Day walks around Leh

For your first couple of days in Leh you can kid yourself that consuming huge quantities of banana and honey pancakes is all part of your rigorous acclimatisation programme. However the time may come when you feel like taking a bit of exercise and fortunately this seems to help speed up the acclimatisation process.

There are plenty of nice places to walk to around Leh and the first on people's list is usually the short climb to the Palace and then on up to Leh and Tsemo Gompas. There are wonderful views of the town from here and you can plan slightly longer jaunts from this vantage point. For instance, you could walk out through Chanspa, up the 542 steps to the Shanti Stupa and then return via Sankar Gompa all within a couple of hours. More demanding is a lovely short day walk from Leh to the village of Sabu (p199). This little used route takes you over a couple of low and easy passes which cross the hills to the north-east of Leh.

PART 7: TRAIL GUIDE AND MAPS

Using this guide

The treks in this trail guide have not been divided up into rigid daily stages since people walk at different speeds. All the possible camping places (or guest houses where available) have been indicated so that you can make your own decision on how far you want to walk each day. Walking times for both directions are given on the maps to enable you to plan your own itinerary; and there are also suggested itineraries on p235 based on the distances usually covered by organised trekking groups. For an overview of each of the treks see pp22-35 and the **trekking routes map** (inside back cover).

ROUTE DESCRIPTIONS

The route descriptions can be followed in either direction. There are advantages, however, in walking some routes in a particular direction. Any information solely relevant to trekkers walking the route in the opposite direction to that described is marked by '▲'.

To make route descriptions clearer, a compass point is given in brackets after the direction, 'left (S)', or occasionally the other way round, 'south (L)'. The geographical terminology has been used when a trail follows a river or stream: the 'left' bank or side means the 'left' bank as you face downstream. To clarify this, the compass point is also included.

ROUTE MAPS
Walking times
In steep mountainous areas, approximate walking times are far more useful than distances in miles or kilometres. These walking times are given along the side of each map and the arrow shows the direction to which the time refers. Black triangles point to the villages between which the times apply. Note that the **time given refers only to time spent walking**, so you will need to add 20-30% to allow for rest stops. When planning the day's trekking, count on five to seven hours actual walking. Allow yourself a few extra days for resting, side trips and for acclimatisation.

Up or down?
The trail is shown as a dotted line. An arrow across the trail indicates a moderate slope; two arrows show that it is steep; a single dotted arrow

shows that it is gentle. Note that the arrow points towards the higher part
of the trail. If, for example, you were walking from A (at 3800m) to B (at
4000m) and the trail between the two was short and steep, it would be
shown thus: A - - - > > - - - B. Dotted arrows signify a gentler slope.

Altitudes
Altitudes are given in metres on the maps and in metres/feet in the text.
They are based on my measurements with an altimeter and where possible have been verified or correlated with other reliable sources. As they
are rough measurements they have been rounded to the nearest 10
metres/feet except where a height is officially recognised as being correct
(for example, by the Indian Mountaineering Foundation). Their prime
purpose is to allow trekkers to work out a safe acclimatisation schedule
for themselves (see p238 for further information).

Place names
As there is no standard way to transliterate Ladakhi names into English,
most place names have accumulated several weird and wonderful
spellings. The most commonly used spelling has been chosen for the
maps and the text; other familiar spellings are also mentioned in the text
so that cross-references are possible with other maps, books and guides.

Camping and sustenance
Possible places to camp are marked with a tent symbol. These are flat
areas of ground where it is possible to pitch at least two lightweight tents.
Unless otherwise specified, they are always by a water source. Some villages on popular treks have official campsites; but these are rare.

Reliable sources of water are shown by a 'W' in a circle. Tent restaurants are also shown but they are seasonal and they won't necessarily be
there all season.

Changes
The Ladakhi landscape is constantly and rapidly changing all the time.
Each year sees bridges swept away, paths destroyed by landslides and
streams changing their course. Follow maps and directions as far as is
practicable and use your common sense when navigating.

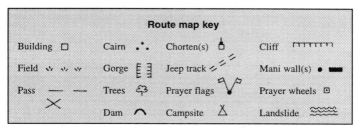

Route map key			
Building □	Cairn ∴	Chorten(s) ♟	Cliff ⊓⊓⊓⊓⊓
Field	Gorge	Jeep track	Mani wall(s) ● ■■
Pass	Trees	Prayer flags	Prayer wheels ⊡
	Dam	Campsite △	Landslide 〰〰

Markha Valley trek

(6-10 DAYS)

GETTING TO THE START

There are buses from Leh to Spituk (7km) every 15 minutes, or for Stok (14km) at 07.30, 14.00 and 17.00. Alternatively you could get a taxi for the short journey; Rs145 to Spituk bridge or Rs245 to Stok. Bring all your supplies from Leh as you won't find much in these villages.

STOK TO RUMBAK (alternative start)

Follow the river towards the mountains from Stok. Where the trail splits take the path that leads right (SW) into a side valley. Carry on up this valley, ignoring the pass on the left (S), until you reach the base camp for the Stok La (or Namling La) (3-4 hours). It's a very steep 3-4 hour climb up to the pass (4800m/15,750ft) with an equally steep descent the other side down to Rumbak. Here you join the trail from Spituk (see below).

SPITUK TO JINGCHAN   [MAPS 1-2]

Spituk/Pitok/Spitok (3200m/10,500ft)

Spituk is the site of the first Gelukpa gompa in Ladakh which is well worth a visit if you have the time, particularly for its commanding views over the Indus Valley.

Pass through the village and carry on along the bumpy road to the bridge across the Indus. There are some flat pastures here where it is possible to **camp** and this area is often used by the pony-men as they await their next group of trekkers.

Leaving Spituk An early start to this stage is important; if you plan to camp at Jingchan it means you will arrive there before the large organised groups and therefore get the pick of the campsite. If you intend to go on to Rumbak on your first day you will need the time to walk the extra 6km (1$\frac{1}{2}$ to 2 hours).

Cross the bridge, follow the jeep track south for 300m and then west (R) to a small village with two impressive houses. You leave all vegetation behind you as you begin crossing a flat and desolate plain at the foot of the Stok mountains. You may witness the impressive skill of Indian Airlines pilots guiding their planes between the mountains as they come down to land at Leh airport; it's reassuring to have your feet firmly on the ground. This may not be your idea of a Himalayan wilderness experience

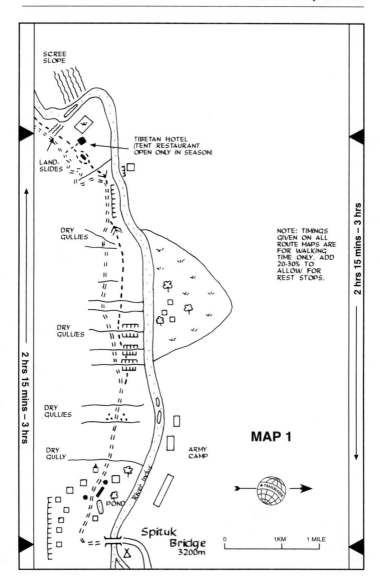

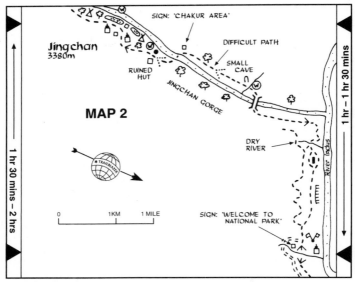

with the busy Leh-Srinagar road on the north bank of the Indus but you will soon be leaving all signs of the 20th century far behind.

After about 1¹⁄₂km across this plain the path splits. The jeep track stays on the higher ground while a pony track cuts a more direct route across the plain. The latter is slightly shorter but crosses a number of small, dry ravines which the jeep track avoids. The two trails meet for about 300m and then split again. This time take the short-cut down the slope to the small shelter that proudly calls itself the **Tibetan Hotel**. You can refresh yourself here with tea and apple juice.

Hemis National Park
The path swings to the south-west following the Indus into a narrower valley. You soon reach a sign on a rock welcoming you to the national park. Just beyond is a chorten and prayer flags from which you get impressive views down the Indus gorge. This stretch of river is popular for rafting and it's exciting to watch the rafts shoot the rapids below from the safety of dry land. There is a choice of two trails from here. It does not matter which you take at this stage, but when you reach a mani wall, move onto the lower trail as they don't meet up again.

(Opposite) Top: The view from the top of a pass is always worth the effort it takes to get there; looking south-east from the Prinkiti La (see p186). **Bottom:** Ponies and pony-men crossing the Markha River between Markha and Umlung (see p170). Rivers are a frequent obstacle on many treks in Ladakh.

Jingchan Gorge (Zinchan/Zinchen/Jingchen) The route gets exciting from here as you leave the Indus behind and head into the mountains along the pretty, willow-lined Jingchan gorge. Follow the stream bed as best you can, sometimes scrambling up the valley side and occasionally fording the stream if necessary.

Jingchan (3380m/11,090ft)

There are two **campsites** here, one just before the village and the more secluded one just after. If you're planning on going up to the Ganda La base camp next day it would be wiser to push on to Rumbak. It's at a much better height for acclimatising as it's 300m higher than Leh (3500m/11,480ft) to which you should already be acclimatised. This is far more sensible than sleeping at Jingchan (3380m/11,090ft) which is 120m lower. However, you may need to be particularly persuasive to get your pony-man to go on to Rumbak the first day, as Jingchan is the usual stop.

JINGCHAN TO YURUTSE [MAP 3]

The route is straightforward as you are simply following the Jingchan Nala upstream. Leave the village on the higher path which avoids fording the stream. Down by the river is a small hut which is the official entry point to Hemis National Park. This is very rarely staffed but if anyone is in residence you may be asked to pay a small entry fee.

The valley soon narrows and you pass between two rock buttresses beneath graffiti on the rock which asks you to 'Preserve Wildlife'. There is a choice of two paths. It's easier and drier to take the trail which rises away from the stream to the right (W). Horses usually take the trail which stays close to the stream but crosses it several times.

Do not get too excited by the sign that says you are in a 'Snow Leopard Area'. Although this is true, your chances of seeing one of these rare creatures are almost nil. You are far more likely to see small herds of *bharal* (blue sheep) clinging to the impossibly steep sides of the gorge, but they can be hard to spot as their colouring merges with the rock. In about 1 ½km you get to another sign that has an arrow pointing to 'Golden Eagle Nest'. You could be forgiven for wondering if you are on a nature trail! The nest is impossible to see but there are lovely views ahead to a spectacular jagged ridge.

The stream forces the path closer and closer to the right (W) side of the valley until you have no choice but to wade across. If you've put on stream crossing shoes, keep them on as there's another crossing in about 10 minutes. When the valley splits at a walled willow plantation, take the

---

(**Opposite**) **Top:** An attractive campsite just before the village of Markha (see p170). **Bottom:** A trekker with the ideal minimal trekking outfit of pony and guide passes through the hamlet of Yurutse.

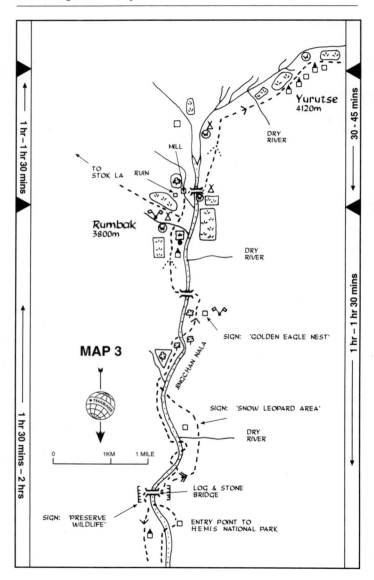

Yurutse
4120m

DRY
RIVER

TO
STOK LA

MILL

RUIN

Rumbak
3800m

DRY
RIVER

SIGN: 'GOLDEN EAGLE NEST'

JINGCHAN NALA

MAP 3

TRAILBLAZER

SIGN: 'SNOW LEOPARD AREA'

DRY
RIVER

0   1KM   1 MILE

LOG & STONE
BRIDGE

SIGN: 'PRESERVE
WILDLIFE'

ENTRY POINT TO
HEMIS NATIONAL PARK

1 hr – 1 hr 30 mins

1 hr 30 mins – 2 hrs

30 - 45 mins

1 hr – 1 hr 30 mins

right fork (SW). The trail carries on up this narrow gorge for $2^{1}/_{2}$km until the valley widens revealing the snow-topped peaks of the Stok mountains.

Rumbak (3800m/12,470ft)

Prayer flags on a wide pasture mark the junction with the trail leading east (L) to the Stok La. You can see the pass to the right of the toothy skyline ridge. This pasture makes a good **campsite** but there are other alternatives a little further up the main valley.

You should consider leaving Rumbak only if you are having no problems with the altitude as it's a further 500m up to the Ganda La base camp and 1000m up to the pass.

Carry on walking upstream to a water mill and a bridge. If you have not inspected one of these mills yet, peer inside. Although this method of grinding barley is simple, the technology is ingenious and has remained unchanged for centuries. The mill is usually used for grinding roasted barley into tsampa.

Cross the bridge and continue upstream until the valley forks. Take the right (SW) fork and follow the path as it cuts up the right (N) side of the valley.

Yurutse/Urucha/Yuruche (4120m/13,520ft) is little more than a large house. You can fill up with clear spring water from a pipe below the main building.

> **Chortens**
> These domed Buddhist monuments, also called *stupas*, are found all over Ladakh, especially at the entrance to villages where they are supposed to ward off evil spirits. They were originally used to hold the remains of the Buddha and other saints; now they don't necessarily contain anything. There are many different types of chorten though most have the features of a square or rectangular base, representing the earth, a spherical central section representing water, a spire representing fire, which is topped by a parasol representing air and ether – thus symbolising all five elements of the cosmos. Like mani walls, you must keep them on your right when you pass.

YURUTSE TO SHINGO   [MAP 4]

Just past the village the valley is split by a beautiful purple band of rock. Take the right branch, past a mani wall and cairn.

Ganda La Base Camp (4380m/14,370ft) There are a number of places where you could camp in this valley, but the stream flows intermittently so it's worth going on to the top camp where there's a spring. Follow the stream up the obvious left (W) valley and not the smaller valley on the right going off to the north-west. The **camp** is 200m on from passing a blue and purple scree slope, before the valley divides again.

There are wonderful views back to the Stok La. If you've come all the way up from Jingchan you may well be feeling the effects of the altitude as you are 1000m higher. If in doubt about your condition descend to Rumbak.

Climb the spur above the camp leaving dry stream beds on your left and right. You are aiming for the left (SW) valley but want to keep above and to the right of the small stream. A clear path soon appears which takes you west towards the Ganda La. Stok Kangri dominates the south-eastern skyline as you climb. You may see yak, brought up here so that the fodder close to the villages has a chance to grow during the short summer.

Ganda/Kunda/Gandha La (4850m/15,910ft)
From the pass you can see the Zanskar Range to the west, while there are views to the Stok Mountains and beyond to the east. If you want better views climb either of the ridges by the pass. The fields of Shingo can also be seen far down in the valley. This is where you are aiming for.

▲ **Opposite direction** Route finding is simple enough from here; you cannot go far wrong if you just head down hill.

Descent to Shingo
Keep an eye out for marmots as you descend from the pass as they seem to thrive in these desolate, high altitude spots. They are remarkably unconcerned about humans and will often just sit watching you pass. If you approach too close they give a shrill whistle of alarm and dive into their burrows.

The trail down to Shingo is straightforward and passes a number of possible **campsites**.

▲ **Opposite direction** The highest camp would make an ideal base camp for the pass.

Shingo (4150m/13,620ft)
There is a **tent restaurant** just before the hamlet where you can rest with a glass of tea and stock up with biscuits. Notice the solar panel on the roof of the main house. These are common in even quite remote villages and can provide power for simple needs.

Apricots
The Ladakhis' use of apricots exemplifies their tradition of wasting nothing. The fruit is eaten fresh or dried for the winter; the sweet kernels are eaten and enjoyed for their almond-like flavour. Bitter kernels are ground for oil, which is then used for cooking, in lamps for lighting, or for putting on the skin and hair. The cake that remains after extracting the oil is used as animal fodder. Dried apricots are even used for cleaning tarnished metals, while the apricot wood from pruned trees is a fine hard wood that is used for making tools and musical instruments.

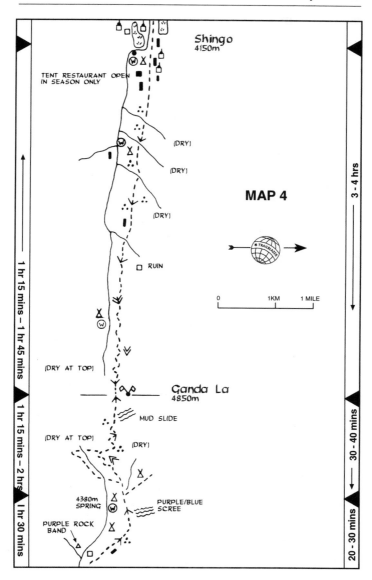

Shingo
4150m

TENT RESTAURANT OPEN
IN SEASON ONLY

(DRY)

(DRY)

MAP 4

(DRY)

3 - 4 hrs

RUIN

0   1KM   1 MILE

1 hr 15 mins – 1 hr 45 mins

(DRY AT TOP)

Ganda La
4850m

30 - 40 mins

MUD SLIDE

(DRY AT TOP)   (DRY)

1 hr 15 mins – 2 hrs

4380m
SPRING

PURPLE/BLUE
SCREE

20 - 30 mins

1 hr 30 mins

PURPLE ROCK
BAND

SHINGO TO SKIU [MAP 5]

Shingri Nala

The next stage takes you through a spectacular gorge with beautifully coloured and eroded rocks. Follow the intertwining streams below the hamlet, crossing and recrossing downstream through the willow grove. There is no path; follow the hoof prints and horse manure. Eventually the trail becomes established on the left (S) bank. You continue down the gorge for 2¼-3 hours, crossing the stream on stepping stones several times. The bottom of the gorge is thick with willows and seabuckthorn, which provides convenient shade from the fierce sun. Water is never a problem as the stream is always close. About 1½km before the end of the gorge the stream disappears underground leaving just a dry bed.

Skiu/Skyu/Skio (3400m/11,160ft)

As you enter the tiny village the towering rock faces ahead of you are awe-inspiring. There is an attractive gompa on top of the cliff on the right (W). Turn east (L) upstream and the pretty campsite is 400m ahead among the trees.

Day trip From Skiu you can make a day trip downstream to the Zanskar Gorge, passing many apricot trees and the village of Kaya. The round trip takes 4-5 hours.

SKIU TO MARKHA [MAPS 6-7]

The trail to Markha is not too strenuous, rising about 300m over the 22km. Being at a relatively lower altitude it can get very hot in the sun.

Markha River Skiu sprawls along the right (N) bank of the Markha for about 1½km and then you start walking through thorny scrub. There are a few clearings here where it's possible to pitch one or two tents but the only source of water is from the silty river. After about 9km on the right bank cross a solid wooden bridge high above the water onto the left (S). The trail goes 100m or so through the scrub and then climbs away from the valley bottom to traverse a steep slope prone to landslides. Descend to a grassy patch which could make a good **camp**. The stream running through the grass is your best source of **water** for a while.

Chaluk/Chalak After passing this hamlet keep your eyes open as the path veers off to the right (SW) cutting through some crumbly cliffs and climbing steeply upwards. Cross the river again at **Tunespa** (Thinlespa), a village with very basic dwellings but well-kept fields. At the top of the rise out of the village you reach a collection of large chortens and mani walls. There are wonderful views back down the valley.

As you approach Markha you get the first glimpse of the snow covered

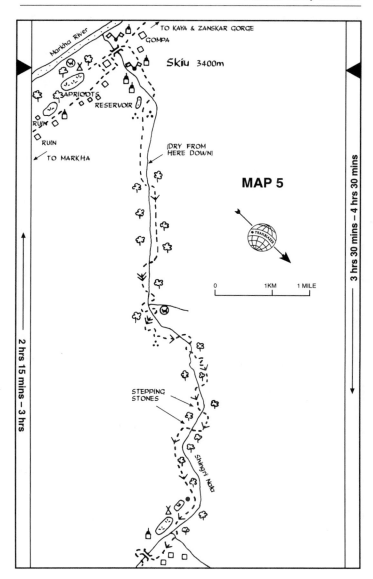

TO KAYA & ZANSKAR GORGE

Markha River

GOMPA

Skiu 3400m

APRICOTS

RESERVOIR

RUIN

RUIN

TO MARKHA

(DRY FROM HERE DOWN)

MAP 5

TRAILBLAZER

0   1KM   1 MILE

STEPPING STONES

Shingri Nala

2 hrs 15 mins – 3 hrs

3 hrs 30 mins – 4 hrs 30 mins

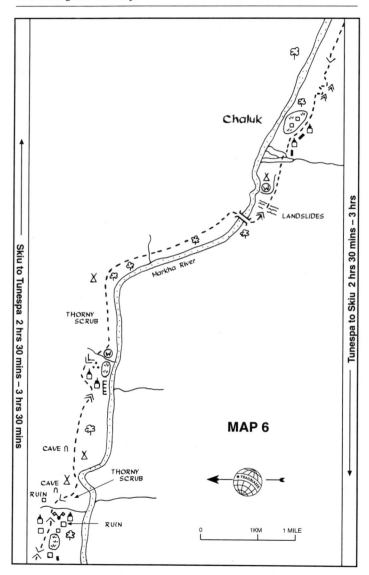

Chaluk

LANDSLIDES

Markha River

THORNY SCRUB

CAVE

CAVE

RUIN

THORNY SCRUB

RUIN

MAP 6

Skiu to Tunespa 2 hrs 30 mins – 3 hrs 30 mins

Tunespa to Skiu 2 hrs 30 mins – 3 hrs

0   1KM   1 MILE

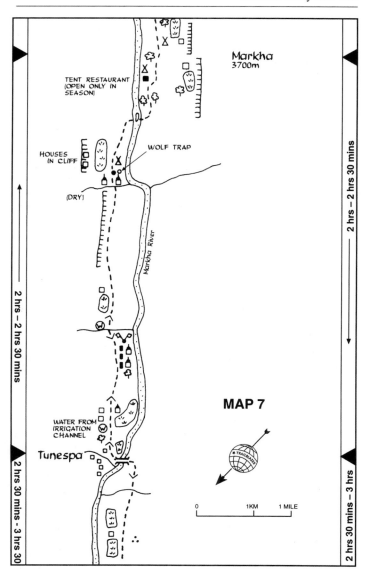

TENT RESTAURANT
(OPEN ONLY IN SEASON)

Markha
3700m

WOLF TRAP

HOUSES
IN CLIFF

(DRY)

Markha River

MAP 7

WATER FROM
IRRIGATION
CHANNEL

Tunespa

0   1KM   1 MILE

2 hrs – 2 hrs 30 mins

2 hrs – 2 hrs 30 mins

2 hrs 30 mins - 3 hrs 30

2 hrs 30 mins – 3 hrs

slopes of Kang Yaze/Nimaling (6400m/21,000ft). This magnificent mountain commands the view for the next two days. There is a wolf trap on the outskirts of the village which may have a carcass at the bottom as bait. The wolf runs up the ramp into the trap and because the sides are sloping slightly inwards it cannot escape. It is then stoned to death by the villagers. During the summer the wolves are not a problem, but as food supplies dwindle during winter they often come down to the villages in search of livestock.

Markha (3700m/12,140ft)

Keep to the trail by the river and in about 500m you will have to ford it. The current can be quite strong so if possible cross with others. Carry on up the left (SW) bank to a **tent restaurant** among some trees. It's possible to **camp** here or beneath the main farm house 500m further on. This is a lovely campsite but finding clear water is a problem and you will probably have to make do with silty water from the main river. Don't pollute the river with soap (see p144) as a channel from it takes water to the other houses.

Cross the river on the bridge by the campsite and follow the path as it climbs up to the main part of Markha village. The remains of a fort lie up to the right. To visit the monastery take the path on the left. Otherwise carry on through the village and fields.

MARKHA TO TAHUNGSTE   [MAP 8]

The trail soon splits, the left (E) fork climbs and then traverses a steep cliff face while the right (S) fork heads down to the river. Unless the river is particularly high it's safer to take the right fork and ford it rather than risk the precipitous cliff path. This path is usable but it is badly eroded in parts; a careless step could be fatal.

If you cross the river, carry on up the left bank, passing a valley on your right (SW). A large rock spire marks the entrance to this valley. This is the beginning of the Zhumlam (Jumlam), an extremely demanding route into Zanskar (see p34). Progress on this side of the river is soon stopped by a rock wall and you are forced to ford the river again. Despite the double river crossing, this route is still safer than the cliff path unless the water is very high.

Umlung Gompa (Dinlung/Humlung/Omlung/Omung) Feeling cool and refreshed after the river crossings you may have the energy to climb to the gompa high up on the left. After slogging to the top consider the poor monks who had to build the monastery and those here today who have to go down and up this path just to collect water. The views are not that amazing but you get a great sense of height as you stand far above the valley bottom. The monastery is often closed during the summer as the

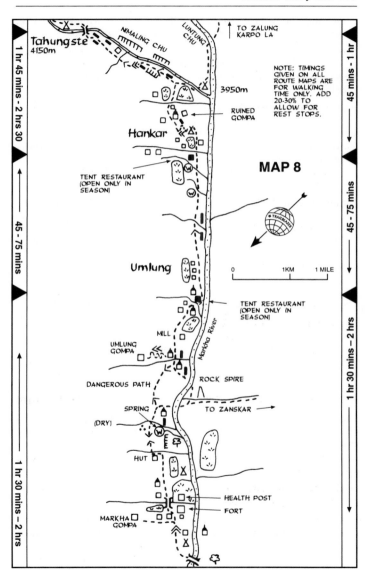

MAP 8

NOTE: TIMINGS GIVEN ON ALL ROUTE MAPS ARE FOR WALKING TIME ONLY. ADD 20-30% TO ALLOW FOR REST STOPS.

TO ZALUNG KARPO LA

NIMALING CHU

LUNTUNG CHU

Tahungste
4150m

3950m

RUINED GOMPA

Hankar

TENT RESTAURANT (OPEN ONLY IN SEASON)

Umlung

TENT RESTAURANT (OPEN ONLY IN SEASON)

Markha River

MILL

UMLUNG GOMPA

DANGEROUS PATH

ROCK SPIRE

SPRING

(DRY)

TO ZANSKAR

HUT

HEALTH POST

FORT

MARKHA GOMPA

0   1KM   1 MILE

1 hr 45 mins - 2 hrs 30

45 - 75 mins

1 hr 30 mins – 2 hrs

45 mins - 1 hr

45 - 75 mins

1 hr 30 mins - 2 hrs

monks have to go back to their villages to help with the harvest. Unfortunately, the only way to find out is to climb to the top!

Umlung As you approach the village keep the fields on your right hand side. There's usually a **tent restaurant** here. It's a wonderful level walk between here and Hankar with the towering peak of Kang Yaze standing over the valley.

Hankar/Hangkar/Hanker There's another **tent restaurant** here and a good **campsite** just beyond the fields. The trail then takes a sharp left turn and climbs steeply to a group of chortens and mani walls. Up on the right, the ruined outline of Hankar gompa merges beautifully with the rocky ridge on which it sits.

The trail then crosses a small stream and winds through some fields before reaching a river.

Nimaling Chu Don't cross this. The trail divides here. If you crossed the river and followed the valley straight ahead you would eventually end up in Pang on the Leh-Manali road (see 'Indus Valley to the Rupshu' trek, p210). Instead, you want to follow the trail to Nimaling which heads up the right (N) bank of the Nimaling Chu through a gateway formed by large rock buttresses.

A little further on there are some fascinating geological creations of large boulders balanced precariously on top of consolidated earth spikes. The trail drops to a bridge; cross, and continue up the other bank.

Tahungste (4150m/13,620ft) In about 300m you reach the walled pastures of Tahungste/Chachutse/Tchatchutse/Thachungtse. This is a lovely valley to **camp** in; you can cool off from a long days' trek in the icy stream. A popular watering spot for bharal, it's a magnificent sight to see a herd slide and bound down the steep cliffs with incredible agility.

TAHUNGSTE TO CHUKIRMO   [MAPS 9-10]

The trail continues to climb up above Tahungste and soon starts heading off to the south-east, away from the main valley. Note the beautifully eroded rock spikes that you can see down to the left (N). Follow a small stream until it starts heading around to the south. The trail then leaves it and zigzags back on itself as it gains height.

▲ **Opposite direction** It can be easy to miss the path down to the stream and continue on a path straight ahead.

You pass several mani walls and suddenly come across the incongruous **Lake View Restaurant**. This tent restaurant on the edge of a small mountain tarn has wonderful views both of Kang Yaze, whose bulk gets reflected in the still waters of the lake, and also of the Markha Valley which you

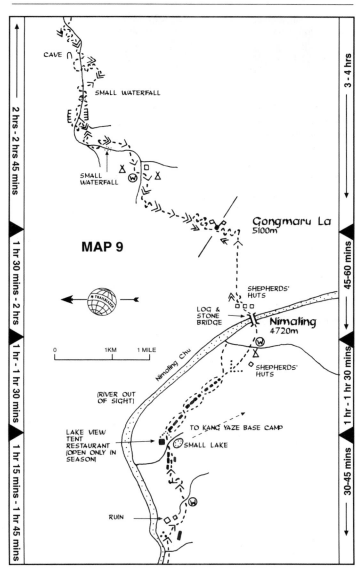

MAP 9

CAVE

SMALL WATERFALL

SMALL WATERFALL

Gongmaru La
5100m

2 hrs - 2 hrs 45 mins

1 hr 30 mins - 2 hrs

1 hr - 1 hr 30 mins

1 hr 15 mins - 1 hr 45 mins

3 - 4 hrs

45-60 mins

1 hr - 1 hr 30 mins

30-45 mins

SHEPHERDS' HUTS

LOG & STONE BRIDGE

Nimaling
4720m

SHEPHERDS' HUTS

Nimaling Chu

(RIVER OUT OF SIGHT)

LAKE VIEW TENT RESTAURANT (OPEN ONLY IN SEASON)

TO KANG YAZE BASE CAMP

SMALL LAKE

RUIN

0   1KM   1 MILE

are now well above. There is a path from the lake to Kang Yaze **base camp**. This peak is a popular mountaineering objective and is usually climbed by way of the north-west ridge. While the climb to the lower secondary summit is not considered particularly difficult, reaching the main summit is far more demanding.

If you are going on to Nimaling, keep the mountain on your right all the time. The trail rises gently past lots of mani walls and then descends slowly to the high altitude valley of Nimaling.

> **Recycled parachutes**
> Parachutes must be the most widely recycled bits of Indian army surplus kit in Ladakh. Not only are they used as temporary restaurants but also as tents by pony-men, shepherds and road builders and as sun-shades by guest houses and for private houses.
>   If you're thinking that there is no way you would jump out of an aeroplane attached to one of those, then fear not, they were used only for cargo drops, not for people.

Nimaling (4720m/15,490ft) This large flat-bottomed valley has a semi-permanent population of villagers who come up from the Markha Valley to graze their livestock on the summer pastures. It is a beautiful and remote place to **camp** and one could easily spend a day or two relaxing or exploring the surrounding ridges and valleys. However, you should be warned that the weather can change rapidly at this altitude and you must come prepared for snow, even in summer.

Sometimes there are one or two **tent restaurants** during the peak trekking season, but don't rely on them being there.

Gongmaru/Kongmaru/Longmaru La (5100m/16,730ft)

The pass lies on the east side of the valley opposite Kang Yaze. There's usually a simple bridge across the Nimaling Chu which is replaced annually by the shepherds. However, it sometimes gets washed away by floods so if you can't find it you'll have to ford the icy stream. The trail climbs steeply from behind a small group of shepherds' huts. The gradient soon eases but the trail becomes a bit vague. Carry on heading east. Soon a saddle in the ridge ahead comes into view; this is the **Gongmaru La**. If there isn't any snow you should be able to make out a path meandering up the slope. As you climb the last short but steep slope to the top there are good views over the Zanskar Range and of the vertical ice walls on the north face of Kang Yaze.

Descent Until Chogdo the descent is particularly difficult for pack animals and very tiring for humans! It starts by descending steeply from the pass for 300m and then more gently down to a stream. Just above a ruin there are some small, flat terraces with enough **camping** space for about five tents. There is a similar camping spot just after crossing the stream. It's a good idea to collect **water** here because the stream gets more and more coloured the further down you go.

▲ **Opposite direction** The camping spot mentioned above would make a good base camp for the pass.

Route finding is easy from now on as you follow this tributary until it meets the Shang River and then you follow that downstream to the Indus. The trail follows the stream as best it can, sometimes in the stream bottom and sometimes clinging to the steep valley sides. It changes from season to season, so you'll have to use your initiative to find the best route. Frequent stream crossings are inevitable, but it's usually possible to keep your feet dry by jumping across at the narrower sections. The boulders are slippery so some kind of stick will make this much easier.

The trail first descends into a valley of pink rock which soon narrows into a mini canyon. Then it follows the stream as it tumbles over boulders and small waterfalls and enters a gorge.

CHUKIRMO TO KARU [MAPS 10-11]

Chukirmo (4070m/13,350ft)

After 5km of hard going you reach a well-stocked **tent restaurant**. There are small terraces for **camping** above it and also down by the stream. It's not the most attractive of camping spots so it may be worth pressing on to the lovely village of Shang Sumdo, about two hours away.

Leave the 'hotel' by taking the path down to the river and not the one rising up a bank ahead of you. The best route among the pebbles and boulders can be hard to find, but it's usually marked by a series of small cairns. Walk in the stream bed until you are almost past the neat village of **Chogdo**, situated up on the north (L) side of the valley. Then cross onto the left (N) bank if you have not already done so. At last there is a good trail that rises out of the river bed up to the left (N); this takes you to Shang Sumdo. There's a short section along the river bed again in twenty minutes, but the rest is easy going.

Shang Sumdo (3660m/12,010ft)

The **campsite** is beautifully situated in front of the farm houses with irrigation channels flowing around the grassy site. There are two **tent restaurants** here so you are well catered for. The village gompa is up the Shang River valley to the north-west, about twenty minutes' walk away.

It's an easy 8km from here to the road at Karu which should take about two hours. There's a bus from Karu to Leh at about midday so there's no need to rush in the morning if you stayed at Shang Sumdo.

Leave Shang Sumdo by walking downstream to a bridge. Cross over onto the right (S) bank and follow the jeep track to **Martselang** (Marcheylang/Merchelong).

▲ **Opposite direction** There is an entry point to the Hemis National

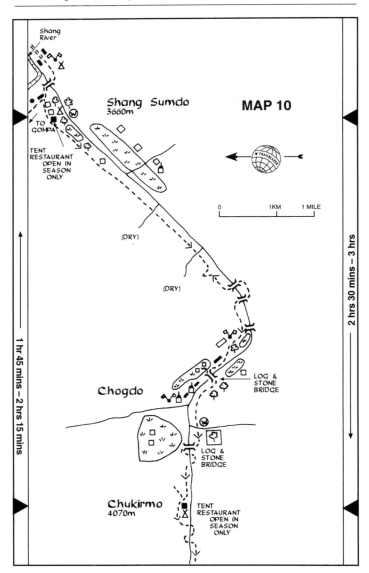

Shang River

Shang Sumdo
3660m

MAP 10

TO GOMPA

TENT
RESTAURANT
OPEN IN
SEASON
ONLY

0   1KM   1 MILE

(DRY)

(DRY)

2 hrs 30 mins – 3 hrs

1 hr 45 mins – 2 hrs 15 mins

LOG &
STONE
BRIDGE

Chogdo

LOG &
STONE
BRIDGE

Chukirmo
4070m

TENT
RESTAURANT
OPEN IN
SEASON
ONLY

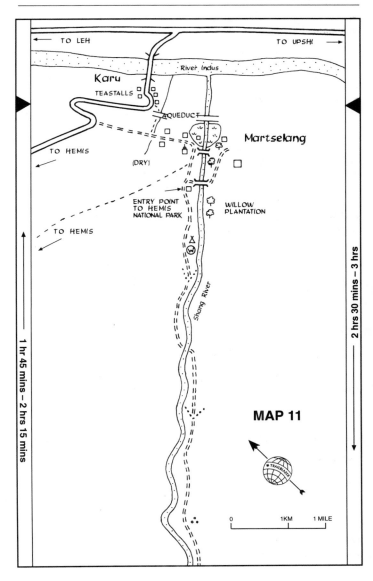

TO LEH

TO UPSHI

River Indus

Karu

TEASTALLS

AQUEDUCT

Martselang

(DRY)

TO HEMIS

TO HEMIS

ENTRY POINT
TO HEMIS
NATIONAL PARK

WILLOW
PLANTATION

Shang River

MAP 11

TRAILBLAZER

0   1KM   1 MILE

2 hrs 30 mins – 3 hrs

1 hr 45 mins – 2 hrs 15 mins

Park here and if it is staffed, which is rare, you may be asked to pay a small entrance fee.

If you want to visit **Hemis** (p134) follow the pony track that leaves the trail to the north-west (L) just as you enter Martselang. It's about an hour from here. Alternatively you could catch the midday bus as it passes through Karu on its way up to Hemis. There is only one bus a day so you would have to stay the night. There is a **campsite** just by the monastery and there are several simple restaurants in the village where you can eat.

As you enter Martselang the track swings round to the left (NW) away from the Shang River. In a few hundred metres you reach a dry stream bed over which an aqueduct passes. This aqueduct is part of a project which plans to irrigate a large amount of the land on the left bank of the Indus. Follow the dry stream bed downhill to the road where you will find a small collection of **tea stalls**. This is **Karu** and is the best place to wait for the midday **bus**.

▲ **Opposite direction** Buses for Karu and Hemis leave Leh at 09.00 and 15.00 daily and take about 2 hours. Taxis cost Rs600 to Karu and take an hour.

Likir to Temisgam

(2-3 DAYS)

GETTING TO THE START

There's a daily privately operated bus from Leh to Likir (Rs30, two hours), which leaves from the main bus stand sometime between 15.00 and 16.00. As Likir lies just to the north of the main Leh to Srinagar highway, you can, of course, get any bus that travels along this route. You reach the village of Likir from the highway by following a side road signposted to Likir monastery. A taxi will cost you Rs760.

LIKIR TO YANGTANG   [MAP 12]
Likir/Lekir (3500m/11,480ft)
This small, spread-out village, situated on the banks of the Likir Tokpo, a tributary of the Indus, is a lovely place to come to after the hustle and bustle of Leh. You can pass the time idling around the gompa (see p128) or exploring further up the valley which eventually leads into Nubra over the Likir La (5350m/17,550ft).

Accommodation There is a campsite and two guest houses in the village. The **Ghap Chow Garden Campsite** (Rs40 per tent) is simple and

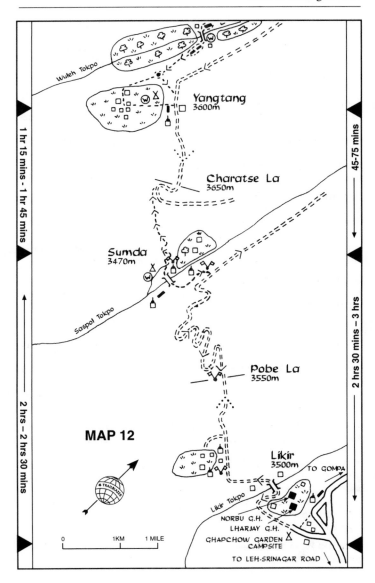

Wuleh Tokpo

Yangtang
3600m

Charatse La
3650m

Sumda
3470m

Saspol Tokpo

Pobe La
3550m

MAP 12

★ TRAILBLAZER

Likir
3500m

TO GOMPA

Likir Tokpo

NORBU G.H.
LHARJAY G.H.
GHAPCHOW GARDEN
CAMPSITE

TO LEH-SRINAGAR ROAD

0   1KM   1 MILE

1 hr 15 mins – 1 hr 45 mins

2 hrs – 2 hrs 30 mins

45–75 mins

2 hrs 30 mins – 3 hrs

adequate, but as it is often used by organised trekking groups it can some-times get quite crowded. The alternative is to stay at either the **Norbu** or the **Lharjay** guest houses in the village. For a modest charge (Rs120) the friendly owners will provide you with somewhere to sleep and will expect you to eat with the family. This is a excellent way of gaining an insight into Ladakhi village life.

Other services There is a very basic **shop** here but don't rely on it for supplies. You should bring everything you need from Leh. You can some-times **hire ponies** or **donkeys** in the village, and also arrange a **guide**. Taking a local guide is the best way to ensure finding accommodation on the trek, as you can often stay with his family and friends. You should allow a couple of days to sort out these arrangements, as it takes time for the word to get around and to bring the animals down from the pastures.

Leaving Likir
Turn left (W) out of the campsite and follow the jeep track as it winds down to the river, over a bridge and up to the **Pobe La** (3550m/11,650ft), leaving behind all greenery and entering an arid moonscape. From here you can either continue on the jeep track or, to avoid its twists and turns, take the steep, slippery short cuts down to the next section of road.

Sumda (3470m/11,390ft)
The green fields and trees of Sumda soon come into view. As you come parallel to the village, leave the jeep track and take the path leading down to the river on the left (W). This path junction is clearly marked by prayer flags and a cairn. Cross the Saspol Tokpo on a wooden bridge and walk up through a lush pasture beneath the village. This makes an ideal **camp-site** and the stream is a good place to fill up your water bottles. The trail heads uphill to a chorten and prayer flags, and then skirts around the left side of the village to begin the ascent of a dry, barren valley. It's a long climb (45-60 minutes) among desolate surroundings, but eventually you join a jeep track leading to the top of the **Charatse La** (3650m/11,980ft).

Yangtang/Yantang/Yangthang (3600m/11,810ft)
The jeep track descends gradually to this prosperous-looking village (35 minutes). Follow a signposted path opposite the primary school down to the village **campsite** (Rs30 per tent), where there are wonderful souther-ly views over the village to the Zanskar range beyond. There are no guest houses as such in the village, but an informal system has developed where you can sometimes stay in a family home for a similar fee. The villagers are under no obligation to let you stay with them and you should not expect this hospitality as a matter of course.

Side trip From Yangtang it is possible to walk down the valley to Rizong gompa (2¹/₂-3 hours).

YANGTANG TO HEMIS-SHUKPACHU   [MAP 13]

From the campsite at Yangtang go back up to the jeep track, turn left (N) and after 50m take a path leading down to the left (W). The route descends to the tree-lined Wuleh Tokpo, crosses it on a bridge and then, between stone walls, climbs the other side of the valley. You soon leave all signs of the village behind as you begin to ascend. As it climbs, the route keeps cutting across the corners of the jeep track to which you are running parallel. That is an alternative route for those who find the climb too steep, but it is much longer.

Sarmanchan/Sermanchan La (3750m/12,300ft)

There are views down to the beautiful village of Hemis-Shukpachu from the pass. Again, don't be tempted to take the jeep track to the village as it's much longer than the good path directly ahead. The trail enters the village through the fields, drops steeply down to cross the Akheur Tokpo, and emerges above the gompa overlooking beautiful pastures (2-2^1/2 hours from Yangtang).

Hemis-Shukpachu (3600m/11,810ft)

Also written as Hemis-Skurbuchan, Hemis-Shukpachan, Hemis Schukpachen, Hemis Skur-buchan and Himis Shukpa, this is a wonderfully tranquil village with a small gompa, green pastures and bubbling brook. It's easy to pass a few idle hours relaxing under the big tree below the **campsite**. There is a very poorly stocked **shop**, but no other facilities.

HEMIS-SHUKPACHU TO TEMISGAM   [MAP 13-14]

To pick up the trail again, cross the pastures in a north-west direction skirting the left (SW) side of the fields. Just after passing some chortens the trail splits. Take the right (N) fork that passes the mature cedar trees (on right) that give the village its name, (cedar is *shukpa*). The trail rises gently over arid ground until you reach a small **pass** (3710m/12,170ft).

The path drops steeply away in front of you and you look across the valley at the pink and mauve coloured mountains ahead; the trail can just be made out as it zigzags up the steep mountainside in the distance. Head right from the pass and drop down to the stream bed where you can pick up a path heading off to the right (N), rather than the one that goes straight down the valley (W). Traverse across the slope to the base of a short but steep climb.

Lago/Meptek La (3750m/12,300ft)

The path winds up the precipitous mountainside to this pass. Walk a little way along the ridge on your left (SW) for magnificent views across to the south side of the Indus Valley. The trail descends steadily along a dry stream bed to the village of Ang (2-3 hours from Hemis-S).

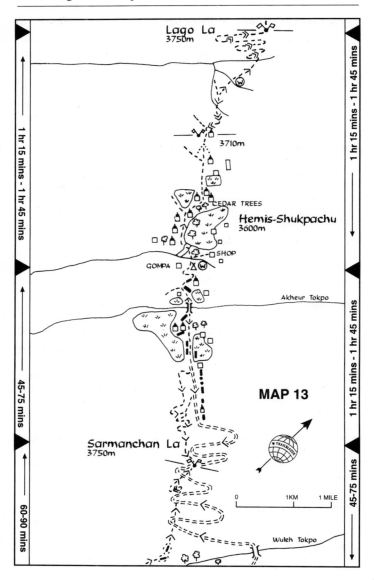

Lago La
3750m

3710m

CEDAR TREES

Hemis-Shukpachu
3600m

SHOP

GOMPA

Akheur Tokpo

MAP 13

Sarmanchan La
3750m

TRAILBLAZER

0   1KM   1 MILE

Wuleh Tokpo

1 hr 15 mins - 1 hr 45 mins

45-75 mins

60-90 mins

1 hr 15 mins - 1 hr 45 mins

1 hr 15 mins - 1 hr 45 mins

45-75 mins

▲ **Opposite direction** Approaching this pass from Ang, keep to the path on the south-west side of the valley as you near the top of the climb.

Ang (3400m/11,160ft)

The villages get more prosperous and fertile the further west you travel along this route. Ang is a fine example, with its beautiful fields and trees. There is a **guest house** here and a good **campsite** on the banks of the wonderfully named, Dangdong Tokpo. You would be better off spending the night here than in Temisgam which, although only an hour away, has neither guest house nor campsite.

The trail crosses the river on a bridge by the campsite and then turns downstream along the right (N) bank. Follow this down the valley where it soon becomes a more substantial jeep track which takes you all the way to the large, spread out village of Temisgam.

Temisgam (3200m/10,500ft)

Also written as Timisgam, Themisgang, Tingmosgang, Tamesgan and Temesgam, this is the largest, most prosperous village on this trek. Set amongst fertile fields and spreading orchards there are some fine examples of large, whitewashed Ladakhi homes. As a result of the division of

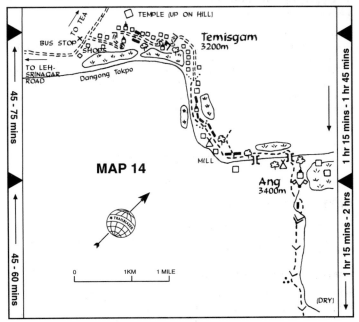

Ladakh in the 14th-15th centuries, the lower kingdom was controlled from Basgo and Temisgam. Little remains of its glorious past; the castle is in ruins but there are still two temples, which can be visited, on the hill behind the village.

Services There are no guest houses and not even a campsite at Temisgam, but it's sometimes possible to stay in a villager's house. You should also be able to make arrangements for **guides** and **ponies** if you are starting your trek from here. As always you will need to allow a couple of days to sort this out. There are two small **shops** and a regular **bus** service to Leh, leaving every morning at about 09.30. If you are going west, or if you miss the bus, you can walk down the road for an hour to Nurla, on the Leh-Srinagar highway, where you shouldn't have to wait long for a passing bus or truck.

> **Treaty of Temisgam**
> In 1684 The village of Temisgam was the scene of the signing of a far reaching treaty between Ladakh and Tibet. It established a border between the two nations (across Pangong Lake) after the Ladakh-Tibet war and it guaranteed that only Ladakhis could buy the valuable pashmina wool (used in the manufacture of cashmere shawls) from western Tibet.

▲ **Opposite direction** Buses from Leh to Temisgam leave Leh at 12.00 every day. Taxis cost Rs1150.

Trek extension
You can make this trek one stage longer by continuing west to **Khalsi** (Khalse/Khaltse) from Temisgam ($3^1/_2$-$4^1/_2$ hours). Instead of turning left (S) down the road to Nurla, turn right (N) up the valley to Tea. From here you cross the Bongbong La and descend via a small pass to the highway. To reach Khalsi from here, try to hitch a ride to save yourself an uninteresting walk of over an hour west along the road.

Lamayuru to Alchi

(4-6 DAYS)

GETTING TO THE START

Lamayuru is 124km west of Leh on the Leh-Srinagar highway. It's a six-hour journey on any of the buses going to Kargil or Srinagar (see p126). A taxi costs Rs1609, plus Rs100 if you want to stop at Alchi as well.

LAMAYURU (3450m/11,320ft)

When you arrive by road you may wonder why everyone says it's such a wonderful place. You are greeted by a collection of run-down tea stalls,

reminiscent of road-side halts all over India. The main village and gompa
(see p129) lie out of sight at the bottom of the valley and when you see
them you'll want to linger here.

Accommodation

Lamayuru is an important stop on the tourist circuit and also the starting
and finishing point for a number of treks. Because of this, there are a surprising number of places to stay. There are two **campsites** (Rs35): the
first is a soul-
less place on a
bare piece of
ground by the
r o a d s i d e
shops. It has
a b s o l u t e l y
nothing   to
recommend it,
e s p e c i a l l y
when   you
compare   it
with the alter-
native below
the   village.
This peaceful
place to camp
is in a mature
willow grove
by a stream.

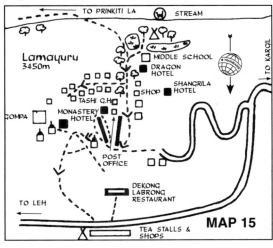

The most popular of the **guest houses** is the **Monastery Hotel and
Restaurant** which is within the gompa walls and run by the monks. If
you can't get a place here, there are other options: the simple **Tashi Guest
House** behind the post office; the **Shangrila Hotel** on the west side of the
village; and the larger **Dragon Hotel** down towards the stream. If all else
fails there is the purpose-built **Dekong Labrong Restaurant** below the
highway. **Food** is available at all these and also at the tea stalls by the
road; choice is limited.

Shops

There is a shop in the main part of the village; you will need to ask a local
where it is, as it has no sign and is usually closed. The shops by the road
are better stocked and it should be possible to scrape together enough
supplies for your trek, including basics such as kerosene and rice. This is
handy if you haven't come from Leh, but prices are higher and you may
have to adapt your diet to the very limited selection. Lamayuru also
boasts a **post office**.

Guides and pack animals

Compared with most Ladakhi villages finding guides or pony-men in Lamayuru is relatively easy. This is because the village is at the end of the trans-Zanskar trek from Darcha or Padum and consequently, pony-men having just finished that trek will be looking for employment at this end. Obviously they prefer trekkers who are going into Zanskar so that they get a paid trip home but they are usually happy to undertake other treks as well. If you are travelling relatively light, there are some local young men with donkeys who are usually more than willing to accompany you on your trek. The advantage with them is that they know the area better than those from Zanskar and Lahaul and they are marginally cheaper. You'll find them by asking around in the village.

LAMAYURU TO WANLA   [MAP 16]

Leaving Lamayuru

Walk down to the stream and follow its bed east (L). After 15 minutes take a path that cuts uphill to some chortens and prayer flags. The trail goes over arid land in a southerly direction following a stream bed (often dry) until it splits. Walk up the bottom of the small gully on the left until that also splits, this time in three directions. Again take the left fork which winds steeply up to the Prinkiti La.

Prinkiti La (3700m/12,140ft)

The climb to this pretty notch in the ridge is easy. From the top you look over the complicated terrain of the Zanskar Mountains to snow clad rock spires and the Konzke La in the east, over which the route passes. Descend steeply into the narrow gully which you follow for over an hour until it deposits you in the Shillakong (Shilakang/Shelakhong) Valley.

Shilla/Sheela

There is a **tent restaurant** at this small village, which is just as well if you are thirsty, as the water in the river is particularly silty. Cross the bridge and continue downstream on the right (S) bank, past a possible **campsite**, as far as Wanla (¹/₂ hour).

Wanla/Wanlah (3200m/10,500ft)

This pretty village, with its eleventh century gompa high up on a crag, makes a pleasant place to stop. The gompa was built during the time of Rinchen Zangpo, the man credited for the revival of Buddhism in this area because of his many translations of Sanskrit texts.

The **Shangrila Hotel** offers food but not accommodation; the **shop** next door has most supplies. The **campsite** is conveniently situated opposite on the banks of the Yapola River. There is a spring with good **water** just after crossing the bridge up the slope to the left.

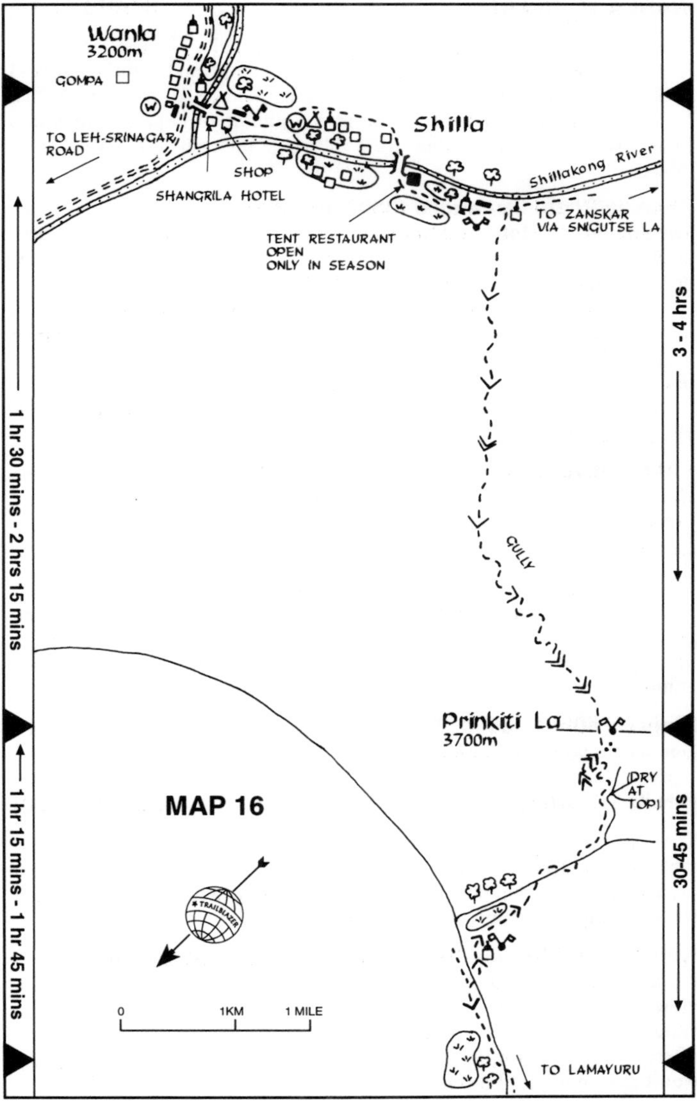
Wanla
3200m
GOMPA
Shilla
TO LEH-SRINAGAR ROAD
SHOP
SHANGRILA HOTEL
Shillakong River
TO ZANSKAR VIA SNIGUTSE LA
TENT RESTAURANT OPEN ONLY IN SEASON
GULLY
Prinkiti La
3700m
(DRY AT TOP)
MAP 16
TRAILBLAZER
0
1KM
1 MILE
TO LAMAYURU
1 hr 30 mins - 2 hrs 15 mins
1 hr 15 mins - 1 hr 45 mins
3 - 4 hrs
30-45 mins

WANLA TO HINJU [MAPS 17-18]

Head upstream on the right (NE) bank of the Yapola. The trail, initially a
jeep track, becomes more arid the further up you go and is totally devoid
of shade. The muddy river is your only water source for over two hours.
Just before a group of houses, you pass a jumble of huge boulders in a
field, which must have fallen from the ridge on your left – a sobering
thought.

Phanjila/Phenjilla/Fangila (3300m/10,830ft)

The **Spangthan Hotel and Shop** has very little to offer apart from a glass
of chai. The trail to Alchi turns north-east off the main trail (which goes
on to Zanskar, p226), up the Ripchar Valley.

After the main group of houses the trail climbs a bank and traverses a
high, steep, unstable slope for 2^1/2km (don't take the level path which
leads to the fields). This section could be dangerous in rain. There are a
few places to **camp** in the meadows below you, by the stream.

The trail drops down to the river and passes a small **campsite** in a willow grove, before crossing a side stream and entering a mini-gorge.

• **Alternative route** Another way to Alchi is to turn north up this side
stream which takes you via Urshi, over the difficult Tar La
(5200m/17,060ft), down through the villages of Tar, Mang Gyu, Gira and
Lardo (3 days).

It's about 1-1^1/2 hours to Hinju from the turn off to Urshi. The Ripchar
Valley gets more and more beautiful the higher up you walk, with its thick
growth of willows and dramatic views back to rock pinnacles on the sky
line. Don't mistake the couple of houses you pass after about 1^1/2km for
Hinju – the main village is marked by prayer flags across the path.

Hinju (3750m/12,300ft) There are pastures just before and after the village where you can **camp** (Rs25).

HINJU TO SUMDAH-CHENMO [MAPS 18-20]

The trail continues up the valley, crossing several side streams and passing a few **campsites**. Follow the main stream all the time. The gradient
increases as you approach the head of the valley where the trail leaves the
stream, climbing steeply up to the left.

Konzke/Chot/Konke/Choke/Konze La (4900m/16,080ft)

It's a strenuous climb to the top of this pass, but you're rewarded with
views all the way back to the Prinkiti La. The initially steep descent to the
valley becomes more gentle towards Sumdah-Chenmo (2^1/2-3 hours).
There are good **camping** places in this valley before the village; you
won't find more until 5-6 hours after it.

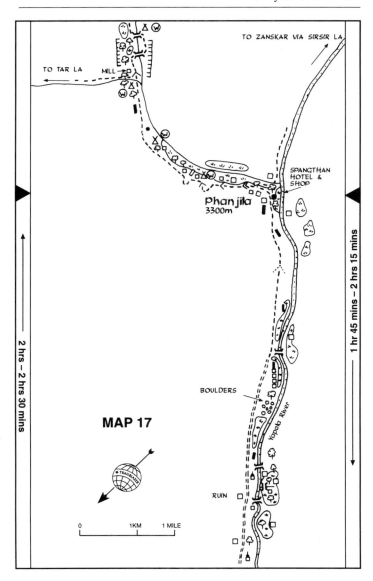

TO ZANSKAR VIA SIRSIR LA

TO TAR LA

MILL

SPANGTHAN
HOTEL &
SHOP

Phanjila
3300m

2 hrs – 2 hrs 30 mins

1 hr 45 mins – 2 hrs 15 mins

BOULDERS

Yapola River

MAP 17

N TRAILBLAZER

RUIN

0   1KM   1 MILE

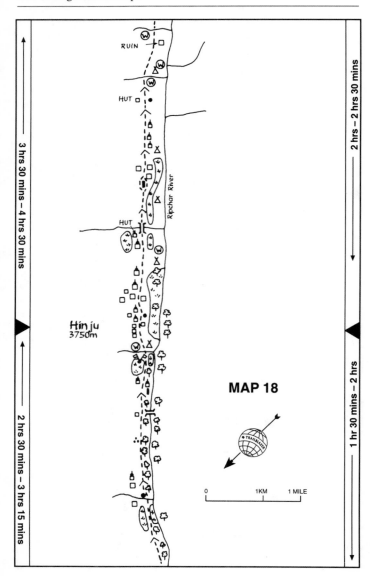

MAP 18

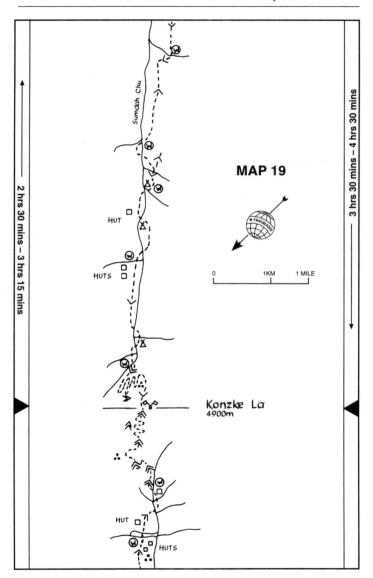

MAP 19

Konzke La
4900m

Sumdah Chu

HUT

HUTS

HUT

HUTS

0   1KM   1 MILE

2 hrs 30 mins – 3 hrs 15 mins

3 hrs 30 mins – 4 hrs 30 mins

During the summer months shepherds from Hinju cross the Konzke La so that they can graze their livestock in this valley. The trail passes some of their huts and enclosures where they spend their time making butter, curd and cheese. You may see the cheese spread out on the ground to dry. It is dried into small white nuggets which will then keep for years; very little is eaten fresh.

Sumdah-Chenmo/Sumda (3900m/12,800ft)

The name literally means great Sumdah. This isolated village shows few signs of change and the villagers are still largely self-sufficient. There is a small gompa here with two resident monks, which comes under the jurisdiction of Hemis. Remember to take your shoes off if you go inside and to leave a small donation.

> **Route to Chiling** (see p198) Two routes that lead to Chiling split off from the Alchi trail just after Sumdah-Chenmo. This link can be used to join the trail from Lamayuru with the Markha Valley, opening up several possibilities for longer treks (see p31).

As you leave the village there is a ruined gompa far below. This is probably of a similar age to the one at Alchi, but the villagers have resisted any attempts to restore it believing it would bring bad fortune on the whole community.

SUMDAH-CHENMO TO SUMDAH-CHOON   [MAP 20-21]

Stay up high on the shoulder out of Sumdah-Chenmo and after about 1 to 1½ hours descend to the river.

Sumdah Chu The trail follows the river as it curves around to the east. After 1km you cross it on a simple log bridge and continue on the right (S) bank. This whole section is difficult and prone to change so keep an eye out for any alterations to the route. In another kilometre you cross back over to the left (N) bank, this time high above the river on an impressive bridge that spans the narrow gorge. Ford the river 1km further on. (If you're wearing stream crossing shoes keep them on as there is another crossing very soon).

The best way now is to scramble up the steep scree slope in front of you, cross over a shoulder and scramble back down to the river. This is far too precipitous for pack animals which will have to wade down the stream instead. Cross back to the left bank for the last time. The path is a little hard to follow as it picks its way through the vegetation of willow, rose and seabuckthorn.

The river rushes through a gorge and the way ahead is on a trail that has been ingeniously built onto a sheer rock face. This is not a place to

---

(Opposite) The monk at Sumdah-Chenmo looks after the small village gompa as well as performing religious duties in the locality. **(Overleaf)** The bare mountainsides are transformed into productive fields below the village and gompa of Sumdah-Choon.

linger. After passing some boulders balanced precariously on top of earth spires the path turns north-east and crosses a small tributary. Leave the main trail (which goes to the Zanskar River and on to Nimu) and follow the willow-lined tributary upstream to the village of Sumdah-Choon.

Sumdah-Choon (3850m/12,630ft)

The inhabitants of this whole area are skilled metal workers and you can sometimes hear the banging of a hammer against metal as you pass the house of a craftsman. *Choon* means small so this is the little relation of Sumdah-Chenmo. The two Sumdahs have in fact linked themselves together as an administrative group along with Chiling.

There is an impressive gompa standing on the hillside above the village, whose design and paintings are very similar to the temple at Alchi. Like Alchi it was constructed at the time of Richen Zangpo, which makes it one of the oldest in Ladakh. If there are no monks in residence, find the gompa caretaker in the village. Remember to remove your shoes before entering the temple and to put a small donation in the box provided.

There are no flat pastures for camping near the village but for Rs20 you can **camp** on the flat roofs of the stables behind the lower houses.

SUMDAH-CHOON TO ALCHI   [MAPS 21-22]

The trail to the Stakspi La

Ascend a valley to the north-east of the village along the side of a small tributary. Opposite some huts there is a small uneven flat which is sometimes used as a base **camp** for the pass. Just above this the stream stops flowing, so you will need to fill up with enough **water** for at least four hours.

The going gets harder as you ascend a series of giant steps formed in a past glacial age. There is not much of a path, but a dry stream bed soon materialises giving you something to follow in the right direction.

As you approach the head of the valley you are faced with a choice of routes to the pass. There is no path so route finding is critical. Both the routes to the top are demanding and involve ascending steep, loose scree. You can either choose the more direct line and ascend to the left of the crags in front of you, or go up to the right of the crags until you reach a rock band, traverse left below this, cross over a shoulder ridge and rejoin the other route as it reaches the top of the climb. As you trudge wearily up the scree wishing for the top, you can keep your mind busy searching for quartz crystals which litter this side of the mountain. The final section to the pass is over rocky ground with the way indicated by a series of

---

(Opposite) Top: Mani stones at Wanla engraved with the mantra 'Om mani padme hum'. Mani walls, chortens and other Buddhist monuments must be passed in a clockwise direction (see p106). **Bottom:** Approaching the Zalung Karpo La from the north (see p211). A reliable guide is essential for Ladakh's remoter trails.

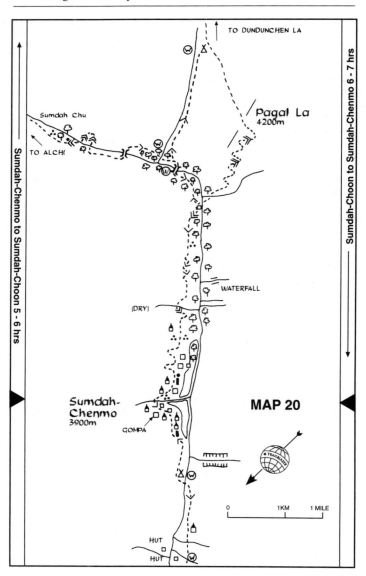

TO DUNDUNCHEN LA

Pagal La
4200m

Sumdah Chu

TO ALCHI

Sumdah-Chenmo to Sumdah-Choon 5 - 6 hrs

Sumdah-Choon to Sumdah-Chenmo 6 - 7 hrs

WATERFALL

(DRY)

Sumdah-
Chenmo
3900m

GOMPA

MAP 20

0   1KM   1 MILE

HUT

HUT

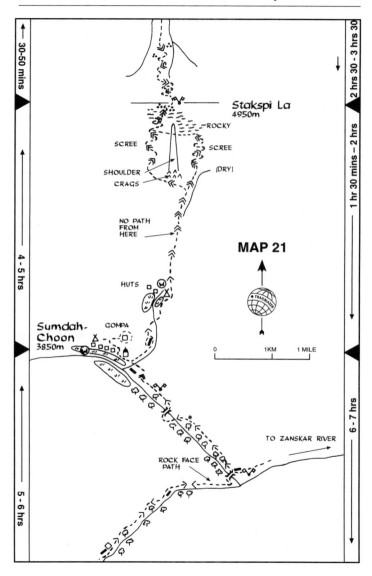

Stakspi La
4950m

ROCKY

SCREE

SCREE

SHOULDER

CRAGS

(DRY)

NO PATH
FROM
HERE

MAP 21

HUTS

Sumdah-
Choon
3850m

GOMPA

0   1KM   1 MILE

TO ZANSKAR RIVER

ROCK FACE
PATH

30-50 mins

4 - 5 hrs

5 - 6 hrs

2 hrs 30 - 3 hrs 30

1 hr 30 mins – 2 hrs

6 - 7 hrs

cairns. The panoramic views that unfold as you climb and the lack of any properly established path over the scree give this route a real mountaineering feel.

Stakspi La (4950m/16,240ft)

The whole of the Likir to Temisgam trek can be seen laid out beneath you to the north. Likir monastery is just about visible and the closer village in the foreground, of which you can only see half, is Saspol (Saspul, Saspool). Descend steeply through the rocky terrain in a northerly direction from the pass. After going down a central spur between two streams cross the stream on the left (W) to reach a shepherd's hut.

▲ **Opposite direction** The roof of this hut is the only bit of flat ground around and is occasionally used as a place to camp before crossing the pass. If you do camp be sure to check that any inhabitants that might be here do not mind. You can see the pass from here; it's the flattened U in the ridge due south. Seeing it from here makes navigating up to it much easier. The trail goes up just to the right of the pass, through the crags, and then traverses below it as it nears the top.

From the hut the trail follows the valley all the way down to Alchi ($2^{1}/_{2}$-3 hours). In half an hour the trail becomes established in a barren and rocky valley devoid of shade. **Water** is no problem at first as you are constantly by the stream but in 3km a side stream enters the main stream and discolours the water making it undrinkable from here on.

Alchi (3150m/10,340ft)

When you reach this large prosperous village carry on down the trail to the road. Turn right (E) to the village and gompa, or left (W) for the main highway and a lift back to Leh.

Most people come to Alchi to see the unique iconography of its famous low-lying gompa. With plenty of accommodation available and its proximity to Likir, Saspol and Rizong, it also makes an ideal base for a few days of sightseeing.

Accommodation Places to stay (Rs100 upwards) are mainly centred around the gompa complex. The **Zimskhang Guest House** is popular with its open air restaurant and also has a **campsite** (Rs30) in the garden. Behind the tea stalls by the bus stand are the **Pota La Restaurant and Guest House** and the **Sandup Ling Guest House**, while opposite them is the **Lotsava Guest House**. If you want to be further away from other tourists then the **Choskor Guest House** along the road towards the river should be suitably isolated.

Guides and pack animals Because most trekkers finish at Alchi there are often guides with animals who are only too happy to be paid for a return trip to Lamayuru.

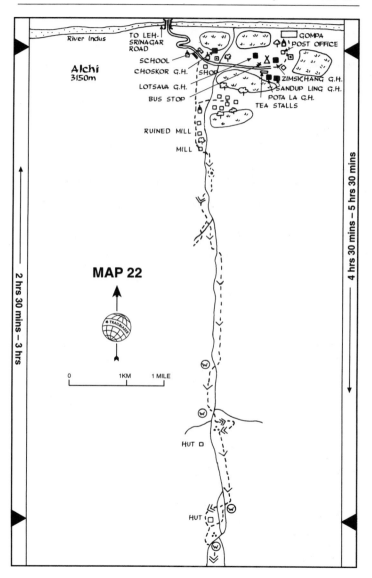

River Indus

TO LEH-
SRINAGAR
ROAD

GOMPA

POST OFFICE

Alchi
3150m

SCHOOL

CHOSKOR G.H.   SHOP

ZIMSKHANG G.H.

LOTSAVA G.H.

SANDUP LING G.H.

BUS STOP

POTA LA G.H.

TEA STALLS

RUINED MILL

MILL

MAP 22

★ TRAILBLAZER

0   1KM   1 MILE

HUT

HUT

2 hrs 30 mins – 3 hrs

4 hrs 30 mins – 5 hrs 30 mins

Shops The tea stalls act as basic shops but it could be hard to find enough provisions for a trek here. There is a **post office** on the path to the gompa and also plenty of souvenir sellers.

Buses Buses to Leh (Rs25, 3 hours) leave at 07.30 from the bus stand in the village. You can also get a bus west from here, to Lamayuru and Kargil. If you miss the appropriate bus then you should be able to pick up a truck or bus on the Leh-Srinagar highway which is only a short walk from the village.

▲ **Opposite direction** Buses leave Leh at 15.00 daily for Alchi or you could get a taxi, Rs805.

Sumdah-Chenmo to the Markha Valley

(LINK ROUTE VIA CHILING – 2-3 DAYS)

SUMDAH-CHENMO TO CHILING   [MAP 20, p194]
Route to Dundunchen/Dungdungchan/Dundochonila La
• **Option 1** Stay up high on the shoulder out of Sumdah-Chenmo and after about 1-1½ hours drop down to the river. A tributary joins the Sumdah Chu from the south, just before it curves round to the east. Ford the Sumdah Chu upstream of the tributary by a building in the river bed. Then cross the tributary. Climb the ridge in an east-south-east direction following a zigzag path to a minor pass, the **Pagal La** (4200m/13,780ft) (1½ hours). There are amazing views from the top. Traverse a steep slope to pastures where you can **camp** (30 minutes). From the campsite it's 1½ hours' steep climb to the Dundunchen La.
• **Option 2** Stay up high on the shoulder out of Sumdah-Chenmo and after about 1-1½ hours descend to the river. The trail follows the Sumdah Chu as it curves around to the east. After 1km it crosses the river on a simple log bridge. The main trail to Alchi continues down the valley; the way to the Dundunchen La is up the slope ahead, following a small tributary to pastures where you can **camp** (as above). From the campsite it's 1½ hours' steep climb to the Dundunchen La.

Dundunchen La (4700m/15,420ft)
There are fantastic views from this pass. Traverse for 30 minutes and then descend into the valley (S). Follow the path and stream down the valley to Chiling (3½ hours).

Chiling (3250m/10,660ft)
This village is famous for producing some of the best metalwork in Ladakh. It is believed that the people may be descended from Nepalese

craftsmen who came to Ladakh in the 17th century to help construct the statue of Buddha at Shey. You'd be foolish not to find space in your pack for the beautiful cups and spoons made here; prices are much lower than in Leh. There's a nice **campsite** (Rs20) where the valley that you descended joins the Zanskar River. The only water available is rather silty, so filtering it would be wise. There's also a **shop** in the village which should be well supplied as there is a road up the Zanskar from Nimu. You should at least be able to find basic supplies such as rice, tea, dal and vegetables, which could be useful if you're planning an extended trip up the Markha Valley.

CHILING TO SKIU

Before you leave Chiling you need to ask for the man who operates the cable-car across the Zanskar. The cable-car is supposed to be free, as the man gets paid by the government, but tourists won't get across without giving a small tip. You obviously can't take pack animals across the river so this is as far as they can go with you. You can sometimes find a willing pony-man in one of the villages on the other side but don't rely on it.

Follow the easy trail past the village of Kaya to **Skiu** ($3^{1}/_{2}$ hours, see p167, Map 5). An alternative to going into the Markha Valley is to follow the Zanskar downstream to the beautiful oasis of Choksti and then on to Nimu. Here you'll be able to pick up a bus or truck going in either direction along the Leh-Srinagar road.

Leh to Nubra

(4-6 DAYS)

GETTING TO THE START

You can either walk from Leh to Sabu (3 hours) or catch a bus. There are J&KSRTC buses from Leh at 08.00, 14.00 and 17.00 (Rs5, 20 minutes). Sabu is a very spread out village, so if you want to avoid a long walk make sure you get on the bus to the top of the village (ask for Sabu Phu). Sabu Phu is also a convenient place to meet your pony-man. If you want to get back to Leh you can get on any of these buses as they all return directly. A taxi to Sabu will cost you about Rs150.

LEH TO SABU   [MAP 23]

One of the advantages of this trek is that you can walk directly from Leh. This three-hour hike to the pretty and prosperous village of Sabu also makes a good day walk. Head east out of Leh above the polo ground towards a small triangular shaped mountain. The first part of the route is not pleasant as it passes an area used for dumping rubbish. The route ahead is visible as it angles up the slope to a small pass. Go down the other side into a quiet, arid valley and then walk south-east to the next pass, which entails a steep but short climb. There is a collection of cairns at the top and good views to the tall poplar trees of Sabu village. Descend the steep winding path, through crags to the valley floor.

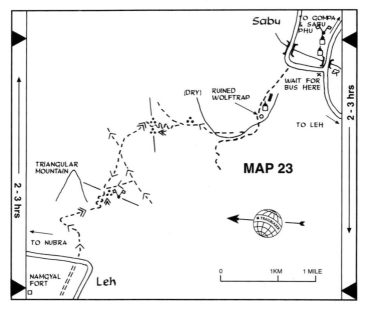

Follow a dry stream bed down to the outskirts of Sabu which is marked by an old wolf trap, a chorten and a mani wall. When you reach a road, turn right and follow it to a junction by a bridge. This is the best place to wait for a bus heading in either direction. To walk, turn left over the bridge and follow the road up to the gompa (2km) and Sabu Phu (5km).

SABU PHU TO THE DIGAR LA   [MAP 24]

Sabu Phu (3700m/12,140ft) The bus turns around where the road ends. Follow the track uphill, past a few houses and fields (possible **camping**). Cross the bridge over the clear, tumbling Sabu River and follow this upstream on the right (W) bank. You walk up through green pastures between high boulder-filled moraines, climbing steadily for about two hours until you arrive at a simple hut on your left and a ruin on the right.

Pulu Digar (4400m/14,440ft)
There's a small flat area here where you could pitch a couple of tents, but a better alternative for **camping** is to head up the steep slope on the left (NW) which takes you up to the main cluster of shepherds' summer shelters (often empty).

The path becomes hard to follow from here on, so just continue along the main stream. When it forks, in about 1km, take the left fork. Keep an eye on the **water** in the stream as it sometimes vanishes underground. Before it does, make sure you fill up as there may be no water higher up.

Digar La Base Camp (4700m/15,420ft)
After walking for 1-1$\frac{1}{2}$ hours up from Pulu Digar there is another possible **camp** on the right (NW) bank of the stream. This is about as close as you can camp to the Digar La and makes a convenient base camp. There are wonderful views over the Stok mountains with Stok Kangri dominating the scene.

Continue up from here until the ground levels off. You are faced with a wall of mountains ahead of you and the easiest way over them appears to be to the north-west. Unfortunately the pass lies to the east.

Digar La (5250m/17,230ft)
You should be able to make out the path as it zigzags up the steep and tiring slope to a string of prayer flags at the top. Follow the stream to the east, skirt a large moraine and begin climbing. As you struggle up the stiff climb to the pass, you'll be glad to know that William Moorcroft found it equally tiring in the early 1820s: 'Being on a steep ascent, it was also very fatiguing, and the difficulty of breathing was more troublesome and painful than I had before experienced: this extended to the animals, particularly the horses; but the yaks were not wholly exempt, and we were obliged to halt repeatedly to give the cattle relief.' (*Travels*)

The views from the pass are excellent. The mountains you can see to the north are the Saser Range of the eastern Karakoram, which contain Ladakh's highest peak, Saser Kangri (7670m/25,165ft), which is the most easterly of the great Karakoram mountains. There has been very little mountaineering activity in this area because of military restrictions and many peaks have not yet been climbed. If you're expecting a glimpse of K2, you'll be disappointed. Unfortunately it lies too far to the north-west to be visible. However, behind you to the south are stunning views of the Zanskar Range.

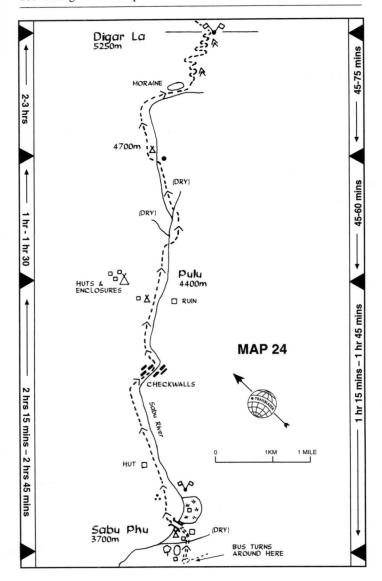

Digar La
5250m

MORAINE

4700m

(DRY)

(DRY)

Pulu
4400m

HUTS &
ENCLOSURES

RUIN

MAP 24

CHECKWALLS

Sabu River

HUT

0   1KM   1 MILE

Sabu Phu
3700m

(DRY)

BUS TURNS
AROUND HERE

2-3 hrs

1 hr - 1 hr 30

2 hrs 15 mins – 2 hrs 45 mins

45-75 mins

45-60 mins

1 hr 15 mins – 1 hr 45 mins

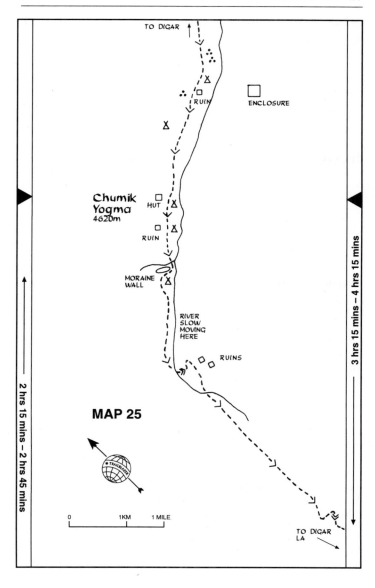

TO DIGAR

X

☐
RUIN

☐
ENCLOSURE

X

Chumik
Yogma
4620m

☐
HUT

X

☐
RUIN

X

MORAINE
WALL

X

RIVER
SLOW
MOVING
HERE

☐ ☐
RUINS

MAP 25

● TRAILBLAZER

0   1KM   1 MILE

TO DIGAR
LA

2 hrs 15 mins – 2 hrs 45 mins

3 hrs 15 mins – 4 hrs 15 mins

DIGAR LA TO CHUMIK YOGMA   [MAP 25]

Head north from the pass descending into the valley. You soon pick up a
small stream which flows all the way to Digar. After descending a short,
steep slope below some ruins, cross onto the left (W) bank as it gets wet
and difficult if you stay on the right. The route crosses a beautiful small
plateau where the stream loses most of its energy forming long, deep,
slow-moving pools. The going is quite hard as the ground is hummocky
and wet but it soon eases at the far end of the plateau where it's flat
enough to **camp**. Though there are more camping places further down the
valley, they get fewer the closer to Digar you get.

Chumik Yogma (4620m/15160ft) The path skirts the right side of a
small wall of moraine that blocks the end of the plateau and then
descends gradually through boulder filled pastures. These are the summer
grazing grounds for the livestock of Digar and you'll find a couple of
shepherds' huts here.

The path begins to move away from the river and becomes harder to
follow. Fill up with **water** if you are running short. As you make your
way down the widening valley, head gradually towards the left (N) side
where you will eventually pick up a more definite trail.

CHUMIK YOGMA TO THE SHYOK VALLEY   [MAP 26-27]

Digar (3900m/12,800ft)

As you near Digar the path drops steeply to a collection of chortens and
prayer flags. The aridity of the Nubra landscape becomes starkly apparent as you see it contrasting with the vibrant fertility of the village fields
in front of you. The stream disappears into a deep gorge on your right
(SE) and flows far below the village. Across on the other side of the valley is a collection of houses whose inhabitants seem to be fighting a losing battle against erosion as the river takes away more of their fields
every year.

Places to **camp** are very limited here but this is your last chance until
you are down in the Shyok Valley. Cross the village's irrigation channel
and follow the stony, walled path between the fields to the main cluster
of houses. Wind through the village passing a rock covered in Buddhist
graffiti and an interesting temple built onto a huge boulder.

As you leave the village you are starting a particularly desolate section of
the route. Make sure you have plenty of **water** as you won't find any for
at least two hours. The scenery gets increasingly barren, with hardly any
vegetation in sight. The trail starts heading in a north-westerly direction
and rises to a mani wall. Its positioning is perfect with sweeping views of
the Shyok flood-plain which stretches into the distance. If you look
behind you can see the lush fields of villages up the Lazun Lungpa. This

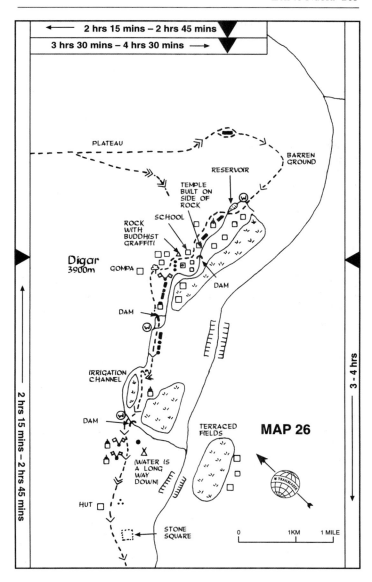

2 hrs 15 mins – 2 hrs 45 mins

3 hrs 30 mins – 4 hrs 30 mins

PLATEAU

BARREN GROUND

RESERVOIR

TEMPLE BUILT ON SIDE OF ROCK

SCHOOL

ROCK WITH BUDDHIST GRAFFITI

Digar 3900m

GOMPA

DAM

DAM

IRRIGATION CHANNEL

DAM

TERRACED FIELDS

MAP 26

(WATER IS A LONG WAY DOWN)

HUT

STONE SQUARE

0   1KM   1 MILE

TRAILBLAZER

3 - 4 hrs

2 hrs 15 mins – 2 hrs 45 mins

remote valley leads via the Chang La to Sakti and can therefore be used as an alternative route into or out of Nubra.

Plateau Drop down to an amazing plateau that sits above the Shyok Valley. You want to head across it in a north-westerly direction, and the 3km trudge can be painfully slow as there are few landmarks by which to mark your progress. The plateau suddenly ends with a precipitous drop to the valley floor, 300m below.

You can now see the route ahead which follows the left side of this vast valley.

▲ **Opposite direction** from the plateau you will see that there are two possible ways ahead. Either the one mentioned above or, a 'short cut' heading steeply up to a pass on the right (SW) side of the plateau. The former is the easier option as the ascent is far more gradual.

Zigzag steeply down from the plateau and then go up a short rise to the top of a sand dune. The descent down the long north face of this dune is great fun as the sand allows you almost to ski as you slip and slide to the bottom. An ascent of this would be extremely hard work, akin to walking on a treadmill!

ALONG THE SHYOK VALLEY TO RONG   [MAPS 27-28]
Shyok Valley (3300m/10,830ft)
There is a small stream on your left (W) and the ground is flat enough for **camping**. There isn't any grazing, which could be a problem if you are using pack animals. Collect **water** if the stream is flowing, it gets dirtier further on and the next source of good, clean water is $2^{1}/_{2}$ hours away.

You need to exercise a certain amount of caution when relying on these desert streams as they do not necessarily flow all year round. If you do run out, the main Shyok River is never far away, but the water needs filtering being heavily laden with silt.

Desert Cross the desert in a northerly direction, heading towards the rocky spur which juts out into the valley. There is no path as such and you may need to cross the stream a couple of times to seek out the best route.

▲ **Opposite direction** you will be able to see the path winding up to the plateau 3km ahead. Aim for the bottom of this path.

Cliff path As you pass the spur, keep an eye out for a trail which climbs up through the cliff on your left (W). There's a stone wall marking its start. This path is steep and difficult in parts, especially for animals, but it saves you several deep crossings of the Shyok river. From the top of the climb, by a cairn and small shelter, there are good views both up and down the valley. You can see the multiple braiding of the Shyok and can

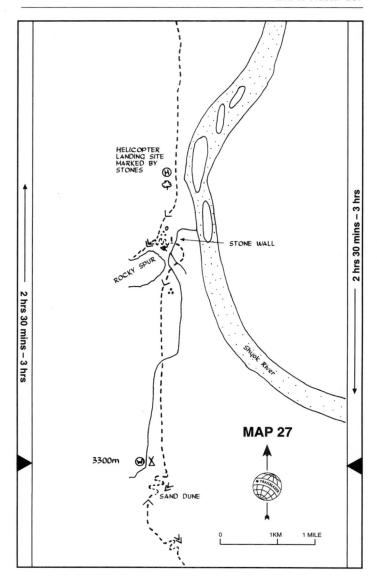

HELICOPTER
LANDING SITE
MARKED BY
STONES

STONE WALL

ROCKY SPUR

Shyok River

2 hrs 30 mins – 3 hrs

2 hrs 30 mins – 3 hrs

3300m

SAND DUNE

MAP 27

0   1KM   1 MILE

appreciate how complicated it would be to find a route along the valley floor. The path gradually descends and you continue along the stony alluvial bed, sticking to the west (L) side of the valley.

Valley floor Again there is no path to follow and the next 5^1/2km are hard and monotonous along the stone and sand of the flat valley floor. If you stay on the west (L) side of the wide valley and are not tempted up onto the valley sides, you won't go far wrong. The monotony is alleviated briefly by a prayer flag and cairn, around which are scattered hundreds of tiny piles of stones. It's a fascinating sight and you have to tread carefully in order not to knock any of them over. They are presumably placed there by passing travellers but one wonders if they are washed away each year by the flooding river. Across on the other side of the valley is the village of Rongdu, whose fields are irrigated by a tumbling mountain stream.

Soon you come to a small stream where it's possible to **camp** if there's enough water. Again, there is little fodder for animals. Follow the stream down for a few hundred metres and then take the large and obvious track which winds up the steep valley side. The gradient soon eases and you walk along an easy path, high above the river. There are a few areas where landslides have swept the path away and you have to scramble around the obstacles.

The Silk Route

Nubra was on a major branch of the Silk Route between Leh and Yarkand until the trading was stopped in 1949. There were two main routes. In winter the traders followed the huge loop of the frozen Shyok River, while in summer they were able to take the short cut over the Saser La (5330m/17,490ft), north-east of Panamik. Although not the highest of the five passes, it was the most feared. Its treacherous glaciers were responsible for the loss of many lives and some recent expeditions have reported the huge number of animal bones that litter this section of the trail.

A typical year would see 300 caravans making the month long journey to Yarkand, each caravan consisting of up to 200 camels, donkeys and horses. The traders were spurred on by the enormous profits that could be made on the silk and carpets from Yarkand or the spices, cotton, hashish and opium that were transported north from India. The only remnant of this past age is a distinctive herd of the two-humped Bactrian camel, which still roams in the Nubra Valley.

You soon reach a section where the road engineers' craft is expertly displayed: they have carved a route across a sheer rock face while the river flows directly below. Keep an eye on the loose rock above, as judging by the debris underneath, large chunks appear to fall onto the track at random.

The trail descends to the valley floor and skirts the right side of a small rocky outcrop. From here the track turns into an extraordinary paved track across the desert which suddenly begins, and just as suddenly fin-

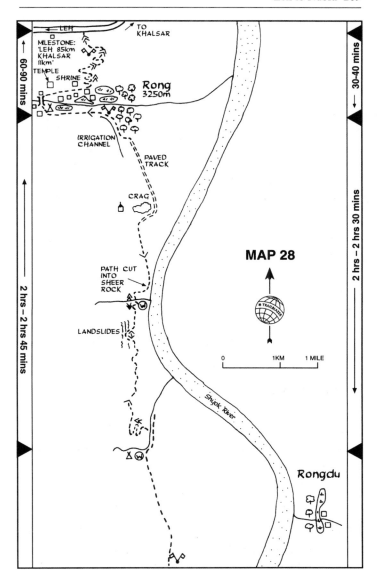

TO KHALSAR

LEH

MILESTONE:
'LEH 85km
KHALSAR
11km'

TEMPLE

SHRINE

Rong
3250m

60-90 mins

30-40 mins

IRRIGATION
CHANNEL

PAVED
TRACK

CRAG

2 hrs – 2 hrs 30 mins

PATH CUT
INTO
SHEER
ROCK

MAP 28

LANDSLIDES

2 hrs – 2 hrs 45 mins

0   1KM   1 MILE

Shyok River

Rongdu

ishes, about a kilometre further on. It is reminiscent of a Roman road, being dead straight and made of large stones. When you see an irrigation channel running parallel to the track, on the far left (W) of the valley, cross over to it. This leads past a large wood to a river. Follow this upstream to the village of Rong.

Rong (3250m/10,660ft)

Just before the bridge there's a beautiful **campsite**. This peaceful village is a wonderful place to stay and rest among the mature poplar and willow trees. Cross the stream and follow the trail that goes above the main part of the village. The trail then climbs steeply above the last house, giving stunning views of the village and of the Shyok Valley. It's a stiff climb, but it's also your last. You eventually reach the main road at the top.

Leh to Nubra road Turn left for the Khardung La and Leh, or right for Khalsar and the rest of Nubra. As long as you arrive at the road quite early in the day you should easily get a lift on a truck in either direction. Buses to Leh will pass by very early in the morning at about 06.00 (Rs50).

▲ **Opposite direction** See p137 for bus times and fares from Leh. If you are starting the trek from here keep your eyes peeled for the mile stone which says, 'Leh 85km, Khalsar 11km'. This is a few hundred metres uphill from the beginning of the trail, and is where you should get off. Alternatively, you could walk from Khalsar.

Indus Valley to the Rupshu

(8-10 DAYS)

GETTING TO THE START

Karu is an hour by taxi (Rs600) from Leh or two hours by bus. The buses leave at 09.00 and 15.00 daily and are bound for Hemis.

KARU TO CONFLUENCE OF NIMALING & MARKHA RIVERS

The first three or so days of this trek follow the last few days of the Markha Valley trek, but in reverse (pp172-178). The altitude gain on the first stage of this trek is rapid; you must be very well acclimatised or you'll have to take the climb up the Gongmaru La very slowly (3-4 days).

CONFLUENCE TO THE ZALUNG KARPO LA   [MAP 29-30]

Up the Luntung/Langtang Chu Upstream of this confluence, the river previously known as the Markha becomes the Luntung Chu. Ford the Nimaling Chu to the flat grassy area between the two rivers; this is a possible **camp** (3950m/12,960ft). It's a good feeling to be turning off the popular Markha Valley route and to be going up this less frequented, inviting valley. The trail stays close to the river, crossing it several times when necessary.

After 1^3/$_4$ to 2^1/$_4$ hours you reach a pleasant **camp** (4200m/13,780ft) below the west face of Kang Yaze (6400m/21,000ft) by a stream that flows from the same mountain.

Mani walls Continue up the valley crossing a few side streams as you go. When you get to some mani walls there are good views looking back towards the steep west face of Kang Yaze and a small mountain further down the valley, that has exposed stratified rock like the inside of a Swiss roll. The mani walls up remote valleys like this are maintained by passing monks. Monks going on this route would most likely be heading for the gompa at Dat.

Moraine wall Further up the valley you cross a main stream and climb up and over a wall of moraine which is immediately ahead of you. There are flats for **camping** either on top of the moraine, by a ruined hut, or down on the other side.

The main valley begins to narrow and the stream becomes smaller and easier to cross, which you have to do several times to pick out the best route. Pass a tributary on the right (W), which squeezes through a narrow opening in the rocks. Soon after this, the stream splits in a perfect 'Y'. Take the right branch that heads south-west. There are lovely views to snow fields up the left branch.

False summit The gradient increases slightly as you climb through stony, barren ground. It looks as though the pass is only just ahead but this is a false summit. Carry on walking easily through this rolling scenery to the pass proper.

ZALUNG KARPO LA TO SORRA   [MAPS 30-31]

Zalung Karpo La (5050m/16,570ft) Jagged rock pinnacles, typical of the Zanskar range, lie to the north, while the Kang Yaze massif fills the skyline behind you. Head west from the pass and descend the steep zigzag trail to the south-west.

Sorra (Kurma) Chu The trail follows the stream all the way down this remote valley. At first the stream bed is dry but as you progress it fills with water, swelling in size when a larger tributary joins from the north-east. There is a nice **camp** (4300m/14,110ft) by this confluence and several others further down on the left bank. Continue to the village of Sorra, fording the stream twice.

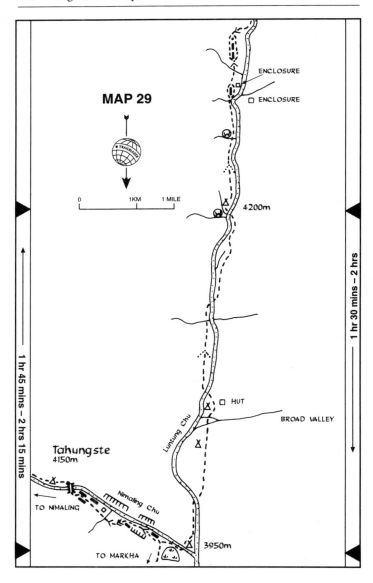

MAP 29

0   1KM   1 MILE

ENCLOSURE

ENCLOSURE

4200m

HUT

BROAD VALLEY

Luntung Chu

Tahungste
4150m

TO NIMALING

Nimaling Chu

TO MARKHA

3950m

1 hr 30 mins – 2 hrs

1 hr 45 mins – 2 hrs 15 mins

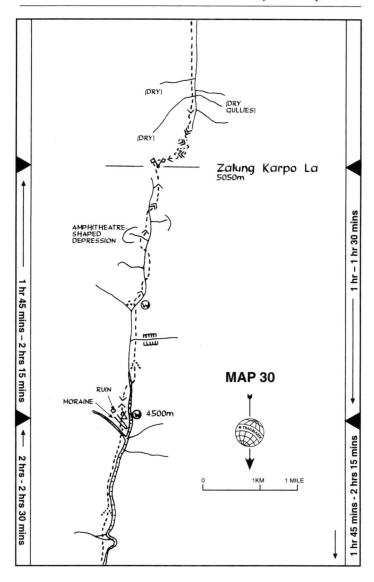

(DRY)

(DRY
GULLIES)

(DRY)

Zalung Karpo La
5050m

AMPHITHEATRE-
SHAPED
DEPRESSION

1 hr – 1 hr 30 mins

1 hr 45 mins – 2 hrs 15 mins

RUIN

MORAINE

4500m

2 hrs - 2 hrs 30 mins

1 hr 45 mins - 2 hrs 15 mins

MAP 30

TRAILBLAZER

0   1KM   1 MILE

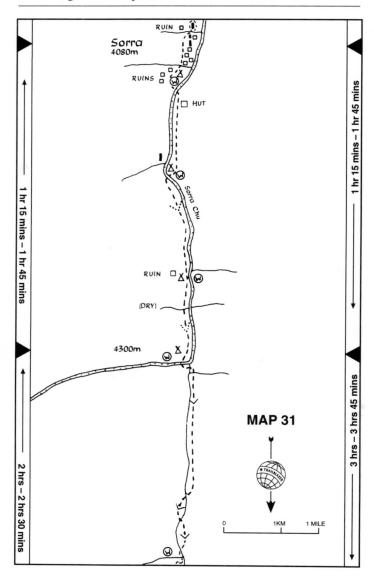

Sorra/Kurna Kur (4080m/13,390ft)

This collection of simple buildings, and small fields of inter-cropped barley and peas is often deserted in the summer months. This is when the inhabitants take their livestock to higher pastures.

SORRA TO DAT   [MAPS 32-33]

Sorra Gorge

Follow the river into a dramatic and beautiful canyon. One can only guess at the magnitude of the river that once formed this magical place. Today only a small clear stream runs along the bottom. The mature willows that carpet the floor of the gorge are highly prized by the locals as so little of this region is wooded. The people of this valley make the most of this natural bounty by selling the wood in Leh and you may pass donkey caravans undertaking the long journey to the capital.

When the canyon splits, ford the Sorra Chu onto the left (S) bank, go over a rise with a ruin on top, then ford the Khurna River and follow this new valley upstream all the way to Dat. The Khurna eventually flows into the Zanskar River about 10km south of Chiling, but you are following it in the other direction.

There are several **campsites** (4030m/13,220ft) in this part of the gorge and spending a night here would be a wonderful experience although it can get very cold, the floor of the gorge seeing little sun during the day.

Eventually the route emerges from the canyon into a broad valley. Keep following the Khurna River through flat pastures – you may need to ford it a couple of times. The valley narrows and then widens again, and tall cliffs tower above you on the left (E). Just before Dat, the trail goes up and over two small rises, both decorated with lots of mani walls, a definite sign that a monastery is nearby.

Dat and Datgo/Khurna (4250m/13,940ft)

These two villages are unlike any in other areas of Ladakh. They are the winter quarters of semi-nomadic herders who leave in summer with their livestock for high altitude grazing grounds. Each simple low shelter is set in a small stone enclosure; there are no cultivated fields and the poor, shabby buildings reflect a harsh lifestyle. Even the gompa looks neglected. If there are no monks to let you in, you can see into the temple by climbing the steps to the roof and peering down through the open ceiling.

There are plenty of places to **camp** on the wide flood plain beneath the villages, although the best is probably by the spring just beyond Datgo (its name literally means 'upper Dat').

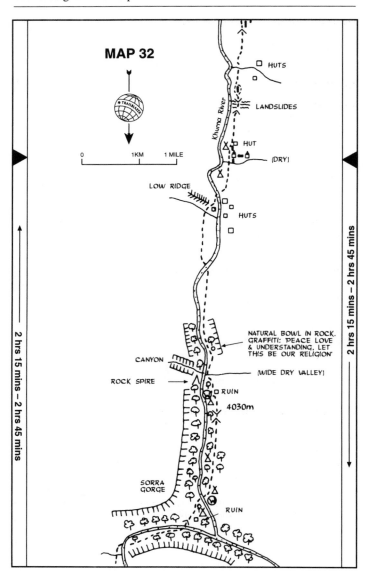

MAP 32

HUTS

LANDSLIDES

Khumo River

HUT

(DRY)

LOW RIDGE

HUTS

0   1KM   1 MILE

NATURAL BOWL IN ROCK.
GRAFFITI: 'PEACE LOVE
& UNDERSTANDING, LET
THIS BE OUR RELIGION'

CANYON

(WIDE DRY VALLEY)

ROCK SPIRE

RUIN

4030m

SORRA
GORGE

RUIN

2 hrs 15 mins – 2 hrs 45 mins

2 hrs 15 mins – 2 hrs 45 mins

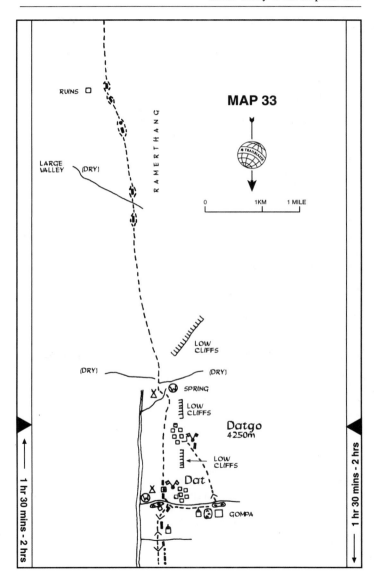

RUINS

RAMERTHANG

LARGE VALLEY (DRY)

MAP 33

TRAILBLAZER

0   1KM   1 MILE

LOW CLIFFS

(DRY)   (DRY)

SPRING

LOW CLIFFS

Datgo
4250m

LOW CLIFFS

Dat

GOMPA

1 hr 30 mins - 2 hrs

1 hr 30 mins - 2 hrs

DAT TO THE YAR LA   [MAPS 33-34]

There is **no water** on this section of the trail until the base of the Yar La,
over three hours away, so take plenty from Dat. The grandeur of the landscape, with its sweeping plains and vast valleys marks the transition
between the Zanskar Mountains and the Rupshu.

Ramerthang

The trail heads south-south-east across a vast flat-bottomed valley known
locally as Ramerthang. The path sticks to the left (E) side of this plain and
is marked at intervals by mani walls. The trail is easy to follow across the
parched earth and the walking is very gentle. This valley is inhabited by
herds of *kiang*, or Tibetan wild ass (see p245), but this shy and fast animal is very hard to spot if you haven't the keen eyes of a local.

As you approach the end of the main valley the trail swings east (L)
into a side valley and follows a dry stream bed. Here you can see some
inviting caves high up on the left (N). The valley soon divides. Don't take
the valley to the north-east; carry on following the main dry stream bed
(east-south-east) to the base of the Yar La. Here you will find a spring and
a small and stony **camp** just large enough for a couple of small tents.

Yar La (4850m/15,910ft)

It's a short and easy climb to the top where you'll find a large chorten
brightly decorated with prayer flags. It's incongruous in this underpopu-
lated area and one wonders who would have built such a monument here.
The rolling scenery of the Rupshu lies ahead of you, while to the north-
north-west you can see all the way back to the Zalung Karpo La.

YAR LA TO POGMAR   [MAPS 34-36]

Descend easily down a sandy spur to the confluence of two streams beds.
Follow the stream down for 1km until a wide green valley appears on the
left. This makes an ideal **campsite** (4580m/15,030ft). Inexplicably a jeep
track is being built up the side of this valley, creating an ugly, damaging
scar. It starts and finishes abruptly; its worth to the tiny semi-nomadic
population is not apparent.

Lungmoche

Carry on downstream to the abandoned village of Lungmoche. Instead of
taking the prominent trail down the left (NE) bank of the stream (which
leads to the Leh- Manali road as it crosses the More Plains), cross over to
a chorten and two mani walls on the right (SW) bank. The trail is ill-
defined but continues along the right (SW) side of the valley.

▲ **Opposite direction** The chorten on top of the Yar La is visible from
here and gives you something to aim for.

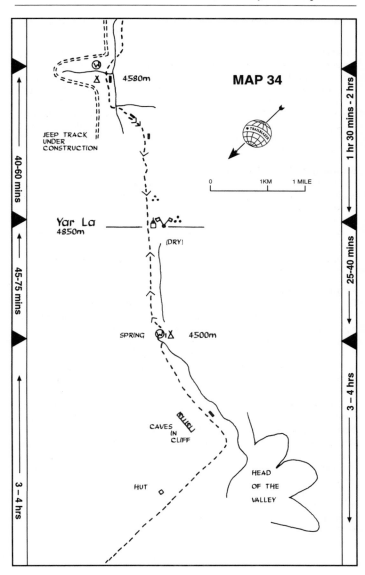

MAP 34

4580m

JEEP TRACK
UNDER
CONSTRUCTION

0   1KM   1 MILE

Yar La
4850m

(DRY)

SPRING   4500m

CAVES
IN
CLIFF

HUT

HEAD
OF THE
VALLEY

40-60 mins

45-75 mins

3 – 4 hrs

3 – 4 hrs

1 hr 30 mins - 2 hrs

25-40 mins

3 – 4 hrs

After passing two mani walls the trail gradually climbs the arid valley side to some prayer flags that mark the top of the rise.

Desert The next stage takes you across an intimidating desert landscape for about an hour. The trail goes in a southerly direction but can be very indistinct. From the flags, go down into the small valley ahead and follow this down until it starts to bend to the south-east and another valley enters from the right (SW). Climb the slope ahead and cross two small ravines. Pass a small cairn and then descend steeply down a small gorge flanked by low cliffs. At the bottom there is a mani wall from which you'll see some white chortens ahead. Walk towards them along a dry stream bed.

Shahang (4300m/14,110ft)
Many of the inhabitants of this small place are Tibetan semi-nomadic herders and so the village is likely to be deserted in the summer. It is situated on the banks of the Zara River and it's amazing to see so much water flowing through this parched land.

Wade across to the other side of the river and pass between the ten white-washed chortens and mani walls. Follow a dry stream bed to the south-east, across more desert. The trail climbs gradually to the green pastures below the village of Pogmar.

Pogmar (4500m/14,770ft)
The inhabitants of this village are Tibetan refugees. This is reflected in the design of the houses, which are very different from the Ladakhi buildings seen in other villages. Not only are they more solidly built but much thought has gone into combating the cold – a constant winter enemy at this high altitude. The buildings are joined together in an 'L' shape, all facing into a central courtyard to provide shelter against the icy winds that blow up the valley. There are no windows on the down-valley side for the same reason.

Despite the harsh conditions in the Rupshu, some of the semi-nomadic people are relatively prosperous. Pogmar is a good example: there are 12 households here and between them they own over 300 yaks, along with horses, sheep and goats. Their lifestyle has, however, hardly changed in centuries, still revolving around the annual migration to the summer pastures, where a black yak hair tent becomes the family home for a few months.

The pastures beneath the village make a lovely **campsite** before crossing the Pogmar La. The main stream is usually dry but the small spring that irrigates the pasture will provide ample water for cooking and drinking. There are wonderful views over the desert to the mountains beyond.

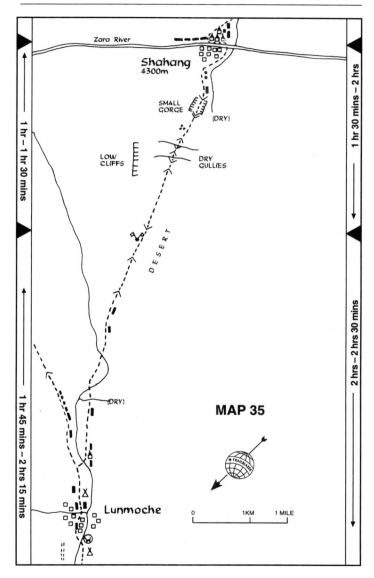

Zara River

Shahang
4300m

SMALL
GORGE

(DRY)

LOW
CLIFFS

DRY
GULLIES

D E S E R T

(DRY)

MAP 35

Lunmoche

1 hr 30 mins – 2 hrs

2 hrs – 2 hrs 30 mins

1 hr – 1 hr 30 mins

1 hr 45 mins – 2 hrs 15 mins

0   1KM   1 MILE

POGMAR TO PANG [MAP 36]

Just above the campsite there is a gully off to the right (S). The trail to the Pogmar La follows this up the steep hillside to a crag on top of the ridge. The trail heads south-east along the ridge, and then more southerly as it gently contours round the head of the valley to the pass (1 1/2 hours).

Pogmar La (4800m/15,750ft)
Below the pass, stretching south to distant mountains on the horizon, is the wide plain of Kanchuthang. This is one of the summer grazing grounds for the people of Pogmar. They usually come here in the second half of the summer and construct a tented village at the bottom of the pass, which they call Narbus.

Halfway across the plain is the Leh-Manali road, only visible if vehicles are travelling along it throwing up a cloud of dust in their wake. The trail descends to Narbus and then crosses the plain in a south-south-east direction, basically straight down the valley. There is no path but the walking is easy over hard desert and scrub until you hit the Leh-Manali road (1 1/2 to 2 hours from the pass).

▲ **Opposite direction** If you are starting the trek here leave the road by a large yellow Himank sign, 'Jule, Namaskar...', and head north-north-west across the plain to the low pass that can be seen on the skyline. That's the Pogmar La.

Pang (4450m/14,600ft)
It's not essential to go to Pang which is a 2 to 2 1/2 hour slog along the road from here. You could try flagging down a passing bus or truck. Pang lies at the bottom of a spectacular gorge through which the road descends in a series of hairpin bends. You can by-pass these if you're walking by taking the steep path down to the left.

Pang itself is a grim collection of five **tent restaurants** and a depot for the army and road builders. However, it's the only place on the highway for some distance where you can get food and a place to sleep. You can **camp** down by the river, but this is not an inviting proposition after the solitude you have been used to.

Buses There are a number of different buses throughout the day going to Leh, Keylong and Manali. Most of these will stop at Pang to give the driver and passengers a break. It's impossible to give accurate times for when the buses will pass through. As a rough guide, buses to Leh should arrive in the morning, which could mean anything from 08.00 to 13.00, while those going to Keylong and Manali should arrive in the afternoon. If you are fed up with waiting for a bus you could always try hitching on a truck. Expect to pay the same as the bus fare and establish the rate before you set off.

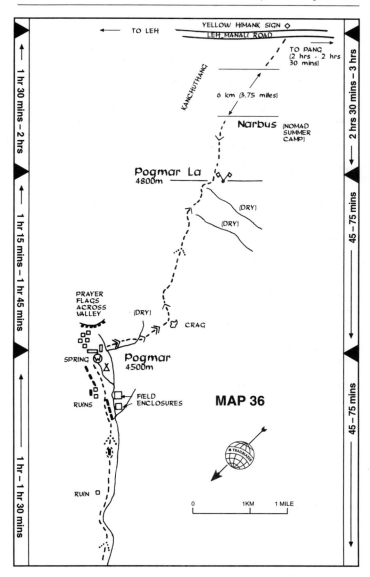

TO LEH

YELLOW HIMANK SIGN ◇

LEH-MANALI ROAD

TO PANG
(2 hrs - 2 hrs
30 mins)

KANCHUTHANG

6 km (3.75 miles)

Narbus (NOMAD
SUMMER
CAMP)

Pogmar La
4800m

(DRY)

(DRY)

PRAYER
FLAGS
ACROSS
VALLEY

(DRY)

CRAG

SPRING

Pogmar
4500m

RUINS

FIELD
ENCLOSURES

MAP 36

RUIN

1 hr 30 mins – 2 hrs

1 hr 15 mins – 1 hr 45 mins

1 hr – 1 hr 30 mins

2 hrs 30 mins – 3 hrs

45 – 75 mins

45 – 75 mins

TRAILBLAZER

0   1KM   1 MILE

Stok Kangri ascent

(4 DAYS MINIMUM)

This elegant 6153m mountain is an ideal peak for amateur Himalayan mountaineers. Competent trekkers with experience using crampons and an ice axe should find the ascent of Stok Kangri a challenging but attainable goal – **given good conditions**.

GETTING TO THE START

Stok is easy to get to from Leh. There are several buses a day (see p132), or you could take a taxi (Rs245) for the short journey. Ask to be dropped at 'Stok trekking point', which is just above the bus stop.

STOK TO THE BASE CAMP   [MAP 37]

Follow the river upstream from Stok and pass through a narrow gorge. Where the trail splits you can either carry on up the main valley, which involves some difficult stream crossings, or take the path that leads off to the right into a side valley. This then climbs steeply to a small pass which takes you back into the main valley higher up. Continue up to Camp 1, an obvious grassy flat (4 hours).

The base camp (about 5000m/16,400ft) is a further 2-3 hours up the valley and this is almost always occupied by at least one large group who are attempting the summit.

BASE CAMP TO SUMMIT

It is possible to climb to the summit from the base camp, and return all the way to Stok in time to catch the 18.00 bus back to Leh. However, most people prefer to spend another night at base camp before returning to civilisation. Another alternative is to start your summit bid from a bivi at advanced base camp, at the foot of glacier 2. However you decide to tackle it, you should aim to be climbing by 5am to make the most of the early morning snow conditions.

Cross the glacier and head up the steep slope to the summit ridge. Scramble carefully up this ridge which will lead you eventually to the summit at 6153m/20,188ft (5-7 hours).

(Opposite) **Top:** Stok Kangri (6153m) is clearly visible from Leh and has become a popular mountaineering objective. **Bottom:** Crossing the desert between Lungmoche and Shahang (see p220).

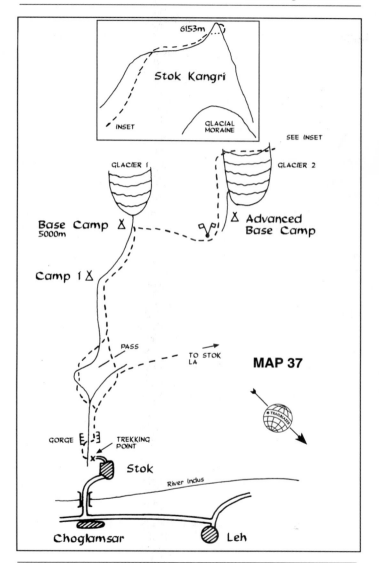

(Opposite) Snow is possible on high passes year round. **Top:** An August storm retreats as trekkers descend to Nimaling from the Gongmaru La (5100m) (see p174). **Bottom:** Crossing the Digar La (5250m) after heavy snow in early September (see p201).

Across Zanskar

(15-21 DAYS)

GETTING TO THE START

See p129 for details of how to get to Lamayuru, p131 for Padum and p92 for Darcha.

PART 1: LAMAYURU TO PADUM (8-11 days)   [MAP 38]

Lamayuru Follow the same route to Phanjila, via **Shilla** (Sheela) and **Wanla**, as described in the Lamayuru to Alchi trek (p184).

• **Alternative trail** From Shilla there's also an alternative route that goes up the Shillakong River, and then over the Snigutse (Sniugutse) La (5050m/16,570ft), to meet the main trail just north of the Sirsir La.

Phanjila/Phenjilla/Fangila Here the trail to Alchi heads north-east, while the trail to Padum carries on along the river and soon enters a gorge. When you reach a bridge, cross over and continue on to the confluence of the Yapola and the Spang Nala.

• **Alternative trail** The water level can sometimes be low enough to allow you to walk directly to Photoksar, up the Yapola and then up the Photang River. This saves you the climb over the Sirsir La. However, this is usually only possible in October when the summer melt waters have eased. Check with locals before embarking on this route.

Turn west up the **Spang Nala** and follow the trail as it rises gently to the large village and gompa of **Hanupatta**. You can camp down by the river. The trail follows the Spang Nala west, and then south-west, up its narrow valley. It starts to climb out of the valley as you approach the pass.

Sirsir La (4800m/15,750ft) There are wonderful views to the Sengge La and the Zanskar Mountains from here.
    Descend steeply at first, then more gently, to the Photang River. Follow this downstream to **Photoksar** (Photosar/Photaksar/Photaskar) (3750m/12,300ft). This beautiful village, situated beneath towering rock faces, is reached after 1½-2½ hours.

It's an easy climb over the **Bramiktse/Bumiktse La** (4250m/13,940ft), from which you follow a wide grassy valley to the base of the Sengge La. It's possible to camp here (4500m/14,770ft).

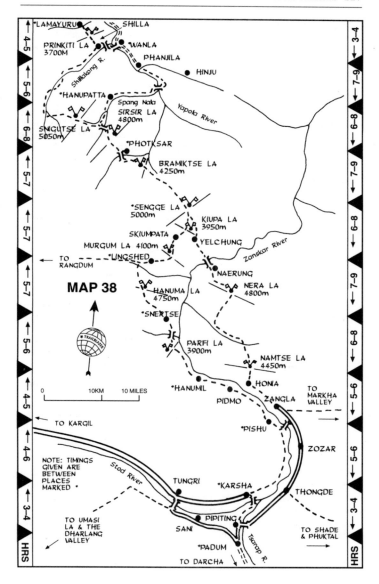

Sengge La (5000m/16,410ft) It's a short climb from the camp to the 'Lion Pass', which also appears on maps as Singi, Senge, Singay, Singila and Singe. This is the highest pass between Lamayuru and Padum, with fantastic views to Zanskar. Descend steeply to a possible camp.

• **Alternative trail** Soon, an alternative route leads from here via the Nera La and Zangla to Padum (see opposite).

Carry on across the small **Kiupa/Khupte/Khyupa La** (3950m/12,960ft), and then descend steeply to **Skiumpata** and **Gongma**, where you could camp. From the village cross easily over the **Murgum/Nietukse/Netuke La** (4100m/13,450ft) to **Lingshed/Lingshot/Lingshet** (3750m/12,300ft), where there's a Gelukpa gompa which you can camp close to.

After a couple of hours of undulating terrain past Lingshed, the trail splits. The difficult trail to the west leads eventually to Rangdum (3-5 days). Carry on along the main trail as it curves south to a possible camp, before the long and steep climb up to the **Hanuma/Hamalun/Haluma La** (4750m/15,590ft). There are good views back to Lingshed Gompa.

Descend through narrow valleys to the meadows of **Snertse** (Nyetse). These are the summer grazing grounds for the livestock of Lingshed village, where the shepherds spend up to three months staying in the small shelters. There's a campsite by a willow grove.

Continue down the steep and difficult trail to the **Jingchan/Zingchen/Oma Chu**. Once you've crossed the bridge you're officially in Zanskar.

Climb steeply to the **Parfi/Purfi La** (3900m/12,800ft), passing a possible camping place on the way up, and then descend steeply to begin with, and then more gradually, down to the raging **Zanskar River**.

The trail is easy to the small but attractive village of **Hanumil/Hanuma** where there's plenty of camping.

Walk across the tiny kingdom of **Zangla**, which stretches from here to the village of **Pidmo** (Pidmu). This small place was once famous for the gold that was found in the waters of a nearby river. Continue to **Pishu**, a large and neglected village where you could camp.

• **Alternative trail** Another trail to Padum, which goes along the east bank of the Zanskar via Zangla, Zozar and Thongde, leaves the main trail near here. Zangla used to be reached by crossing the longest hanging bridge across the Zanskar, and possibly the longest in the Himalaya. This is half an hour upstream from Pishu and although it's not in use any more, it can still be seen spanning the 60-metre gap to Zangla. Such bridges are made by local families and are replaced regularly as they rot over the years. The river is now crossed on a temporary footbridge.

Walk through pastures keeping close to the Zanskar River all day.

Karsha This is a large village with a beautiful Gelukpa gompa which sprawls down the near vertical hillside. This is the largest monastery in Zanskar with about 140 resident monks. It's well worth a visit, not least for the wonderful views across the wide Zanskar Valley. This was probably the site of the original gompa at Karsha, before the one you see today was built in the fourteenth century. There's also a nunnery here, on top of a hill to the west of the main monastery. You can camp here.

Cross the Stod (Doda) River on a good bridge below the village. This river and the Tsarap join just downstream to form the Zanskar River. Go via the hilltop gompa at Pipiting, to Padum.

Padum/Padam (3500m/11,480ft)
The capital of Zanskar is little more than a large village. It has a surprisingly large Muslim population, mainly Baltis from the Kargil area, who have settled here since the mid 17th century. The settlement itself has little charm but it's situated in a beautiful valley and is well-equipped for the trekker. There are hotels, restaurants, tourist bungalows, camping, and a super-efficient tourist officer. Arranging pack animals and guides here is usually simple and you can also buy most basic supplies for a trek, although prices are higher than outside Zanskar. There is nowhere to change money so make sure you bring enough with you. There's a helipad should you have the misfortune to need to be evacuated.

Bus You can get to Kargil by bus or truck. There is usually a bus every other day which departs at about 07.00 (Rs100, 16-18 hours).

Alternative route: Sengge La to Padum via Nera La & Zangla
This alternative route takes about the same time as the main route via Karsha. It's much harder, route finding being tricky and parts of the trail very dangerous for pack animals. Take a guide with you as there are few settlements along the way. The optimal conditions are usually found at the end of August or beginning of September when the snows have had time to melt. Don't attempt the route if there has been recent heavy rain.

Near **Yelchung** the trails split, the more travelled trail going on to Lingshed, while this route crosses the Zanskar River, and then climbs to the village of **Naerung** where you can camp. From the village climb over the double pass of the **Nera/Nerag La** (4800m/15,750ft) and then along the complicated and demanding trail to the **Namtse/Shing La** (4450m/14,600ft). Descend steeply from the pass down a narrow gorge to the village of **Honia** (camping).

Zangla (3400m/11,160ft) It's an easy walk along the Zanskar River from here to Zangla. This is where the King of Zangla (king in name only) lived up until his death a few years ago. The palace is very similar to the other large houses in the village. A ruined fortress that was once the royal residency sits high above the current village on top of a precipice. The Hungarian scholar, Csoma de Koros, spent a cold and miserable winter here in 1823.

The route from Zangla to Padum follows a jeep track all the way. Before you reach the village of Zozar, there's an amazing rope bridge across the Zanskar which is sadly not used any more.

• **Alternative trail** Cross over the new foot bridge if you want to visit Karsha, and then continue to Padum on the west bank.

Zozar/Zazar/Tsasar/Chazar (3500m/11,480ft) has a small gompa with some interesting wall paintings in it. Carry on to **Thongde** (Tongde/Thonde/Stongde), where the second largest monastery in Zanskar sits on a cliff high above the village. This attractive Gelukpa establishment has about 60 resident monks. From here you can trek to Phuktal Gompa over the Thongde La but this is a very difficult route (see Padum to Phuktal to Padum trek, p34).

The jeep track follows on along the east bank of the river, which soon becomes the Tsarap. Cross over to Pipiting on a good bridge and then on to **Padum**.

PART 2: PADUM TO DARCHA (7-10 days)   [MAP 39]

Padum is about halfway on the trek from Lamayuru to Darcha. The start of the trek is an uninspiring 10km walk south along the jeep track to **Bardan**. Rising high above the roaring Tsarap River, isolated on its crag, is the seventeenth century monastery. This houses a gigantic prayer wheel which stands over three metres high.

Continue along the undulating bank of the Tsarap River until you reach the village and monastery of **Mune**, where the valley widens. You could camp here. The friendly monks will show you round this small Gelukpa gompa.

South-west of this village is a trail that leads to both the Kang La (5450m/17,880ft), a difficult route to the beautiful Maya Nala in Lahaul, and the Poat La (5400m/17,720ft), an even harder, glaciated pass into the Dharlang Valley.

Raru/Reru There is good camping near here. Cross the stream beyond the village and carry on up the narrowing valley past the pretty village of Ichar (Itchor) on the other bank. Continue past **Surle** (camping) to Purne.

Purne Cross the Kargyak River on the good bridge to reach this popular village at the confluence of the Tsarap (or Niri) and Kargyak rivers. There is a good campsite here but it tends to get crowded with trekking groups. The village has two well-stocked shops.

Side trip Phuktal/Phugtal This spectacular gompa cannot be missed. It's a fantastic sight with the monastery buildings built on to the sheer face of the rock, while the temple itself disappears into the dark cave above. This Gelukpa monastery is built around a sacred spring which issues from the depths of the cave. Nobody is quite sure who founded it, but it's most likely that it was the prolific Rinchen Zangpo, also known as the 'Great Translator'. However, there's also a legend that a lama called Chansen Cherap Zampo decided that it was a suitable place for a gompa, after finding three Indian holy men living in the cave. They complained that it was far too small to house lots of monks. Undaunted, the lama miraculously increased the cave to its current size.

It's an easy 1 1/2 to 2 hour walk to the gompa. Head up the left bank of the river through a beautiful gorge, and then cross a bridge onto the right bank. The gompa is a little further on. There's an alternative route which crosses the Tsarap after Surle and goes through the village of Char. However, this route is quite difficult at times and impossible for pack animals. There is no space for tents at Phuktal but it's sometimes possible to stay overnight at the gompa for a small fee. If you walk just 20 minutes north of the gompa (go through the gompa complex, not down to the river) there are wonderful views into other valleys.

It's possible to return to Padum from here by way of Shade and Thongde but it's a hard route (see p34).

From Purne, follow the Kargyak River up a broad valley, past the villages of **Testa/Teta** (camping) and **Karu/Kuru** (camping), before crossing over the river on a bridge to **Tanze** (camping). The houses in these high altitude villages look very basic compared to the elaborate architecture found elsewhere in Zanskar. In this harsh environment aesthetics have to give way to practicality – the rooms are built slightly below ground to keep them insulated during the long cold winters, but this gives the houses a hovel-like appearance. Continue along the right bank to Kargyak.

• **Alternative trail** About 30 minutes past Tanze you pass a narrow gorge up which the trail to the Phirtse La goes. This is the alternative route to Lahaul, (see below).

Kargyak (4000m/13,120ft) is the last and highest village in this valley. There is good camping at two sites, one before and one after the village. There is a small temple at the village of Shi, across the river from here.

Continue up the valley past the beautiful sheer-sided mountain called **Gumburanjon** (5900m/19,360ft). Wade across the wide Kargyak river to reach the meadows of **Lakang/Lakong** (4400m/14,440ft), which make an ideal base camp for the Shingo La. This river crossing can be difficult if there has been a lot of snow melting during the day, raising the height of the water. If this is the case, cross early in the morning.

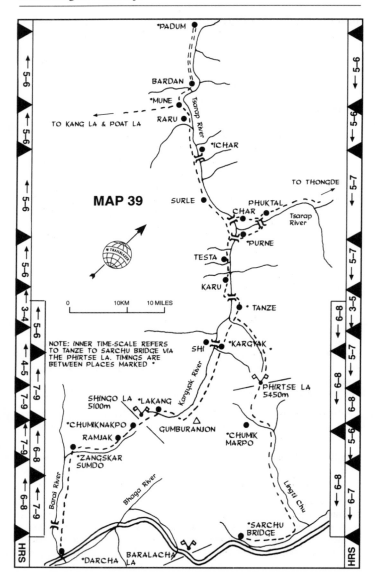

Shingo/Shinkun La (5100m/16,730ft) It's about 2 hours in a south-west direction to the pass. The last section is steep. From the top there are wonderful views over the peaks of Ladakh.

Descend across a snow field and then steeply down beside a stream along the right bank. The first camp is a pasture called **Chumiknakpo** (4050m/13,290ft), or you could go on a little further to **Ramjak** (3750m/12,300ft). Descend to **Zangskar Sumdo** (Zanskarsamdu/Jankar Samdo) (camping) (3580m/11,750ft) where the once dangerous river crossing has been made safer by a modern suspension bridge. The pack animals can't cross on it and therefore must be unloaded so that they can swim through the river. This is the boundary of Zanskar and Lahaul. The trail is vague and demanding, crossing lots of boulders, but essentially follows the Barai River all the way to Darcha.

Darcha (3300m/10,830ft) can provide the trans-Zanskar trekker with the dubious luxury of a cooked meal and endless glasses of chai at one of its many 'hotels'. Unfortunately, there are no guest houses here but there is a well used campsite. Travelling north to Leh or south to Manali is relatively simple as buses and trucks pass through frequently.

▲ Opposite direction If you are starting from Darcha hire ponies and buy all your food in Manali. You will need to allow two days for the ponies to get from Manali to Darcha. If you are thinking of trekking into Zanskar from here and are not yet used to the altitude, it is vital that you take the first section up to the Shingo La very slowly. It's not unreasonable to take four days to the pass, walking gently for about four hours a day. See p234 for recommended rates of acclimatisation.

Alternative route: Tanze to Darcha via Phirtse La

This is a less used route out of, or into Zanskar. It follows the more popular trail as far as the village of **Tanze**. From here it heads east up a steep, narrow gorge to the base of the **Phirtse La** (camping). Cross the pass (5450m/17,880ft) and descend steeply to the pastures and shepherds' shelters of **Chumik Marpo** (camping). From here the trail follows the Lingti Chu down to its confluence with the Tsarap River. Follow the Tsarap upstream to **Sarchu Bridge**. You can now either trek along the Leh-Manali road over the **Baralacha La** to **Darcha** (2-3 days), or catch a lift on a bus or truck.

Bihari road menders
Travellers on Himalayan roads are often struck by the image of these tough, dark skinned workers, whose camps resemble something out of a Mad Max movie. The occasional memorial stone on the side of the road is a testament to one of the hardest jobs in India. Yet the Rs80 per day that they receive is enough to lure them away from the poverty-stricken lowlands of Bihar to the high altitude and appalling weather of the western Himalaya.

APPENDIX A: INDIAN EMBASSIES

Australia: Canberra
3-5 Moonah Pl, Yarralumla
Canberra, ACT 2600
(☎ 06-273 3999)

Australia: Melbourne
13 Munro St
Coburg, Vic 3058
(☎ 03-9384 0141

Australia: Perth
195 Adelaide Terrace
East Perth, WA 6004
(☎ 09-221 1207)

Australia: Sydney
153 Walker St
North Sydney, NSW 2060
(☎ 02-955 7055)

Belgium
217 Chaussee de Vleurgat
1050 Brussels
(☎ 02-640 9802)

Canada
10 Springfield Rd
Ottawa, K1M 1C9
(☎ 613-744 3751)

Denmark
Vangehusvej 15
2100 Copenhagen
(☎ 045-3118 2888)

France
15 Rue Alfred Dehodencq
75016 Paris
(☎ 01-40 50 70 70)

Germany
Adenauerallee 262-264
53113 Bonn 1
(☎ 0228-54050)

Israel
4 Kaufman St, Sharbat House
Tel Aviv 68012
(☎ 03-58 4585)

Italy
Via XX Settembre 5
00187 Rome
(☎ 06-488 4642)

Netherlands
Buitenrustweg 2
252 KD, The Hague
(☎ 070-346 9771)

New Zealand
180 Molesworth St
Wellington
(☎ 04-473 6390)

Norway
Niels Juelsgaten 30
0244 Oslo 2
(☎ 2255 2229)

Spain
Av Pio XII 30-32
28016 Madrid
(☎ 91-345 0406)

Sweden
Adolf Fredriks Kyrkogata 12
11183 Stockholm
(☎ 08-10 7008)

Switzerland
Effingerstrasse 45
3008 Berne
(☎ 031-383 3111)

UK: London
India House, Aldwych
London WC2B 4NA
(☎ 0171-836 8484)

UK: Birmingham
19 Augusta St
Birmingham B18 6JL
(☎ 0121-212 2782)

USA: New York
3 East 64th St
New York NY10021-7097
(☎ 212-879 7800)

USA: San Francisco
540 Arguello Blvd
San Francisco, CA 94118
(☎ 415-688 0662)

USA: Washington
2107 Massachusetts Ave NW
Washington DC 20008
(☎ 202-939 7000)

APPENDIX B: ITINERARIES

The preceding trail guide was deliberately written without specific daily stages in recognition that trekkers walk at very different paces and have varied objectives. However a suggested itinerary for each trek is given below purely to help you plan your trip. Most of these are based on itineraries commonly used by trekking companies and would suit people who walk at a moderate pace. If you are a strong walker you could reduce them by a day or two, but remember that none of these itineraries include rest days. Note that some of the daily stages climb higher than the recommended altitude gains for each day. To work out a safer rate of ascent read the advice on p238 and use the altitude figures in the trail guide.

Markha Valley Trek
Day: 01 Spituk to Jingchan
      02 Ganda La base camp
      03 Skiu
      04 Markha
      05 Tahungste
      06 Nimaling
      07 Shang Sumdo
      08 Karu

Likir to Temisgam
Day: 01 Likir to Yangtang
      02 Ang
      03 Temisgam

Lamayuru to Alchi
Day: 01 Lamayuru to Wanla
      02 Hinju
      03 Camp before
         Sumdah-Chenmo
      04 Sumdah Choon
      05 Alchi

Leh to Nubra
Day: 01 Sabu Phu to Pulu Digar
      02 Chumik Yogma
      03 Shyok Valley
      04 Rong
      05 Khalsar or Leh by bus or truck

Indus Valley to the Rupshu
Day: 01 Karu to Shang Sumdo
      02 Gongmaru La base camp
      03 Nimaling
      04 Luntung Chu
      05 Sorra Chu
      06 Dat
      07 Camp before Lungmoche
      08 Pogmar
      09 Pang

Across Zanskar
Day: 01 Lamayuru to Wanla
      02 Hanupatta
      03 Photoksar
      04 Base of the Sengge La
      05 Lingshed
      06 Snertse
      07 Hanumil
      08 Pishu
      09 Padum
      10 Mune
      11 Camp before Surle
      12 Purne
      13 Purne to Phuktal to Purne
      14 Tanze
      15 Kargyak
      16 Lakang
      17 Chumiknakpo
      18 Zangskar Sumdo
      19 Darcha

APPENDIX C: HEALTH AND MOUNTAIN SAFETY

'Travel broadens the mind and loosens the bowels' goes the old adage. Judging from the fact that the latter subject features prominently in conversations whenever travellers get together you might think that stomach problems are altogether unavoidable. This is not true. Similarly, it is easy for trekkers to get the hazards of the mountains out of all proportion. Although infectious diseases are much more common in India than in the West and there are inherent dangers of travelling in high and remote mountains, if you follow a few simple guidelines for reducing the risks you should have a trouble free trip.

YOUR RESPONSIBILITY

It is impossible in this section to give more than basic advice on the most common and easily preventable health problems. On the majority of treks in Ladakh you are likely to be at least two or three days away from any rescue/medical facilities (see below) and should therefore be able to deal with situations that are beyond the scope of basic first aid, which is only designed to assist or treat a casualty until a doctor arrives. In the mountains the doctor won't arrive! A rudimentary understanding of basic medical care, the ability to deal with injuries resulting from impact (falls and falling objects are one of the most common hazards in the mountain environment), knowing when and how to perform CPR (cardio-pulmonary resuscitation) and how to recognise and respond to altitude illness should be part of every mountain traveller's repertoire.

Many trekkers get by with little or none of this knowledge, but if you want to minimise the risks take along a handbook written for medical amateurs in wilderness situations (such as *Medicine for Mountaineering* by James Wilkerson) and consider booking yourself onto a short first-aid course designed for people going to remote areas (in the UK contact the British Mountaineering Council, ☎ 0161-445 4747, 177-179 Burton Road, West Didsbury, Manchester M20 2BB).

EATING AND DRINKING

Good health can be maintained by taking care over what you eat and drink:
• Food can be considered safe if it has been freshly cooked, boiled or is piping hot.
• Local dishes are generally safer than attempts at Western cuisine because the cooks know how they should be prepared.
• Only eat raw fruit or vegetables if you peel them yourself; don't eat salads.
• Avoid ice and ice cream.
• Avoid anything that flies have been on.
• Don't drink tap water. Purified water, bottled mineral water (check that the seal has not been tampered with), carbonated bottled drinks and hot drinks are usually safe.
• Chang is not usually safe to drink as untreated water is used in its preparation. Illegally distilled *arak* sometimes contains poisonous wood alcohol – stay clear.
• If you can't avoid eating or drinking something that you suspect to be unsafe, have less of it: the chances of getting sick are proportional to the amount you ingest.
• Keep your hands clean!

WATER PURIFICATION

There are a number of waterborne parasites, bacteria and viruses that can cause illness in the unwary traveller. No water in India should be assumed safe to drink or even to clean your teeth in, until it has been purified. This rule is just as important while trekking as it is in towns. Sparkling mountain streams could have been polluted further upstream by human or animal faeces.

The first step before purifying is to collect water from the cleanest available source. Most guest houses have filtered water available for the asking, which is cleaner than tap water (but not safe to drink), and when trekking try to use spring water or water from the cleanest stream (the fastest current in a stream is best avoided as the water contains more sediment). If the only water available is heavily silted then make sure that you either filter it (using a Millbank bag or coffee filter paper) or allow the sediment to sink to the bottom of your container, then decant the clearer water from the top. This is necessary because fine sediment, 'rock flour', in glacial meltwater can irritate the gut, thus causing diarrhoea.

Boiling
This is the most effective way to make water safe to drink, but is not practical for all your water requirements as it is time-consuming and means carrying extra fuel for your stove. Water only needs to be brought to the boil (even at high altitude where water boils at a lower temperature), not continuously boiled, to ensure that it is safe.

Chemical purification
Iodine-based purification methods are reliable, cheap and convenient and are better than chlorine-based methods, because iodine is more effective against amoebic cysts, acts faster and is less pH-sensitive. Iodine is not thought to be harmful when used for purifying water, but to be on the safe side, it is recommended that you don't use it for more than about three months at a time. If you will be travelling for longer than this you could alternate between iodine and using a portable water filter.

The standard concentrations that you should use are given below. If the water is particularly cloudy or cold you should double the contact time, or double the normal concentration. If you dislike the taste of iodine in your water then you could use half the normal concentration (which won't taste as strong) and double the contact time. The alternative is to add fruit juice powders to mask the taste, but as these can sometimes react with the iodine and stop it working, it should only be added after the iodine has had a long enough contact time. Iodine is available in various forms (none of which is available in Leh):

• **Tincture of iodine** This is the cheapest method and the most widely used by trekkers. It is usually sold as a 2% solution, but you must verify this to determine the concentration to use. Buy it in the West where such information is reliable and buy plenty. To dispense the correct amount you will need to buy a dropper as well. For a 2% solution use four or five drops per litre of clear water and leave for 20-30 minutes. Tincture of iodine must be kept in a glass bottle; wrap it in lots of plastic bags in case it breaks. The tincture will resist freezing.

• **Iodine tablets** There are a number of brands of tablets containing tetraglycine hydroperiodide (eg Potable Aqua). One tablet should be left for 10-15 minutes to purify one litre of water. Once the tablets are exposed to air the amount of iodine begins to decrease, so opened bottles should be used or discarded within a few months.

• **Iodine solution** Iodine crystals (eg Polar Pure) are dissolved into a solution in a tiny bottle and then the solution is added to your drinking water. A temperature indicator on the side of the jar helps you determine the correct dose.

Micro filtration devices (water filters)
These can be a convenient way to purify water; there are many makes on the market whose capacity and intended use varies widely. If the unit does not combine filtration

with chemical treatment, you will need to add iodine or chlorine at some stage in the process in order to destroy any viruses. The main thing against them is that they are bulky, expensive and some are fragile.

ACUTE MOUNTAIN SICKNESS (AMS)

Travellers to Ladakh must be continuously on their guard against this sometimes fatal sickness. Anyone is potentially susceptible to its serious consequences above altitudes of about 3000m or 10,000ft. The height at which individuals are affected varies enormously from person to person and with each time a person goes to altitude but is not related to their physical or mental strength. Its cause is not the altitude itself but rather a result of getting to that altitude too quickly. Atmospheric pressure decreases with height and it is that pressure that our bodies rely on to drive the oxygen from the air into our blood. For instance, at 5500m or 18,000ft (the same height of Everest base camp or the Khardung La) there is half the amount of pressure than there is at sea level; humans are perfectly capable of living at that height, and higher, as long as the body is given enough time to adapt. The body adapts in a number of ways including breathing more, producing more red blood cells and making the heart work faster (especially in the first few days of being at altitude). This process takes about two months to complete fully, but about 80% is finished after about 10 days. Therefore, by choosing the appropriate rate of ascent for your body, the illness is entirely preventable.

Prevention
• **Follow a safe rate of ascent** The safe rate of ascent for each person is different and varies every time that person goes to altitude. However, various rates have been recommended and act as useful guidelines:

The standard recommendation for ascent is that before reaching 3000m/10,000ft you should spend at least one night at an intermediate altitude of 1800-2400m/6000-8000ft (eg Manali 2050m/6700ft), and when above 3000m/10,000ft, sleep no higher than 300m/1000ft above the previous night's altitude. After every 1000m/3000ft gain above 3000m/10,000ft you should have a rest day and spend two nights at the same altitude. This regime should be followed whenever possible. It is practical for those trekking into Ladakh from Manali and for following while on your trek.

An alternative for those travelling faster to sleeping altitudes of between 3000m/10,000ft and 4200m/14,000ft (eg on a bus) would be to spend three or four days exercising gently at an intermediate altitude (1800-2400m/6000-8000ft) first. A similar two or three day stop at 3700-4000m/12,000-13,000ft would be sensible before going to between 4600m/15,000ft and 5500m/18,000ft.

The third option for those going rapidly to about 3500m/11,500ft without stopping (eg from Delhi to Leh by air) is to rest and do very little for three or four days after you have arrived. Then build up your daily activity slowly and follow the first example if you want to go any higher.

To help you work out your own rate of ascent, the altitudes of popular stopover towns are as follows: Delhi 216m/710ft; Manali 2050m/6730ft; Keylong 3350m/10,990ft; Leh 3500m/11,480ft; Kargil 2650m/8690ft; Srinagar 1730m/5680ft.

• **Sleep low, climb high** This mountaineers' maxim emphasises that it is the altitude you sleep at that is more important than how high you climb during the day. Therefore, you can climb as high as you feel comfortable during the day as long as you return at the end of the day to your previous night's sleeping altitude, or no more than 300m/1000ft above it.

- **Drink lots of water** Avoid alcohol. (See 'dehydration' below),

- **Eat well** A good appetite at altitude suggests you are acclimatising well and by eating well you can promote good health. It is quite common to lose your appetite at altitude though this does not necessarily mean you are getting AMS. It can sometimes be a warning sign, so be on your guard.

- **Avoid over-exertion** as this can lead to HAPE (see below). Pace yourself so that you don't have to keep stopping to rest.

- **Keep warm** This will lessen your chances of getting HAPE.

- **Look out for symptoms of AMS** If you feel ill you should assume that you have altitude sickness (unless you can prove otherwise) and take the necessary action.

- **Using Diamox** Acetazolamide (Diamox) can reduce some of the symptoms of AMS and help to promote acclimatisation. Its benefits must be weighed against the possible side effects which include tingling sensations, altered taste and increased urination. It must not be taken by those allergic to sulfas, or those with liver or kidney diseases. You may consider taking it if you have to ascend rapidly to altitude by road or air, or if you have suffered from AMS on previous occasions. The usual dose is 250mg every 12 hours, starting one or two days before ascent and continuing for two or three days after arrival. However, it has been shown that taking 125mg instead of 250mg is just as effective and causes fewer side effects. You may find it preferable to wait until you arrive at altitude before making a decision (based on how you feel) as to whether to take the drug or not. This has little effect on its performance.

MILD AMS – NEVER GO HIGHER!

Any of the following symptoms can indicate mild AMS: **headache** (which gets better after taking a mild painkiller eg aspirin or paracetamol), **nausea**, **loss of appetite**, **difficulty in sleeping** (never take sleeping pills at altitude), **dizziness**, or generally **feeling unwell**.

If you suffer from any of these symptoms assume it is because of AMS. While these are not serious in themselves, they provide vital warnings of a possible progression to serious AMS. If the symptoms do not go away you must remain at the same altitude for a day or so, until you feel better. If they get worse, you should descend to the last altitude where you felt well. When the symptoms disappear you can begin ascending again.

Diamox can be helpful with some of these symptoms. 125mg taken at bedtime can help sleep, or take 125mg every 12 hours until you feel better (see side effects and warnings above). No drug should ever be a substitute for descent.

SERIOUS AMS – DESCEND IMMEDIATELY!

This is life-threatening and death can follow rapidly. There are two types of serious AMS: high altitude pulmonary edema (HAPE) which is a build up of fluid in the lungs; and high altitude cerebral edema (HACE), which is a swelling of the brain. They can occur together or on their own.

Symptoms to look out for include: **headache** which does not disappear after administering medicine; **ataxia** (loss of co-ordination and balance) – test for this by drawing a straight line on the ground and getting the subject to walk along it heel to toe and compare this with someone who has no symptoms (ataxia is often followed by a coma); **altered mental state** characterised by the subject not speaking, thinking or acting clearly or normally; severe **fatigue**; **nausea**; frequent **vomiting**; **shortness of breath** after very little activity; **rapid breathing** at rest (more than 20 breaths per minute); **rapid pulse** at rest (above 110 beats per minute); **cough** which can be dry or producing sputum; **blueness** of the lips and the beds of the fingernails; and occasionally **fever**.

Any of these symptoms, either together or on their own, can indicate the onset of serious AMS. They can sometimes be hard to detect in yourself so warn your companions at the first sign that things are not well and keep a careful watch on everybody else.

Descend immediately if serious AMS is likely, even in the middle of the night. A descent of 300-1000m/1000-3000ft can sometimes see improvements, but the lower you go the better. Do not wait for the subject to make this decision for themselves; make it for them even if it's against their will. Similarly, if you are with a group you may have to go against the wishes of the leader who might not want to disrupt their schedule. If you have made the decision early enough the subject should be able to walk down (always accompanied), but it may be necessary to carry them or put them on a pack animal.

Diamox may help reduce the symptoms of severe AMS (250mg every 12 hours), but **descent must always be the priority** as it is the only sure way of saving someone's life.

Other effects of altitude
• **High altitude systemic edema** This is a swelling of the feet, hands and face which affects about 20% of high altitude travellers. Women are more susceptible than men, but it is not a serious condition and will clear up when you reach lower altitude.
• **HAFE** High altitude flatulence/fart emission. This genuine syndrome is more annoying for your tent companion than you!
• **Birth control pills** Taking oral contraceptives could theoretically increase the risk of blood clots at altitude, but there is no evidence to suggest that this is the case. The consequences of coming off the pill may involve more risk.
• **Acclimatisation wears off as quickly as it is gained** Therefore most of the benefits disappear after 1 or 2 weeks at sea level.

DIARRHOEA

Diarrhoea is a common problem in India and many travellers suffer from mild forms of it. It is often accompanied by nausea, vomiting, fever and chills. It is usually passed on in contaminated water and food and is mainly caused by bacteria, viruses, parasites (giardia or amoeba), or by toxins in food you've just eaten. The best way to prevent it is to follow the guidelines under 'eating and drinking' and 'water purification' above.

Initial treatment
If you are unfortunate enough to get a bout of diarrhoea then you should rest assured that it is rarely life-threatening and urgent treatment is not necessary. The diarrhoea will often clear up on its own within a few days, so the best course of action to begin with is just to wait and see what happens. Drink plenty of water to offset the dehydrating effect of the illness and if possible add an oral rehydration salt solution (available from most pharmacists in India). Soft drinks that have been allowed to go flat, weak tea and soups are also useful. Eat plain food if you are hungry (avoid greasy or spicy food and most raw fruits apart from ripe bananas) and be as active as you like – if you feel your body needs a rest then do just that. Taking drugs which are designed to block you up, such as Imodium or Lomotil, can prolong the illness by not allowing

your body to get rid of the infection. However, situations occasionally arise when their use is preferable to intense embarrassment (on a long bus journey) or discomfort (stuck in a tent with a blizzard howling outside).

Stool test

If the diarrhoea doesn't get any better after a few days and particularly if it is severe (10 stools or more a day); contains blood, mucus or pus; or is accompanied by a fever or chills, you should get a stool test to determine what the cause of the illness is. These are available in most towns in India and are cheap and usually reliable – film canisters make excellent containers for your sample. It must get to the laboratory within two hours.

Self treatment

When trekking you will be a long way from any such facility and will have to rely on treating yourself. Self-diagnosis is not as easy as some books suggest which is why you should get a stool test if at all possible. The best way to go about self treatment is to work through the most likely causes and deal with each in turn. This isn't as hit and miss as it sounds as two drugs can cure most frequently-encountered causes of diarrhoea.

• **Onset of diarrhoea** Do not take antibiotics at the first sign of diarrhoea because the illness will often clear up on its own in a few days. Antibiotics tend to be indiscriminate about which bacteria they kill and so a course of them will often kill off many harmless bacteria which naturally live in your gut and keep you healthy. The absence of these friendly bacteria can increase the risk of further illness later. If the cause of your diarrhoea is food poisoning or a virus (both common) antibiotics will have no effect on them anyway and the only cure is to wait until your body has got rid of the offending agent – five or six hours in the case of food poisoning or up to a week or so if it's a virus. Just drink lots and keep your strength up by eating if you are hungry.

• **No improvement after three or four days** If there has been no improvement in three or four days and particularly if the diarrhoea is severe (10 stools or more a day); contains blood, mucus or pus; or is accompanied by a fever or chills, then you should begin more active treatment. A **bacteria** of some sort is the most likely cause of the illness and ciprofloxacin is very effective against these. The dose is 500mg twice a day for three to five days. Take this two hours after eating, if possible.

• **Still no improvement after three more days** If there is still no improvement after three days of taking this drug the cause is likely to be either a parasite or a virus. As there is no treatment for a virus (apart from making sure you don't become dehydrated) you should begin treatment for a parasite infection. The two likely culprits are giardia and amoeba which can both be treated with metronidazole. However, different doses are required for each parasite and so some kind of diagnosis is necessary.

Giardia is far more common and the onset of the illness begins one or two weeks after ingesting the parasite. It is characterised by foul-smelling sulfurous burps and wind, and three or four soft (rather than liquid) stools a day which don't have any blood, mucus or pus in them. Take 250mg of metronidazole three times a day for five days. You must not drink alcohol while using this drug or for a day after.

Amoebic dysentery is rare among trekkers and usually starts slowly with just a mild diarrhoea that sometimes comes and goes in cycles. As it gets more serious so does the diarrhoea, with liquid stools often containing blood and mucus. The person will often tire easily, feel aches and pains in their body and may have a slight fever. Treatment is 750mg of metronidazole three times a day for five days. As this is a large dose it is advisable to get a stool test and seek medical opinion if at all possible before commencing the treatment. You must not drink alcohol while using this drug or for a day after. Metronidazole does not always eradicate the parasite and further treatment may be deemed necessary after a medical examination. Complications can arise if this parasite is allowed to spread to the liver or lungs, so if you suspect you had any contact with amoeba while on your trip, you should have a proper examination when you return home.

OTHER HEALTH PROBLEMS

Bedbugs, scabies and lice

These can be a nuisance to travellers but rarely carry diseases. Bedbugs and scabies can be avoided by using your own sleeping bag rather than a borrowed blanket, or using a clean sleeping bag liner in a rented bag. Frequent airing of your sleeping bag in the sun will also reduce your chances of being irritated by these night-time companions. Lice are spread by direct human contact. Head lice can be kept away by frequently combing your hair and can be killed (along with scabies) by using an insecticide lotion (available in India).

Blisters

Care of your feet will stop blisters developing in the first place. If you feel any 'hot spot' on your feet while you are walking, stop immediately and apply adhesive tape, moleskin or Second Skin to the area. If you catch it too late and a blister has developed you can either surround it with moleskin or the like, so that it is protected, or if it is too painful, clean the skin and burst the blister with a needle (hold the needle in a flame for a few seconds to sterilise it). Apply Second Skin or any other non-adhesive dressing and hold that in place with adhesive tape.

Gynaecological problems

The menstrual cycle can be upset by travel and exercise so periods may become irregular or even stop altogether. This is not a cause for concern.

If you are susceptible to urinary tract/vaginal infections then you should bring a course of treatment in case it recurs.

Sore throat and cough

The dry air in Ladakh can sometimes cause a sore throat and a dry cough. Sucking boiled sweets is the best way to relieve this irritation. If the cough is persistent and produces green and yellow sputum then the cause could be bronchitis. If you are a long way from medical help a broad spectrum antibiotic should probably be given to prevent a possible progression to pneumonia (indicated by a high fever along with obvious sickness). If pneumonia is suspected then immediate descent to lower altitude is essential, along with medical help.

ENVIRONMENTAL HAZARDS

Dehydration

It is extremely easy to become dehydrated while trekking in Ladakh and it is vital that you replace the lost fluid to maintain good health and to avoid heat illnesses. Much of this is lost through perspiration owing to the heat and the high level of physical exertion but another significant factor is the loss of fluid while breathing. Not only does your body have to moisten the extremely dry air that you inhale but because of the altitude and the exercise you also tend to be breathing with increased rapidity. Up to four litres a day can be lost through the lungs alone. Unfortunately, thirst is not a particularly reliable indicator of your need for water and it is better to judge your condition by the frequency and colour of your urine. Frequent passing of clear or pale yellow urine is a good sign. If it becomes darker and is passed less often then you must drink more. Drinking at least four litres a day is a good rule of thumb, the bulk of which should be made up from water, fruit juice, soft drinks or soup, but not coffee, tea or hot chocolate which contain diuretic agents. If you become dehydrated then adding a sachet of oral rehydration salts (available in India and Ladakh, often called electrolyte solution) to a litre of water can be very helpful.

Water is not abundant in the mountains of Ladakh and every opportunity to fill up your water bottle should be taken.

Heat exhaustion

A long trek in the heat of the day coupled with not enough to drink can cause nausea, headache, dizziness, vomiting and even fainting. It is important that this is not allowed to progress to heat stroke. The individual should lie down in the shade and drink lots of water, preferably with oral rehydration salts added.

Heat stroke

This is a very serious condition which can progress to being life-threatening very quickly. The body temperature will rise dramatically and is sometimes accompanied by a lack of sweat in proportion to the amount of exercise that has been performed. The person's mental state will also be altered and this will be the most obvious sign to others, walking will be difficult because of poor co-ordination, and fits and unconsciousness are common. The body temperature must be cooled rapidly either by immersing the victim in water, or by covering in wetted clothing and then fanning the body. Rehydration is also important.

Hypothermia

This condition, also known as exposure, results when the body can't generate enough heat to maintain its normal temperature, and the body-core temperature begins to drop. It is caused by not wearing suitable clothing for wet, cold and windy conditions and by not eating high-energy foods regularly enough. Other important causal factors include exhaustion, dehydration, high altitude and low morale.

It is important to recognise it early on and take appropriate action. As it is almost impossible to recognise hypothermia in yourself all members of a group should keep an eye on each other. Early warning signs are feeling cold and tired, with involuntary shivering. This is soon followed by strange behaviour, poor co-ordination, slurring of speech and problems with vision. If these signs are left unattended the individual will stop shivering and unconsciousness, coma and death will follow quickly.

Treatment of the early stages is simply a matter of finding shelter and then rewarming with a hot drink and some food. If the hypothermia is more serious a tent will have to be pitched and the victim warmed as quickly and thoroughly as possible. Often the best way to do this is with bare skin contact – another person getting into a sleeping bag with the victim.

Frostbite

High altitude trekkers frequently come across conditions where frostnip (the early stages of frostbite) and even frostbite could occur. By wearing warm gloves, hats, socks and boots most people easily avoid these hazards. With frostnip your extremities (feet, hands and face) become cold and painful and then lose their feeling and go white. You must heat them up by putting them on a warm part of your (or anyone else's) body – armpits, groins and mouths are all good heat sources.

Frostbite occurs when the cells actually freeze and this can lead to permanent damage. The skin will look similar to frostnip but will feel frozen and blisters may form. Rewarming (in hot water at 40°C) should not be attempted until there is no chance that refreezing could occur, as this will cause even more damage.

Snow blindness

This is not a serious medical condition but it can be very painful, frightening and potentially dangerous if you temporarily lose your sight. It is caused by over-exposure to UV light and can even occur when there isn't any snow on the ground because of the high concentrations of UV light at altitude. It feels like having sand in your eyes and can cause temporary blindness. It is treated by resting your eyes in the dark. The obvious way of avoiding it is to wear good quality sunglasses with 100% UV protection. Emergency protection 'goggles' can be made by cutting thin slits or pinholes in card shaped like glasses.

Landslides

As much of the ground in Ladakh is steep and dry with little vegetation to stabilise it, landslides are fairly common. They are most likely to occur during and after heavy rain when travel through narrow, steep-sided valleys would be very unwise. However, they can occur at any time so one should always be on the lookout in areas that are potentially dangerous. Quick reactions and a fast pair of legs are your best allies.

River crossings

There are few treks in Ladakh which don't involve a river crossing or two. While there is always some element of risk, you can make the crossing as safe as possible by following some simple guidelines:

If the river looks dangerously high wait until the water level drops. Most streams in Ladakh are fed by melting snow and glaciers and will be at their lowest first thing in the morning. However, if the water level has obviously been affected by a recent downpour of rain, the level should drop within a few hours of the rain stopping.

It's tempting to cross at the narrowest place, but this is usually where the stream is strongest and deepest. Cross where it's wide and shallow. Don't cross the river barefoot as it will be very hard to keep a secure footing on the sharp and uneven river bed. If you are trekking with pack animals then it's worth bringing along a pair of running shoes or sports sandals to prevent your walking boots getting soaked. Otherwise, take your socks off but keep your boots on. Your rucksack will provide quite a lot of buoyancy, especially if the contents are in sealed polythene bags, so keep it on as you cross; have the waist strap undone and be ready to slip it off one shoulder should you slip.

When crossing always face upstream so that the flow does not buckle your knees, keep your feet wide apart and shuffle slowly across. A rope provides the most security, particularly if you use the continuous loop method by tying both ends together. The person crossing ties the rope around their chest, another person stands on the bank upstream feeding the rope out, while a third member stands downstream, ready to pull the crossing member into the bank should they take a swim. However, not everyone carries a rope. A stick placed upstream can also give much needed support to an individual or a whole group.

There are various methods for groups of people to get across using each other for stability. Two or more people can link arms together and cross in a line parallel to the direction of flow. Or alternatively, all face upstream, one behind the other, holding on to the waist of the person in front, then move across sideways together. It's useful if the first person uses a stick for support. Another method, if there are three of you, is to form a huddle by holding on to the shoulder strap of each other's rucksacks. Make sure you all face upstream. If you have ponies, it's sometimes possible to ride them across. Finally, if you do fall in, hang on to your rucksack, float feet first downstream and slowly work your way over to one side. Do not fight the current.

RESCUE

Medical and rescue facilities are few and far between in Ladakh and it is best to assume that you will have to get yourself out of any difficult situation you get yourself into. As pack animals are commonly used in the mountains these are your most reliable form of evacuation. On many treks there will also be villagers and other trekkers who can lend a hand, but some areas are very remote and you may not see anyone else for days – yet another reason to take pack animals rather than backpack.

There are basic health posts in some of the main villages, but for serious incidents you will need to be evacuated to Leh. If land travel is impossible, Indian Air Force helicopters can be summoned from principal villages and towns along the Indus Valley or from Padum and are co-ordinated by J&K Tourism. The helicopter won't leave the ground until payment has been guaranteed which is why it is so important that you take out medical insurance which includes evacuation costs, and leave at your embassy in Delhi details of people who can be contacted and who will be prepared to foot the bill. The service doesn't come cheaply either, costing in the region of Rs10,000 (£200/US$300) per flying hour. As an example, evacuation from anywhere in Zanskar will take at least 5 hours. Flying conditions in the region are extremely hazardous and in bad weather you may have to wait several days before the pilot is prepared to fly. Never request a helicopter unless the situation is life-threatening.

AFTER YOUR TREK

If you have been ill while in India it is important that you get a medical check-up when you return home and let your doctor know where you have been and what you have been doing. Some people advise check-ups even if you haven't been ill as some diseases can lie dormant for a considerable amount of time. If you become ill within a year of returning home, it is worth reminding your doctor that you have been in India, as this may help diagnosis. Malaria, for instance, can often be misdiagnosed as flu.

If you have been taking anti-malarials it is important to carry on taking them for at least four weeks after leaving the malarial area.

APPENDIX D: FLORA AND FAUNA

Ladakh's flora and fauna are more similar to those of Tibet than to the main Himalaya and are a product of the dry climate, cold winters and short growing season. An outline of what you can expect to see is given here; for more detailed information you will need to consult some of the books listed on p44.

FLORA

The main plants in the temperate and subalpine zones are willow and poplar trees which grow wherever there is water, which is usually along man-made irrigation channels. Conifers can also occasionally be found.

In the alpine zone you may find bushes of wild roses and seabuckthorn and sometimes junipers which are usually clinging to steep cliffs, out of reach of the wood cutter's knife. Alpine meadows with wild flowers are rare in this arid landscape and this zone is characterised by scrub and low shrubs. However, even when crossing high passes the trekker will notice plants that have adapted to the harsh environment by growing hairy leaves which capture any moisture in the air. Where there aren't any other signs of life you can still find the occasional lichen clinging to the rocks.

MAMMALS

Although there are quite a few species of wild mammals in Ladakh, trekkers are unlikely to see many. The most commonly encountered is the **marmot**. This member of the squirrel family lives in deep burrows on mountain sides and will allow you to get quite close before giving a whistle of alarm and disappearing under ground. **Martens**, **weasels**, **hares** and **pikas** (a relative of the hare, but with round ears and no tail) are other small mammals which are occasionally seen. **Red foxes** are sometimes seen along the trails in summer, but the **wolves** which also inhabit the mountains, only come into view when they descend to the villages to prey on the villagers' livestock in the cold winter months.

Among the various wild sheep and goats, **bharal**, or blue sheep, are the most likely to be seen. These horned, grey-brown goat-like animals prefer rugged steep terrain and herds are often encountered in the Hemis national park on the Markha Valley trek. **Ibex** are also found in the region, but their preference for steep and high ground means that they are rarely spotted by trekkers. Other species include **markhor**, **urial**, and the huge **argali** sheep.

Herds of **Tibetan wild ass**, or kiang, are not as common a sighting as they once were, but trekkers in the Rupshu and Chang Tang areas are still likely to see groups of this beautiful horse-like ass. Other animals of the grasslands and steppes of the Chang Tang are the **Tibetan gazelle** and the rare **Tibetan antelope**.

Every trekker hopes to stumble across the legendary and endangered **snow leopard**, but the chances of doing so are extremely small. This solitary high altitude cat is found in Zanskar and in the Hemis national park where it preys mainly on bharal. It's about the size of a large dog and has a grey coat with black spots; sightings are very rare because of its depleted numbers and ability to blend into the landscape. There are a few **lynx** in Ladakh's wilder areas and also **Pallas's cats** which are about the size of a domestic cat. Other rare creatures of Ladakh include the **brown bear** and **wild yak**. Any yak you do see will inevitably be the domesticated version.

BIRDS

A large variety of both resident and migratory birds are found in Ladakh and some 240 different species have been recorded. Most visitors will see **magpies**, **sparrows** and **crows** which are all common around villages. Other common birds include various species of **lark**, **twite**, **finches** and **snow pigeon**. In the mountains you are likely to see the **chukor partridge** and the occasional **kestrel**, while soaring high on the thermals are huge scavenging **lammergeyer** (bearded vulture), and also **Himalayan griffin vultures**, **buzzards** and the occasional **golden eagle**.

Of the migratory birds, the **black-necked crane** is one of the rarest, its numbers have been reduced to just a handful of breeding pairs in the Chang Tang lakes. This area is also the breeding ground for the **barheaded goose** and the **great crested grebe**. Another visitor is the **hoopoe**, which is easy to spot with its long curved beak, and pink and black crest. This bird's arrival traditionally heralds the beginning of summer.

APPENDIX E: LADAKHI WORDS AND PHRASES

It is well worth making the effort to learn even a few words of Ladakhi as this will positively affect the attitude of the local people towards you and you will be made to feel all the more welcome. By being able to communicate with local people, you will not only be able to learn more about their culture, but will be able to give them a first-hand account of the realities of life in the West and how it differs from the stereotyped image portrayed in the cinema and on TV.

The few words and phrases below will serve only as a very basic introduction to the language but will give you something to practise before you reach Ladakh. It was compiled from the excellent phrasebook, '*Getting started in Ladakhi*' by Rebecca Norman (with kind permission from the publishers, Melong Publications). Try to get hold of a copy so that you can learn more. It's widely available in Leh, or you can write to the publishers (Melong Publications, c/o SECMOL Compound, PO Box 4, Leh, Ladakh, 194101, India).

The pronunciation is based on English, except that Ladakhi makes a difference between aspirated (*t'*, *p'*, *ch'*, *k'*, and *ts'*) and unaspirated, or soft (*t*, *p*, *ch*, *k*, and *ts*) consonants, whereas English makes no difference. English speakers usually aspirate, which means there is a little puff of air after the sound. For example, the 'p' in 'positive' is aspirated, but unaspirated in 'opposite'.

Capital *T*, *D*, and *S* are pronounced with the tip of the tongue curled back into the palate as if to say *r*, so they have a faint hint of an *r* sound in them.

Ju-le
This is the first word that most foreigners learn and is used as a general greeting: hello, goodbye, good morning, good night, please, thank you, etc.

General words
Are you well?	*k'amzang?*
I'm well	*k'amzang*
I don't understand	*hamago*
I understand	*hago*
Yes, please	*o, ju-le*
No, thank you	*man, ju-le*
That's enough (thanks)	*Dik-le*
Ladakh is very nice, beautiful	*ladak ma-ldemo duk*

Family
mother	*ama (ama-le*)*
father	*aba (aba-le*)*
grandfather	*me-me (me-me-le*)*
grandmother	*abi (abi-le*)*
older brother	*ach-o*
older sister	*ach-e*
younger brother	*no*
younger sister	*no-mo*
uncle/aunt	*azhang/ane*

Terms of address
It is considered polite to call people *ama-le* or *acho-le* etc. Choose the appropriate term to reflect the difference between your age and theirs. * Always add -*le* for respect.

Questions and answers

What's your name?	*nyerang-i minga chi in-le*?*
My name is ...	*nge minga ... in-le**
Where are you from?	*nyerang ka-ne in-le*?*
I'm from America	*nga america-ne in-le**
What is it? (gesturing to something)	*chi in-le*?*
How much is it?	*tsam in-le*?*

Food and drink

Please give me Ladakhi food	*ladaksi k'arji sal-le**
Is there water?	*ch'u du-a -le?*
(Yes) there is water	*ch'u duk*
(No) There isn't (water)	*mi-duk*
I don't eat meat	*nga sha za-met*
tea (common: your own tea)	*cha*
tea (honorific: anyone else's tea)	*solja*
butter tea	*gur-gur cha*
fresh barley wine/ 'beer'	*ch'ang*
water	*ch'u*
boiled water (always served hot)	*ch'u skol*
meat	*sha*
milk	*oma*
yoghurt	*zho*
rice	*das*
roasted barley flour	*tsampa/ngamp'e*
noodle soup	*t'ukpa*
pasta dishes	*skyu/ch'u-tagi*
common apricot	*chuli*
dried apricot with edible nut inside	*p'a-ting*

Animals

male yak	*yak*
female yak	*Dimo*
cow	*balang*
bull	*langto*
cross between yak and cattle	*dzo/dzomo*
donkey	*bungbu*
horse	*sta*

Time

hour, time	*ch'uts'ot*
day	*zhak*
morning	*ngatok*
evening	*p'itok*
night	*ts'an*
yesterday	*dang*
today	*dering*
tomorrow	*tho-re*

* You should always add *-le* to names or sentences to show respect.

Trekking

What is the name of this village?	*i-yul-i minga chi inok?*
How far to the next village?	*yul stingma tsam-zhig thakring yot?*
How far to ...?	*...-a tsam-zhig takring yot?*
Where is the path to ...?	*... lam karu yot?*
Where does this path go?	*i-lam karu ch'anok?*
Is there a shop there?	*deru hati yoda?*
left	*yoma*
right	*yospa*
straight	*k'aTang*
uphill	*gyen*
downhill	*thur*

Numbers

In the market in Leh more people use the Hindi numbers than Ladakhi.

	Hindi/Urdu	**Ladakhi**
1	*ek*	*chig*
2	*do*	*nyis*
3	*tin*	*sum*
4	*char*	*zhi*
5	*panch*	*nga*
6	*chhe*	*Tuk*
7	*sat*	*dun*
8	*at*	*gyet*
9	*nau*	*gu*
10	*das*	*chu*
11	*gyara*	*chuk-chig*
12	*bara*	*chuk-nyis*
13	*teran*	*chup-sum*
14	*choudan*	*chup-zhi*
15	*pandara*	*cho-nga*
16	*sola*	*chu-ruk*
17	*satra*	*chup-dun*
18	*atra*	*chop-gyet*
19	*unis*	*chur-gu*
20	*bis*	*nyi-shu*
25	*pachis*	*nyi-shu-tsa-nga*
30	*tis*	*sum-chu*
40	*chalis*	*zhip-chu*
50	*pachas*	*ngap-chu*
60	*saatt*	*Tuk-chu*
70	*sattar*	*dun-chu*
80	*assi*	*gyet-chu*
90	*naebe*	*gup-chu*
100	*sau*	*gya*
200	*doso*	*nyip-gya*
1000	*hazar*	*stong chig*
10,000	*das hazar*	*Thi chig*
100,000	*lakh*	*bum chig*
1,000,000	*das lakh*	*saya*
10,000,000	*crore*	

APPENDIX F: GLOSSARY

arak	distilled spirit
bharal	blue sheep
bivi (bivouac)	to spend the night in the open
bivi bag	simple and lightweight overnight shelter
bodhisattva	an enlightened being who has renounced nirvana
cairn	pile of stones to mark a path
chai	tea
chang	barley or rice beer
chapati	flat Indian bread
chorten	Ladakhi/Tibetan word for stupa
crampons	spikes which fix to boots for walking on snow and ice
dal	lentils
dhaba	small, basic restaurant
dhobi-wallah	person who washes clothes
dzo	cross between a yak and cow
ghat	steps on a river bank
gompa	Tibetan Buddhist monastery
gur-gur cha	butter tea
kangri	snow mountain, or glacier
kiang	Tibetan wild ass
kushok	head of a gompa
la	pass
lama	Buddhist monk
mani stone	stones engraved with mantras
mani wall	wall faced with mani stones
mantra	Buddhist incantation
momo	Tibetan stuffed dumpling
moraine	debris carried down and deposited by a glacier
nala	stream
ngamphe	Ladakhi word for tsampa
nirvana	the Buddhist aim to be free from the cycle of rebirth
pashmina	fine soft wool used for cashmere shawls
perak	turquoise studded head-dress
phu	high pasture
ri	mountain
Rinpoche	high lama
sham	Lower Ladakh
stot	Upper Ladakh
stupa	hemispherical Buddhist monument
tar-chok	prayer flag
thanka	Tibetan Buddhist religious painting on cloth
tokpo	stream
tsampa	roasted barley flour
tsemo	summit, or peak
tso	lake
wallah	person who does something (a dhobi-wallah washes clothes)
yul	village
yura	irrigation channel

APPENDIX G: MOUNTAINEERING IN LADAKH

If you want to climb any peak in India you need to contact the Indian Mountaineering Foundation (IMF, ☎ 671211) Benito Juarez Road, New Delhi, 110 021, for permission. You must also be accompanied by a liaison officer, unless you are climbing a designated 'trekking peak', of which Stok Kangri is the only one in Ladakh.

Peak fees (US$)
These are biased towards large groups. It's the same price for two people or twelve. If your group is larger than twelve people then it is an extra $300 per additional person.

Below 6000m	$750
6001m-6500m	$1125
6501m-7000m	$1690
7001m and above	$2250
Nun and Kun	$2815

IMF recognised peaks in Ladakh area

Peak	Height
Stok Kangri	6153m
Parcha Kangri	6065m
Gulap Kangri	5900m
Mashiro Kangri	5397m
Kantaka Kangri	5275m
Kang Yaze	6400m
Cumberland	5227m
Yan	6230m
Matho Kangri	6090m

IMF recognised peaks in Zanskar area

Peak	Height
Nun	7135m
Kun	7077m
Pinnacle	6930m
White Needle	6500m
Bobang	5971m
Z2	6175m
Z3	6270m
Z1	6181m
Z8	6050m
D41	5813m
Unnamed peak north of Gulmatang	5934m
N8	6392m
Bien Gnapa	6006m

Trekking peaks
The only difference between these and other peaks is that you don't have to be accompanied by a liaison officer. The highest trekking peak and the only one in Ladakh is **Stok Kangri** (6153m). The others are all north-west of Manali around the Solang Valley. They are **Hanuman Tibba** (5928m), **Ladakhi Peak** (5342m) and **Friendship Peak** (5153m).

INDEX

accommodation
  Delhi 76-80
  Leh 109, 112-14
  Manali 89-90
  Lamayuru 185
  see also place name
acute mountain sickness 238-40
air services 17-18, 57-8, 73,
  75, 81
  Leh 86-7, 108, 117, 125
  Manali 92
Alchi 25-6, 188, 196, 198
Alchi gompa 128
Ang 183

backpacking 10
baksheesh and bargaining 62
Baralacha La 233
Bardan 230
bicycles and cycling 60, 88, 122
Bongbong La 184
books 44-6, 81, 118
Bramiktse La 226
budgeting 18-19
Bumikste La 226
buses 58, 87-8, 92, 126
  Delhi airport 73, 75

camping *see* place name
camping and cooking gear 43
car hire 59
Centre for Ecological Develop-
  ment 124
Chachutse 172
Chaddar 35
Chaluk 166
Chanspa 109
Charatse La 180
Chazar 230
Chemre gompa 134
Chiling 192, 198-9
Chogdo 175
Choglamsar 132
Choksti 199
chortens 163
Chukirmo 175
Chumik Marpo 233
Chumik Yogma 204
Chumiknakpo 233
climate 20-1, 51
  Ladakh 94
clothes 38-9
culture and trekkers 140-2

Darcha 32-3, 233
Dat 215, 218
Datgo 215
dehydration 242-3
Delhi 71-86
dentistry 48, 118
departure tax 75
Deskit gompa 136
Dha-Hanu 138
diarrhoea 240-2
Digar 204
Digar La 201, 204
Digar La Base Camp 201
Dinlung 170
drinks 67-8
Dundunchen La 198

eating out
  Delhi 80-1
  Leh 115-17
  Manali 90, 92
economy 100-3
economy and trekkers 146-8
education 103
electricity 62-3
embassies 234
environment and trekkers 142-6

Fangila *see* Phanjila
festivals 63-5
flora and fauna 44, 245-6
food 66-7
  for trek 152-5
footwear and foot care 37-8

Ganda La 164
Ganda La Base Camp 163
geographical background 51, 93-4
Gongma 228
Gongmaru La 174
Gumburanjon 231

Hankar 172
Hanuma La 228
Hanumil 228
Hanupatta 226
health 47-50, 236-45
  see also medical
Hemis 134
Hemis gompa 134, 178
Hemis National Park 160, 161,
  175
Hemis-Shukpachu 181
Heniskot 33-4

high altitude and health 47-8, 238-40
Hinju 188
history
India 51-3, 72
Ladakh 95-100, 108
holidays 63-5
Honia 229
Humlung 170
Hundar/Hundat 136
hypothermia 243

Ice Path 35
Indian Mountaineering Foundation 82
Indus River 127, 160
Indus Valley 28-9, 34, 93, 210
Inner Line 56-7
inoculations 48-9
insurance 50
itineraries 235

Jankar Samdo 233
Jingchan 158, 161
Jingchan Chu 228
Jingchan Gorge 161
Jumlam 170

Kanchuthang 222
Kang La 230
Kang Yaze 170, 172, 174, 211
Kang Yaze Base Camp 172
Kanji 226
Kargil 131
Kargyak 231
Karsha gompa 229
Karu 175, 178, 210, 231
Kashmir 50, 53
Kaya 166, 199
Khalsi 33-4, 184
Khardung La 136
Khurna 215
Khurna River 215
Kiupa La 228
Kongmaru La 174
Konzke La 188
Kunda La 164
Kurna Kur 215

Lago La 181
Lakang 231
Lamayuru 25-6, 32, 33-4, 129, 184-6, 226
language 60-1, 247-9
Lazun Lungpa 204
Leh 26-8, 107-26, 199
Leh-Manali Highway 135
Leh-Srinagar Highway 130

Likir 24-5, 178
Likir gompa 128
Lingshed 228
local transport 57-60, 122
Longmaru La 174
Lungmoche 218
Luntung Chu 210

malaria 49-50
Manali 89-92, 233
maps 46
Markha 170
Markha River 166, 210
Markha Valley treks 22-4, 34, 158-78, 210
Martselang 175
Matho gompa 133
Maya Nala 230
medical clinics 82, 118
medical books 45
medical kit 40-1
   see also health
meditation 119
money 44, 61-2, 81, 117
motorbikes 59, 122
mountain safety 236-45
mountaineering 251
mountaineering equipment 43
Mune 230
Murgum La 228

Naerung 229
Namgyal Peak 123
Namtse La 229
Narbus 222
Nera La 229
NGOs 119
Nietukse/Netuke La 228
nightlife 122
Nimaling 170, 174
Nimaling Chu 172
Nimaling River 210
Nubra 26-8, 30, 136, 199-210
Nyetse 228

Omlung/Omung 170
overland to India 18

pack animals 10, 148-50
Padum/Padam 32, 34-5, 131, 228, 229, 230
Pagal La 198
Panamik 137
Pang 222
Pangong Lake 137, 138
Panikhar 131
Parfi La 228

Index

Pensi La 131
peoples 103-5
Phanjila/Phenjila 188, 226
Phirtse La 233
photography 42, 119
Photoksar 226
Phuktal 34-5
Phuktal gompa 230, 231
Phyang gompa 128
Pidmo 228
Pipiting gompa 229
Pishu 228
Pitok *see* Spituk
Poat La 230
Pobe La 180
Pogmar 220, 222
Pogmar La 222
polo 125
pony-men 10, 148-50
postal services 65, 119-20
Prinkiti La 186
protected areas and permits
    56-7, 120
Pulu Digar 201
Purne 230

rafting 120
rail services 58, 88
Ramerthang 218
Ramjak 233
Rangdum 33, 131
Raru 230
religions 53-6, 105-6
rescue 245
restaurants 80, 90, 92, 115-17
Ripchar Valley 188
river crossings 244
Rizong gompa 129, 180
Rong 210
Rongdu 208
route maps 156-7
Rumbak 158, 161, 163
Rupshu 28-9, 30, 94

Sabu 199, 200
Sabu Phu 199, 200
Sankar 109
Sankar Gompa 124
Sarmanchan La 181
Saser Kangri 136, 201
security 69
Sengge La 226, 228, 229
Shade 231
Shahang 220
Shang River 175
Shang Sumdo 175

Shanti Stupa 124
Shey 132
Shilla 186, 226
Shillakong Valley 186
Shing La 229
Shingo 163, 164, 166
Shingo La 233
Shingri Nala 166
shopping 68, 82, 121
Shyok Valley 204, 206, 208
Siachen Glacier 136
Silk Route 208
Sirsir La 226
Skiu 166, 199
Skiumpata 228
Snertse 228
Snigutse La 226
Sorra 211, 215
Sorra Gorge 215
Spang Nala 226
Spituk 30, 158
Spituk gompa 128, 158
Srinagar 87
Stakna gompa 134
Stakspi La 193, 196
Stok 30, 132, 158, 224
Stok Kangri 29-30, 164, 224
Stok La 30, 158, 163
Sumda 180
Sumdah Chu 192, 198
Sumdah-Chenmo 188, 192, 198
Sumdah-Choon 192, 193
Sumur 137
Surle 230

Tahungste 172
Taj Mahal 86
Tak Tok gompa 135
Tanze 231, 233
Tar La 188
taxis 58-9, 73, 75, 92
    Leh 123, 126
telecommunications 65, 82, 120
Temisgam 24-5, 183, 184
Testa 231
Thinlespa 166
Thongde 230, 231
Thongde gompa 230
Tikse/Thiksay/Thekse gompa 132
time 61
tourist offices 47, 82-3, 121
trekking gear 36, 43, 121,
    151-2
trekking groups and agencies
    11-16, 121

trekking season 19-21
Tsasar 230
Tso Kar, Lake 137-8
Tso Moriri, Lake 137-8
Tunespa 166

Umlung 172
Umlung Gompa 170
Urucha 163

vaccinations 48-9
visas 16, 56, 122

Wanla 186, 188, 226
water 40, 236-8
Western Ladakh 94
women travellers 69

Yangtang 180, 181
Yapola River 188
Yar La 218
Yelchung 229
Yurutse/Yuruche 163

Zalung Karpo La 210, 211
Zangla 34, 35, 228, 229
Zangskar Sumdo 233
Zanskar and treks 31-5, 50,
  94, 131, 226-33
Zanskar Gorge 166
Zanskar River 228, 229
Zara River 220
Zhumlam 34
Zozar 230

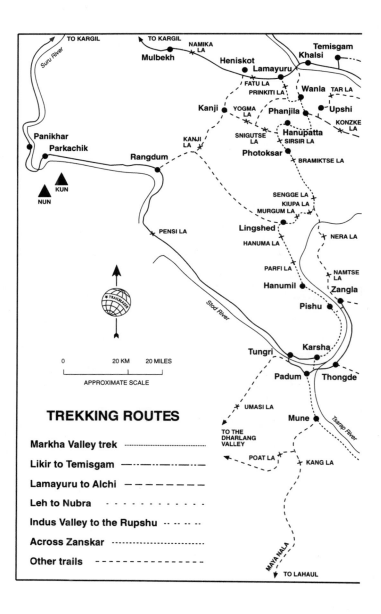